The Passionate Heart

The Passionate Heart

Zoe Ann Nicholson

Lune Soleil Press
Newport Beach, California

The Passionate Heart

Published by
Lune Soleil Press
3419 Via Lido, Suite 614
Newport Beach, CA, 92663
www.lunesoleilpress.com

Art Direction & Cover
By Phillip Tommey

Thanks to all who have given
permission to use their names.
"Elizabeth" and "Adam" are names
which have been changed.

Heartfelt gratitude to
The Witter Bynner Foundation
for permission to reprint material.
Santa Fe, New Mexico, 2003.

Printed & bound in
The United States of America

Library of Congress Control Number: 2003090777
ISBN 0-9723928-2-3

The Passionate Heart
Structure

*For Patty
and her Passionate Heart.*

Appreciation (2003)

David, I am a student of your compassion.

Ann, your heart is the safest place on earth.

Everett, resilient, strong, steadfast inspiration.

I love you, Jennifer & Patrick.
You are the children I wished for.

Though they did not know it,
the Valeriotes lifted me out of many lonelinesses.
Thank you.

Laura & Maria, I miss you everyday.

A choir of angels brought this book into print:
Jordan Ausman, Dina Bitton,
Janet Buehler, Rob Klopp,
Anne Linford, Nikki Myers,
Elizabeth Powers.

Someone recently told me that when I die
Rama and my mother will be waiting for me,
to help me make the transition.
For good or for ill, they are my teachers.

Preface

On August 31, 1993, I pulled back my last row chair, stood up, bowed as deeply, visibly and intentionally as possible, and walked out of the room forever. In a focused daze, after I made the forty feet to the escalator, I collected enough courage to turn around, fully expecting to see fifty or more people behind me. There was no one. I was alone.

Many times I have made such a move, a simple and obvious move. Once I swim to the irreversible side, I pause to discover again and again, that it was a bold and, maybe even, a dangerous move. I suppose Catholics might call it my Guardian Angel advising me. Mystics would say it was the Hand of God. To me, it is just the only move. That is the agenda of a passionate heart -- to follow a course, regardless of the risk, stopping for no one, knowing it is their only choice. Publishing this book comes from such a place.

These 40 chapters in their entirety were written in 1993. I was asked to write it, as the story will explain. It was a task, in the Buddhist sense, given to the student by the teacher. It is holy. It is a gesture of devotion. It is written from the heart and mind of a devotee. I genuinely hope that you can put aside any judgment that *you* would *never* be in such a position; as I believe there is something important to learn here.

Here is a passionate story, filled with passionate people.
I love these people passionately.

Zoe Ann Nicholson
October, 2003

To Rama,

Because he is right.
And the world is wrong.

Acknowledgements (1993)

If you are reading this and you are female, you are sincerely honored here. I am deeply privileged that you are reading this book. It comes from One, far larger than myself, who is working tirelessly for our liberation.

For the women who went before me and paved my path.
For the women who hunger and walk with me.
For the women who will walk on the path we have left behind.

Forgive me for saying that it is your pain that has inspired me. It is your endurance and unbroken hopefulness. It is generation after generation that looks around and insists that it must change. It is the women who have served time in man-made prisons; prisons of lies, poverty, unbridled harassment, legislated biology, violence, and most unforgivable, the prison of isolation.

It is the women, who in the midst of darkness, have seen clearly, shouted loudly, reported honestly and told the truth. Please know, you have been seen, felt and heard. I guard your courage in my heart.

Nancy W, thank you for sharing your strength, your kindness, and intuition. I never would have finished, if it wasn't for you.

I have always viewed with suspicion any feminist book that has acknowledgments to men. Maybe now, I have learned my lesson. My thanks to Ananda, for pointing the way.

To the apprentices, who reach for the Light; never stop. You forced me to unearth what my Teacher has planted in my soul.

My lifelong friend, Patty, told me recently that my love is just too overwhelming and people simply don't know how to deal with it. To which I must tell her, how can I help it when I have such a friend as you?

Author's Note

I am asking for the reader's patience in that I have discarded a major rule in proper English syntax throughout this book. I have consistently used the third person plural pronoun in sentences referring to an individual person of either gender. At first, it may feel foreign. I am hoping that after stumbling upon it a dozen times, it will feel natural and eventually, become invisible.

I have had the miserable experience of reading an author's note of apology that they used *he, him,* and *his,* even though, the reference applies to both a woman and a man. Some even go so far as to toggle the genders, as if that is some type of compensation. To which I say, "Apology not accepted."

Finally, I would like to invite the reader to join me in this syntactical revolution. Maybe if authors weeded out sexism in this fashion; *they, them,* and *their* would become the accepted usage for gender bias-free writing.

Chapter 1

Chuck was standing in front of the science fiction section of my bookstore when he called me over to him. He spoke as if he was imparting a great secret. "Now that you have been accepted as a student, your life will go beyond anything these authors have ever imagined," he said as he scanned the works by Barker, Tolkien, Bradbury, etc.

At the time I had no idea what he meant, except that Chuck knew things, saw things, and I trusted him. He had walked into the bookstore several years before this day. He was a Vietnam war veteran, a Ph.D. candidate, a voracious reader, and an aspiring magician. He ordered the most esoteric books and actually read them.

On our first meeting he was wearing an army fatigue jacket, had long hair, and smoked Marlboro cigarettes. I was at the height of my feminist separatism and downright hostile towards all males. He wanted to be friends. He wanted to talk of things which mattered. I had only contempt for inquiring men. They did not deserve to know our mysteries. He insisted on pushing the issue further. I finally told him that being born a woman was a higher birth. Women were seeking liberation and men were only looking for more insidious ways to oppress. Men were pressing downwards and women moving upwards. Women were growing towards the light, men were promoting darkness.

Frustrated and irritated, Chuck blared at me, "If being castrated means that I would have a better chance at Enlightenment, I would do it in a minute!" What more could a man have said to me? What more could I have demanded from the oppressor to strike a relationship than renounce their weapon of oppression? And so began one of the most astonishing and important friendships of my life.

In the Bahai faith there is a name for a person who announces the coming of the Enlightened one; the Bab. It means the gate. Chuck was my Bab, my Saint John, my gate.

The Passionate Heart

For fourteen years prior, the principle study of my life had been liberation. The very word held all truths for me. I did not just want it for myself. I wanted to know everything about the process of liberation. What led to oppression? What was the nature of the struggle for freedom? What was happening to a soul who oppresses or the soul who is oppressed? I investigated astrology, mathematics, metaphysics, history, and religion.

With a B.A. in Roman Catholic Theology, I knew the machinery of oppression in a male-dominated church. I also knew that the founder of the faith was not an oppressor. But how could women find liberation if they accepted a male for their god? The liturgy, the scripture, the structure of the church had to be rejected fully for women to discover their power.

I had found one significant ideology in Catholicism: Liberation Theology. Father James Gutierrez had written a book by that title and his theory was that God would always join on the side of the oppressed. God could not be a party to oppression. The sides on which one fought would reveal who is fighting on the side of goodness. That side must be the one seeking liberation. I became obsessed with it, reading King, Gandhi, anything about a person fighting on the side of freedom.

While I was working on an M.A. in Religion, a student mentioned to me that I might enjoy a particular book, *The Dialectics of Sex*, by Shulamith Firestone. And so began the wildest, most intense reading adventure of my life. He (!) had opened a door that would point me to my magnetic north.

I could not get enough: Daly, Steinam, Freidan, Dworkin, Greer, Stone, Bunch, DeBouvoir. I was hooked. I haunted woman's bookstores. I ordered from esoteric publishers. I wandered through libraries. I was buried in woman's books: morning, noon, and night. I had found my fight, my beachhead, my life's purpose: the liberation of women. I wrote my graduate exams on Liberation Theology as applied to the American Women's Movement.

I bought and read hundreds of books. I was spending over half of my income at bookstores and publishers. The only sensible thing to do was to sell the house and open a woman's bookstore. I would be able to buy any and all of the books I wanted to read and then sell them. In just a few months the task was done and I opened "The Magic Speller." It was a beautiful little alternative bookstore with special sections on women and metaphysics.

Women came in everyday looking for the best book on battering, on child abuse, on woman's history. They phoned with questions about local political groups, concerts and networking. I had my dream come true. My apartment was over the bookstore. My work and my interest were one and the same. I was self-employed and provided a service in which I believed fully. I was poor but fortunate. I could read anything I wanted. I knew about books being published months in advance.

There were meetings of every type at the bookstore. Women performed, read poetry, signed books, hung posters. I became an officer in the local chapter of the National Organization for Women. I was lecturing any place that would have me, from Woman's Unions at universities, to luncheons for business women. No boss could complain about my time off or personal phone calls. No management could require pantyhose. My cats and dogs came to work with me.

Then one day in early May the phone rang as it had never before. It was Sonia Johnson calling. We had met months before through an autograph party I held for her first book, "From Housewife to Heretic." We talked of the deadline for the Equal Rights Amendment which was July 1, 1982. I had been folding flyers, licking envelopes and hosting fund-raisers for years. Both of us wanted to do something more. We didn't know what it was going to be but we pledged that we would do it together.

"We are going to fast for the ERA," she calmly explained to me. "We are going to go to Illinois, sit in the capital rotunda, live on water only and win the ERA." Of course. It was obvious. It was the only thing to do. We could not lose. We agreed. We set the date and hung up. I slumped into the wall. What had I done? What had I agreed to do? I could die fasting for 45 days on water.

3

The Passionate Heart

A week later I left the Magic Speller and went to Illinois. Seven of us began the fast a couple of days after arriving. We sat on folding chairs in the rotunda. We were interviewed and photographed. We were courageous. We were hungry. We were making history. We would win. Fasting could not lose. NOW put us up in a hotel. Gloria Steinem rented a van for us. And, women from around the world felt hope.

Thirty seven days later it was over. Florida fell and finally Illinois. On June 24, 1982, the ERA was over and so was the fast. I rejoined the world of eating people, the world of oppressed people, the world of unequal people. I was depressed beyond comprehension. I had lost the ERA. I had lost it for every woman.

Returning to my bookstore, I started a new speaking tour. We could not ask the boys' network for permission any more. We would have to start our own laws, our own culture, our own world. I told the groups that I was looking for midwives for the new age. It would be an age by, for, and about women. I wanted to start a community of women who would not accept the status of being unequal. We would seize our equality, with civil disobedience if necessary.

In late August, Chuck walked through the door. He had a stack of newspapers he wanted to drop off. He told me that while he had been getting his hair cut and leafing through a People magazine, he saw my picture. "You are tilting your sword at windmills and I believe that I have found someone who can help you." With this he handed me a hundred copies of Self-Discovery magazine and left.

The cover was an outrage. It was a picture of a pretty blond woman sitting on top of a Porsche. The headline read, "Samadhi is loose in America." The copy was story after story of people seeing miracles. They saw this teacher disappear or grow thirty feet in the air. They said that he was Enlightened.

Why would I care about such a thing? I had seen many a customer over the years insist that they had found a master and I didn't see any big change in their lives. The people in white would come in, the people in saffron would come in, the people in sunrise colors would come in and insist that they had found a real teacher. I was not looking for a teacher.

Secondly, it was a man. I had no use for men, certainly not men who said that they could help women. Women had to help themselves. This man could be no different than the rest considering the sexist picture on the cover of his promotional brochure. In spite of my judgments and doubts, I left the stack of Self-Discoveries on the magazine rack.

A couple of weeks went by and Chuck called asking if I wanted to attend a series of seminars on seven consecutive Thursday nights given by this teacher, Atmananda. He said that there were lots of feminists who were his students, one in particular that he would like me to meet. I wasn't sure. I had nothing to lose. I was curious. How could Chuck be so off about this man who advertises with sexist pictures?

I called my closest friend, Patty, and asked if she would go with me. I was still on shaky footing from the fast. In the time since Illinois, I could only eat things that were white and in very small quantities. My driving was unsure. Nevertheless, my hopes were reassembling. My lectures were not going very well since most women really did not want to hear about women's rights for a while. They needed time to heal.

Patty and I drove to the Sheraton Miramar in Santa Monica on a Thursday night in late September. I would look for myself, but I would never accept a teacher, certainly not a man. The seminar was held in a large ballroom with beautiful chandeliers. The chairs were arranged in precise rows. People were milling around. Electronic music by Jarre was very loud. I was not impressed. The people were classic examples of sexism. The men were wearing suits, dealing with tickets and money. The women were all wearing dresses selling books and tapes. The gender lines were definite and Victorian.

In front of the room was a stage surrounded with flowers and burning incense. Chuck saw me and came over to say hello. He turned and introduced me to his friend, the supposed feminist. She was wearing a flowered silk dress. She tried to defend her politically incorrect outfit saying, "I guess this doesn't look like I am a feminist." I avoided the question and sat down in the third row on the right with Patty.

Finally this man entered the room, walked to the stage, and sat down. People shuffled in their seats, sitting bolt upright. He was in his early thirties, American, tall, and handsome with curly hair. He was wearing trousers and a blue silk embroidered jacket. He began to talk. He explained about the art of meditation. He led several meditations. I was not impressed.

He was articulate. He was funny. He spoke with purpose. But, in the course of the talks, he said that Gandhi had made one grave mistake, allowing himself to be shot and thereby creating bad karma for his assassin. He said that Gandhi should have had armed security for his ashram. I was most definitely not impressed.

After a couple of hours, he got up and walked to the right of the stage. He was standing just fifteen feet in front of me talking. He said that certain people had incarnated at that time to be spiritual "midwives." I heard it. He said it. MIDWIVES!

I left the meeting very confused. I found his students, the music, the incense to be totally unacceptable. Many of the things he said were in direct opposition to my position of pacifism. But what did he mean about midwives? Why did he use that word?

It was clear to me that women did not need meditation. They needed just laws, equal rights, child care, health plans, and shelters. Stopping thought could not change the world for women. This was all nonsense. I decided that night that I would not go to any more seminars.

The next Thursday night arrived and as I sat on my couch watching the rain pouring outside my window, I felt a loss of missing something, or not finding something. This feeling was deeper and more desperate than any of the losses of the summer; it spread across lifetimes. I knew I had to get something from him.

He had something I needed. He had something that was mine by necessity. He had something I had earned by wanting it so badly. I must have it. I wrote him a letter. I told him that the Goddess had told me to find the blueprints for what was to come. I knew that he had them and he was to give them to me. It was a very short letter. I was very sure. He would have to give them to me. I was the one searching for the midwives, and I needed the blueprints.

Chapter 2

Although "Meditation Intensive Seminars" met on seven consecutive Thursday evenings, I was determined to not go back ever again. Atmananda would simply have to answer my letter. I could not imagine myself sitting with those women and men again; certainly not with the electronic music, incense, and ceremony. Why did it have to be a man that had what I needed? There was no doubt in my mind that he had what I was looking for, but I hoped that we could exchange information quickly and with as little interaction as possible.

On the second Thursday night in the series, I sat home alone. My two room apartment above the bookstore was very cute. Everything was hand-made. I loved to sew sweet floral prints which covered windows, cushions, pillows, two love seats, the bed and I even sewed a floral elephant, named Isabel. My teddy bear collection was impressive, international, and rivaled only by my collection of music boxes.

This was far different from the house I grew up in. It was filled with heavy French antiques, oriental rugs, and expensive, although never appreciated, art. Upon leaving my mother's house, she asked if I wanted anything in particular. I asked for the Mary Cassatt which had hung unnoticed on the wall all my life. She said that she had no idea who the artist was and that she didn't care. It had been a cultural waste land. Mitch Miller records were the only ones in the house until I turned old enough to buy my own.

I discovered classical music at 21, the ballet at 22, art museums at 23, Herman Hesse at 24, Laura Ashley at 25, and had my first orgasm at 26. I had a husband, boyfriends, and girlfriends, in that order. My apartment was as far away as I could get from all that had been suffocating me throughout my childhood. It was sweet, innocent, and very humble. It was just enough for me, my dog, Lickie, and my cats, Alice and Jammers.

What was innocent on the inside, was very different on the outside. I had made a name for myself in several different communities. There was no cause too radical for me to take a public stand on. I had lectured widely, been written about, and had been mentioned in the Congressional Record for outstanding political courage. My bookstore was a meeting place for gay rights activists, feminists, astrologers, anti-nuclear people, anyone who was on the left. And, in Orange County, California, that included almost everyone with minimal social consciousness. Since I was self-employed, I could do as I pleased, and I did. More than once, I had hung a "Gone to the Circus," sign on the front door of the bookstore and went off to some political activity.

But something was different on that particular Thursday night. The store was closed and I was surrounded with my furry friends, teddy bears, and thousands of books - but something was desperately wrong. I sat on the couch for hours, watching the rain, and drinking amaretto; something I had never done alone before. Almost as if without my agreement, I picked up the phone and called Patty. I told her that, although I could not explain why, I had to go back to the seminars. She replied that she was just about to call me and say the very same thing. We both were surprised. We both were embarrassed. We both felt we had no choice but to go back again.

On the third Thursday night, I drove up the coast in my VW bus and picked up Patty. We paid our $7.00 each and sat in a sea of well-dressed, educated Yuppies. Fabulous chandeliers hung overhead. Jean Michael Jarre music blared from large black speakers on either side of the stage. There were dozens of vases filled with flowers. Incense drifted everywhere. In the center of the stage was a table, the size of banquet table. It was covered with a beautiful silk cloth, very carefully pinned in place. Catching my eye, Chuck walked by and nodded with a quiet smile.

Finally, a half hour after the announced time, Atmananda entered the ballroom. He walked to the table and in one graceful movement, he placed himself in the center of the table in a half lotus. His posture was extreme, erect, steadfast, but he looked totally comfortable. Unconsciously, the toes on his left foot were occasionally wiggling. His hair was most impressive, one large curly halo. And, although younger than me, he seemed much older, much wiser than anyone was or could be at the age of 32.

9

The Passionate Heart

As he talked, it was clear that he was very American. The jokes were colloquial, news was up to the minute, and popular music was often referenced. In particular, current movies were regarded as a principle tool for instruction. He could be hilariously funny, but the people laughed wildly at every joke, every nuance. At times it was irritating, as if they were making it clear that they were on some inside track. As I sat there, in my straight back chair, I disliked this sanctimonious group. What were their politics? What were they doing about the social conditions of the world they occupied? These women were not feminists. These men were not pacifists.

But as hard as I tried, I could not discount this beautiful man sitting on the stage. His words were more resounding than the contents. The attraction was outside of my control. It was not rational. I had intentionally been living with as little male influence in my life as possible. In my home, no music was played, books read, or paintings hung that were by men. Just as Thoreau searched for nature, I was trying to find what it meant to be a woman in as pure a way as I could construct while living in cosmopolitan USA. But, now I was sitting in a gender mixed group listening to every word a man was saying. To add to the conflict, I hardly agreed with everything that he was saying. His taste in movies included ones with violence. He obviously liked synthetic music. Why were some of his women students wearing saris? Indian customs regarding women were nothing to emulate.

Regardless of all the trappings, the audience's politics (or lack thereof), I knew that essentially Atmananda wanted to teach men and women to meditate, and something inside of me wanted to learn. The form that he taught was called kundalini meditation. It was done for the purpose of waking up an energy, which in the East is called kundalini energy. It originally resides coiled up in the base of the spine and for most people it lies there, dormant. By practicing various exercises, it is awakened and rises up the spine through a tube called the shashumna. As it awakens, a person evolves and goes through a transformation which eventually leads to Enlightenment. Atmananda recommended that each day we should sit alone and still for twenty minutes and concentrate fully on a particular point. It could be a candle flame or flower; it could be a yantra, which is a specialized geometric pattern; or it could be focusing on something called a chakra.

I had heard about chakras once before. In the book, *Joy's Way,* by Dr. Brugh Joy, he described doing surgery one day and suddenly being able to see the patient's energy swirling throughout their body. The vortexes of energy were different sizes, colors, and brightness. But, more importantly, there appeared to be a definite relationship to the areas of the patient's illness. In the diseased areas, the energy was dark and discolored. Dr. Joy had developed what I later came to know as psychic vision.

Atmananda explained that there are seven major chakras and many more minor ones throughout the "subtle" body. This is a network of strands of energy, or light, which is slightly larger than the physical body. The energy that flows throughout one's subtle body is kundalini. The amount and quality of kundalini one has directs every part of one's life; their health, their economics, their sphere of influence, their very state of awareness.

His talk continued, "The major chakras in the subtle body are located from the base of the spine to the top of the head." They act as principle "switching houses" for all of this life-giving energy. In ascending order, the first one is at the base of the spine, the next one is associated with the sex organs, next is the navel, the heart, the throat, the center of the forehead, and, finally, the "crown" chakra, just above the head. In the course of each seminar, we always meditated on the same three; the navel, the heart and the forehead chakra, usually referred to as the third eye.

Atmanada said that meditating on an individual chakra will release an energy of a specialized nature. The navel center, which is located about two inches below the physical body's navel, is the center of raw power. It is the focal point in the practice of martial arts and sports. Beginning each meditation there brings the kundalini up through the lower two chakras and gives the person a power which helps them live in this aggressive and abrasive world. He suggested that we not focus on the lower two chakras at this time, as the energy they release is not easily understood or directed. But raw power from the navel center would aid us in every part of our lives, from school, work, and athletics to avoiding conflict and gaining emotional control.

To show us how to locate the heart chakra, Atmananda said that if you close your eyes and say "me" while pointing to yourself, you will always place your finger on your heart chakra. While meditating on the heart center, he said that we might imagine a rose in the constant motion of opening, or we could picture something we dearly cherished. He went on to recommend that we might want to keep our finger placed lightly on the spot for a few weeks until we actually begin to feel it by merely concentrating on it. He assured us that in time, we would be able to actually "feel" these centers just as we could feel parts of our physical body. Focusing on the heart center releases an energy which will develop balance, compassion, and love.

The throat, the fifth chakra is the center of creativity. We were told that we would pick up this energy when we meditated on the "third eye." This, the sixth chakra, is located between the eyebrows and just slightly above, near the center of the forehead. It is the seat of discrimination, of knowledge from past lives and insight. Meditating here releases the power to discern wisely, to develop intuition, and to see deeply into one's life.

Placing his hand over his hair, Atmanada said that the seventh, and final of the major chakras, is located just above the head. It is known in the East as the "thousand petaled lotus," which symbolizes the unfolding of Enlightenment. In order to connect the crown chakra to the lower six, one has to have reached Samadhi, a state which is beyond all thought.

Each Thursday evening for the next five weeks, Atmananda patiently and enthusiastically led us through three meditations; focusing on the navel, the heart and the third eye. Although he had been teaching for sixteen years, and had shown hundreds of thousands of people all over the world how to do this practice, he explained it as if it was the first and the most important time ever. During the meditations, he played either Jarre, Tangerine Dream, or Vangelis. Playing the music for meditation at home wasn't recommended, but he played it in seminars to smooth out the natural noises and energies that occur while sitting among that many people. I hated the music, but loved the feeling.

Early in the series, it was announced that on the evenings of the sixth and seventh seminar, Atmananda would be accepting student applications. I had no idea what that meant. I didn't know what the process would entail, what it meant to be his student, or what it meant to have Atmananda as a Teacher. But nonetheless, on the sixth, (I could not wait for the seventh) Thursday, I applied to be a student of Atmananda.

There were only twenty four of us filling out applications that night. Patty wanted to wait and see how she felt about it on the seventh night, so she did not join in this little gathering. After the formal seminar we stayed in the Grand Ballroom, sat in a semi-circle, and filled out a very simplified form which inquired, "What is your favorite flavor of ice cream?" Atmananda sat on a chair in front of us, and one by one, looked at each of us for a long time. What was he doing? What was he looking for? Would I be accepted?

So once again, I went home and waited for a letter from Atmananda.

The Passionate Heart

Chapter 3

It was December in the bookstore. It was make it or break it time of the year for retailers. To be successful, it was necessary to do the same amount of business during December as the other eleven months combined. I liked being a retailer at Christmas time. In the course of one season, I would wrap well over 3,000 gifts for my customers, always for free. What could be more fun than helping pick out presents for hundreds of people from my carefully selected inventory. I knew each and every book or record. No list, no relative, no unusual reader escaped my knack to find the perfect package for under their tree.

The presents were on the up side, but as with most things on planet earth, there was always a down side - the bills. It seemed that in the seven years I had my bookstore, I never saw a profit. If I just covered the accounts payable, it was a good year. 1982 was not a banner year for the Magic Speller Bookstore. It was the year of chain discount bookstores and they were selling big hardbound books at retail for less that I could buy them wholesale. Each morning I would wade through the mail trying not to let the huge bills from Random House or Harper and Row ruin my holiday spirit.

One day when the mail arrived, the bills were quickly put aside. There was a letter from Atmananda! My heart was racing. I could not explain why, but being accepted as a student had become very important to me. There was a longing inside me that had grown since the first night that I saw him. He was the most intelligent person I had ever known or read about. He was deep and intense. He was serious about life and yet not obsessed with himself. I wanted him to be part of my life. I wanted him to accept me. It was all happening inside of me without the slightest effort, without any convincing.

I opened the envelope and read it as fast as I could. I had been accepted as his student. I had been accepted as a member of his organization, Lakshmi, named after the Goddess of beauty and good fortune. There were eight hundred students attending classes in three separate centers:

San Diego, Los Angeles, and San Francisco. I would be attending weekly classes in Santa Monica, at a Unitarian church, Unity by the Sea. Tuition was $127.50 a month. I ran to the phone, Patty got accepted too! We could go to our first meeting that very week.

I didn't care about the other students. I didn't care what they wore, what they said, what they did. I only cared that I would be able to see him again. I couldn't wait to see him again. I had been trying to meditate everyday. I sat on the couch, with my eyes closed for twenty minutes, and tried to focus on one of my elusive chakras. Nothing much was happening inside of those twenty minutes, but I seemed to be getting happier and happier everyday. I knew that seeing him again would make it even better.

Patty and I arrived on time and found a parking place. We walked into the church with no idea of what was going to happen. It was a beautiful building. There were rows of pews filled with close to five hundred students waiting for their Teacher. We sat in the middle, joining in the anticipation. He arrived wearing a new exquisitely embroidered silk shirt, walked to the front of the room, sat on a blue floral couch, and began to talk. He told us that he was no longer Atmananda. He had a new name: Rama.

He told jokes. He talked about what was going on in the world. He told us about the movies he had gone to that week. He said that he had seen *The Year of Living Dangerously*, the latest Peter Weir film, and although it was a good movie, the ending was flawed. How could he say that? I loved that movie. It was perfect. The ending was perfect. It could not have ended any other way.

After a long talk, we took a break. Students had brought fruit juice and various treats that were served in the basement of the church. Everyone milled around. Rama was walking through the crowd, chatting casually with people as he passed by. I spotted him just a few feet away and marched right up. "How could you criticize *The Year of Living Dangerously*? It was a wonderful movie and the ending was the most important part." I blathered on to explain my point of view in great detail. He could hardly get a word in edgewise. He stood there smiling at me, nodding from time to time. Finally, he escaped my ambush. I fell back in total shock. What had I done? Who was I to tell this person my puny point of view? I hadn't waited for him to say hello or even look my way. I simply foisted my self and my opinion on him, as if I should have the final word.

Socializing with strangers was not easy for me, so I was uncomfortable with the break. I went downstairs, I got some juice, stood against a wall, and waited impatiently for the others to take their seats. It was at least forty five minutes before they reassembled and I was relieved to be back in my pew. Rama sat down and the first thing he said was that he did not dislike *The Year of Living Dangerously*, and didn't want anyone to misunderstand. He thought it was a good movie. I couldn't believe my ears. He was addressing my objection. He didn't embarrass me. He didn't laugh at me. He didn't dismiss me either.

It was time to meditate. There were no beginners instructions that had been given at the public seminars. He simply told us to meditate and watch him. Rama turned on the music and went into a deep meditation. We must have sat for close to an hour. Then he asked people what they had seen. The answers were astonishing. People saw different historical figures sitting on the couch. They saw an ancient Chinese man with long finger nails. They saw an Egyptian priest. Some said that they saw a woman.

Most of the answers were that they saw light, great golden streams of light emanating out of Rama's body that filled the entire building. They saw him disappear or in something like photo reverse. For others, he grew thirty feet high and back again. During the meditation, Rama made hand gestures called mudras. I had seen some of these exact gestures in Chinese sculpture and Oriental paintings. Students said that while Rama was moving his hands, they saw beams of light shooting from his palms. With each change in the gesture, the quality or property of the light changed. They referred to it as a change in the dimensions in the room or "shifting dimensions."

I didn't see anything. I watched, but I didn't see anything. More curious to me was that I didn't care that I didn't see anything. I wanted to see it all, wished that I had, but the fact that I hadn't seen any phenomena did not throw me into doubt. I knew that these people were telling the truth. Everything that they were saying was true. The states of meditation that Rama was passing through were affecting the entire room and every person in it, regardless of their ability to perceive it.

Rama began to meditate again and this time he kept his eyes open. He turned his head to the far right and began looking at each one of his students. He slowly worked his way through the entire audience. Going from right to left, up and down each row, blinking often, Rama gazed out across the room. The entire process must have taken ten minutes. The students sat incredibly still, each waiting for their moment. I too waited, although I did not know what it meant. When he got to me, I saw that his eyes were very different from what I had seen before. It was as if, in the back of his head, his eyes were connected to all of eternity. Looking into his eyes, there was no resting place. They were endless, bottomless, non-physical. It was as if there was no one in there. The man had disappeared and his body had become a gate to some place I did not know.

It must have been as late as 11:30 when Rama asked all of the new students to come up to the front of the church. I was very nervous and didn't want to walk up there in front of everyone. Not having a choice, I got up and joined the others. We formed a line up the center aisle and, one by one, said hello. Rama smiled and welcomed each of us. Then we returned to our seats. At this point I had no idea how long the meeting was going to last, but I didn't care. I felt as if I was sitting in a vat of whipped cream, extra heavy whipped cream. I never wanted to feel anything else again.

It seemed that the class was over. Rama had nothing else to say. It felt as if it was time to go, but no one moved. Rama closed his eyes, sat perfectly still, and went very far away. He was in Samadhi. He was smiling. He wasn't breathing. Although I did not know why, no one, including myself, was about to leave.

The Passionate Heart

Had I been born in the East, I would have understood immediately. Since I was born in Wisconsin, to a Catholic family, it took me years to know what was happening. Rama was in the Enlightenment process. He was going into higher and higher states with each meditation. He was unfolding right in front of our eyes. To simply look at someone in Samadhi, to stand outside of their house, or offer them a gift, can change a person's future entirely. In India, Japan, Tibet, people know that to be in the presence of someone who is in Enlightened states of mind can bring health, good fortune, and actual miracles into their lives.

Rama was going to be thirty-three in just a couple of months. He was in the final stages of his full Enlightenment cycle. We were sitting in the presence of Enlightenment itself and the light that was flowing through him was touching us and would affect us forever. And so, class after class, week after week, Rama was allowing his students to not only witness his transformation, but also to transform with it.

Eastern traditions explain that a student and a Teacher enter into a special karmic relationship. There is an agreement struck between the two which lasts for all eternity. Rama explained that it is much like helping a student who has to work their way through college. The student has to go to class all day, work at night and then study in the little time remaining. If someone supported the student so that they didn't have to work, they could apply themselves to their studies completely. A spiritual Teacher loans their energy, their states of attention, to their students and actually mitigates the student's karmas so that they can progress at a rate much faster than if they were seeking the light all on their own.

I had thought that karma was a simple mathematical equation; you rob a bank, you will be robbed. You hurt someone, you will be hurt. You abuse power, you will be powerless. To me, it sounded the same as the Christian axiom; "Do unto others as you would have them do unto you." But Rama explained that karma is really the sum total of everything that has led up to any point in one's life. It is the accumulation of all of the states of mind that a person has traversed in this and other lives. If you are a generous person, you will live in states of generosity. If you are angry or full of hate, you will live in a state of mind filled with anger or hatred.

But the students of an Enlightened Teacher live in states of mind far beyond those that they could have possibly accrued on their own. Their Teacher loans them refined and heightened states of attention. It is the responsibility of the student to try to sustain those states of mind and to match them to their own. In other words, the student has a palette of advanced mind states to carry forward for all eternity.

So there I sat until almost 2 A.M. in the presence of Enlightenment itself. Where would it take me? How would it affect my life? My life, as it would have been without this new relationship, I would never know.

Chapter 4

When I was twenty years old, I was a high school teacher. It was 1969, the Vietnam war was on, and the draft was affecting much of my life. Actually the first time the draft made a wave in my life was my freshman year of college. Most people had never heard of the name Zoe. They certainly weren't sure if it was a boy's name or a girl's name. Upon my arrival at college, I discovered that I was registered for the boy's dorm and the school wanted to know my draft status. I was offended, but then, I was easily offended.

After graduation, I got a contract at the local Catholic boys high school teaching a variety of religion classes: New Testament, Old Testament, Morality, Catholic Marriage, and my nemesis, senior home room. My very first morning, in the teacher's lounge, I got the most valuable advice of my career. Ms. Hamilton, the veteran English teacher told me, "You can be nice the first day and spend all year trying to gain control, or you can be a bitch the first day and spend the rest of the year teaching." Thank God for Ms. Hamilton.

The small all-boys school was built in a circular fashion with all of the classroom doors opening to one round sea of lockers. At 8 A.M., when the first bell rang, my room was filled with boys just barely younger than myself, staring at me, plotting my demise. There I stood in my new blue linen dress, full of ideals, politics, and religion, convinced that I was going to change their lives.

The first order of the day was roll call. The names were alphabetical and mostly unpronounceable. Standing at the podium, expecting to elicit the expression, "Here," I called, "Anderson." Thirty-five strong male voices bellowed: "Fuck." Never had the word been said so clearly, so precisely, so intensely. Although I was mortified, I didn't flinch. I didn't move. I didn't breath. I called, "Bailey." Again the chorus responded, echoing throughout the corridor. I had no idea of what to do. The only thing I did know was that my entire teaching career rested on the next exchange. "Baker." The F word must have been heard on the moon.

It wasn't that I was above using the word. I used it often in my everyday life. I was married and certainly not above doing it often in my everyday life. But this particular usage was not in my repertoire. What were the other teachers thinking, especially the members of the Christian Brothers order? I asked my senior home room if they had a football team. Oh, yes, they did. I asked if they had after school practice. Oh, yes, they did. How many practices can you miss before you are kicked off the team, I inquired. Only three. Is the team quarterback in this home room? All eyes turned to one handsome, muscular, grinning boy. Yes, he is. Fine, and would you come here to the front of the room? Chatten stood up and proudly strolled to the podium. I calmly noted that each and every time I heard a single voice say the word "fuck" again, Mr. Chatten would miss football practice. I motioned for him to return to his seat.

With total assurance that I could now proceed, I called, "Chatten." The single solitary voice respectfully announced, "Here." It was over. I was tested. I had passed. And now we could get on with the business of falling in love. I loved them all: the freshman, sophomores, juniors, and mostly the seniors. They loved me. I was not their usual teacher. These were not the usual classes. I bought them condoms. I took them to movies. We read the gospels and sang the score to *Jesus Christ Superstar*. I told them all I could about God and they wrote me poetry. After all, it was the '60s.

I wrote letters to the draft board explaining that, being their religion teacher, I was qualified to identify my students as Conscientious Objectors. Some boys who did not get a CO rating left for Canada. Naturally the only people who were less than pleased were the parents. They held a meeting to discuss the fact that I took their boys to see the movie *Catch 22*. I pointed out that they signed the parental forms. They were still angry. The boys are old enough to go war, they should be able to see war movies, I told them. It was not for viewers under 18, the parents, mostly moms, replied. I didn't care what the parents thought. I just wanted the boys to stay home, stay alive.

Much to the relief of the parents, I moved to California immediately after the senior boys' graduation. My husband

The Passionate Heart

and I lived at the beach. The dogs got terrible fleas. My husband got stoned. I got bored. Leafing through the Beach Cities recreational summer catalog, I found an astrology class for beginners. I knew absolutely nothing about the subject except that the popes sought astrological advice and the Magi were actually astrologers who followed a predictive star foretelling the birth of an avatar. The class was $35. I took a chance.

I don't remember what I expected, but it wasn't Susan. She was my age, a triple Scorpio, very dark, and beautiful. She had two little girls, one Virgo and the other, a double Virgo. Susan was too busy for house work and so these two little Virgos did what Virgos are best at: incessant house cleaning. She painted, had a green thumb, and deeply loved astrology. She wasn't funny, but so interesting that I could listen to her for hours.

All summer long, on Tuesday mornings, I would go to the beginner's class. After that, I took the intermediate class followed by the special topic advanced class, three times. Then we were just friends. We still are. Patty's birthday was in late November, a Sagittarius. I gave her the beginner's classes as a present. Susan looked at Patty's chart and said to me, "One day she will be teaching us." Patty was a natural. She understood the most complex planetary relationships immediately. She could see the chart as a whole and calculate aspects in a flash. At eighteen, she was an accomplished astrologer.

I became, and remain, what I call a cookbook astrologer. I can see dozens of components in a person's chart and seldom see the whole. I love to look at charts, but interpreting them is always piecemeal and unsatisfying for all involved. But philosophically, metaphysically and spiritually, astrology changed the world for me.

The universe is one great symphony of energies, constantly changing, evolving, merging, separating, moving. The planets, people, elements, everything is involved, participating fully, with or without consent. A birth chart is a mirror image of the configuration in the sky at the moment of one's birth, and as a person draws their first breath, everything joins in agreement to carry out a contract filled with the lessons which that soul requires. It isn't that the planets drag a person along some predetermined road. It isn't that a person pulls the planets around the sun. Everything in the universe joins in the concert; harmony or cacophony, chaos or order, there is unity.

The twelve signs of the Zodiac indicate certain proclivities; some positive, some negative. Each sign has what I call a birth defect. Once understood, there is no reason to be angry when the Sagittarius is late or the Leo is center stage - it is simply a characteristic of a person's birth. In Europe, many employers consider an applicant's birth chart along with their resume, knowing chances are that the Capricorn will be responsible and the Taurus will be good with finance. Raising children could be greatly enhanced if you knew that Sally will be drawn to the creative arts or that Bill will do much better in college than in grade school. Astrology gave me a new-found tolerance and appreciation for the complexity of each person walking the earth.

The indicators for a person's evolutionary pattern are the transits. As the planets travel around the sun, changing signs and aspects to each other, they are also circling around a person's birth chart. The geometric relationships between the planets' birth positions and the planets' current positions are called transits. The most obvious transit is one's birthday. It is the day of the year when the sun returns to the exact position of the sun at one's birth. We celebrate, not just because the greeting card companies insist, but because it is a day of light, energy, and regeneration for the birthday boy or girl. We want to get close and feel the warmth of this annual transit.

Transits vary, as do the rates of the planets. The moon travels a full revolution in just twenty eight days, affecting the tides, fertility, and emotions. Pluto, the smallest, most powerful and furthest planet charted to date, takes as long as two hundred years, creating transformation along the way. Saturn moves around a birth chart, ticking off rites of passage towards adulthood and responsibilities. Jupiter circles around bringing gifts and abundance. Uranus always brings a surprise, while Neptune offers insight.

The Passionate Heart

Over the ages, men have been hailed for such information although admittedly, the Church was not quick to honor Copernicus. But women have been burned for knowing such things. Women certainly weren't supposed to be privy to astronomy or mathematics. If women spoke openly about astrology, they were witches, destined for the stake. Americans are still in the Dark Ages about astrology, clearly illustrated by voters' judgments upon hearing about any US president consulting an astrologer. It isn't that presidents don't consult their astrologers, they simply must keep it from the general public, particularly around election time.

In the East, astrology is a matter of course. It is part of business, family rituals, agriculture, financial markets, health, etc. What Americans prefer to dismiss as parlor games or nonsense, Asians rely on openly after centuries of experience. Each culture has their own calculations, mathematics, titles, and methods, but the conclusion remains the same: everything in the universe is in a relationship. If you look deeply at one segment, you will find information about anything else, everything else.

Hindu astrology, ancient and wise, is very different from that of the Western world. Western charts are round, while Hindu charts are square. Because of the knowledge of reincarnation, the Hindu looks at a chart as one map in a series of thousands that an individual soul will journey before they get off the Wheel of Dharma. Known throughout India, the greatest day of the year is the solar return or birthday celebration of an Enlightened Master. Families close their farms or businesses and walk hundreds of miles just to stand outside the ashram of a known holy person. They know that just being in the perimeter of such a person on his or her birthday will bring their entire family successful crops, health, good fortune. Should they be so lucky as to see such a person and receive "Darshan," it can permanently alter their entire evolutionary profile for lifetimes to come.

Celebrations last for days and presents are as extravagant as possible, for the family knows that it is part of the transaction. To bring a gift shows respect. If the gift required sacrifice, the Master knows and responds generously with favors, called boons. To someone from Wisconsin, it may appear to be a bribe, but to the educated Oriental, it is only proper and of benefit to all involved. Just as the Japanese Salaryman knows that if he works hard for his corporation, his corporation will take care of him, so is built the basis for respect and mutual growth in which both parties constantly and consistently benefit.

February 9, 1983, Rama was going to turn 33. It was my Teacher's birthday. It was the day of his solar return. It was going to be a special celebration with his students from all three centers coming together in Los Angeles for one big party. Eight hundred students brought flowers and the stage was more beautiful than ever before. Not knowing what was appropriate, I brought a tiny gift; one of my favorite books, *The Phantom Tollbooth*, wrapped as perfectly as I could. In addition, I contributed to a birthday fund for one big present; a Ford Bronco.

Some of the women students were wearing saris. I hated the reference to the subservient position women held in India, but they were beautiful. If only I could turn off the political analyst who constantly whispers (often shouts) in my ear. Sita, Saraswati, Lakshmi, all of the Indian Goddesses were wonderful images of courage and excellence, but Indian women knew that theirs was a lesser birth, a birth to be reconciled and hopefully, prayerfully overcome. They waited for a male birth, believing that as a woman, they had no chance for advancement. The most they could aspire to was marriage, male children, and finally, suttee.

Rama arrived wearing a white silk jacket embroidered in gold. He was radiant. He was never funnier. He was in love with life. He was becoming the radiance of my life. Students saw golden light pouring from him, filling the room. They saw manifestations of Rama's past lives. I sat, not knowing what was happening except that I was happy, no, ecstatic. I was traversing a range of feelings that I had never known before. There was no pain. There was no world crying for liberation. There were no genders or races. There was only joy, light, and timelessness. The earth had stopped on its axis and the sun was shining in and through him. How can I explain such a thing? I knew it was true and yet, could never explain it. I was in love with my Teacher and it was his birthday.

The Passionate Heart

Rama was born in San Diego, California, on February 9, 1950. Many times he explained to us that his first choice would have been the Himalayas in Tibet. It had been the purest spot on the earth and therefore the best place to bring back one's Enlightenment. But in 1950, the Communist Chinese invaded Tibet, killing hundreds of thousands of Buddhist monks, raping and killing Buddhist nuns. So, Rama took a radical turn and selected San Diego for its consistently clear warm climate. As fate would have it, his parents moved to the East coast when he was only two. One time he told us that he remembered playing in his backyard and beginning to enter Samadhi. He said that he had no understanding that this was not a normal state for five year olds.

I loved it that Rama was totally versed in astrology. I asked him once about my favorite astrologer, Isabel Hickey, and he told me that she had read his chart once. His mother was an astrologer and it clearly had been a reference point his entire life. Much of Rama's teaching revolves around astrology. Desert trips are often on the Solstices and the Equinoxes. Rama composed an entire album called, "Retrograde Planets." He pays close attention to his students' Saturn returns.

Rama was born at 4:49 P.M. His Ascendant is Leo, no surprise when you see his curly hair. Pluto is in the first house, Saturn in the second, Mars and Neptune in the third, and the moon is in the fourth. The sixth house, the house of service, has Mercury and Venus. In the seventh house is Jupiter and the Sun in Aquarius. Finally, Uranus is in the eleventh. Many times over the last ten years, I have gotten out his chart in hopes that I would see something, understand something more about him, but I never do. It is taught in India that if a person receives Darshan, a blessing from an Enlightened being, their birth chart is completely reset from that moment. How could one possibly interpret the chart of an Enlightened being?

At the break, we went to the banquet room upstairs. There were more cakes than I could count, one more beautifully decorated than the next. Each one was at least two feet in diameter and ineffably delicious. With help from some of the students, Rama served the cake himself. He walked among us, listening to eight hundred "Happy Birthdays." He smiled like any child enjoying his birthday party. It must have been the happiest place on earth.

When we all sat down again, Rama went deep into meditation. I found myself wanting to sit up straighter than ever before in my life. I wanted to sit so quietly that I would never move again. I wanted my body to stop sending demands and let me float away. Rama slowly turned his head to his right and began giving Darshan to each and every one of his students. His eyes moved inch by inch, centimeter by centimeter, throughout the audience, missing no one. It must have lasted over forty minutes.

One time a student asked Rama how he could get the moon and the stars to move across the night sky in the desert, right before our eyes. He explained that he and the planets and the stars are all friends, they find delight in doing things for each other. Surely that night the sun was beaming for a special friend on his special birthday.

Chapter 5

Although 1983 began with a desert trip, I did not go for two reasons. One was that Rama was emphatic that it would be a very long walk, maybe ten miles in soft sand, and if there was the slightest chance that one wouldn't be able to keep up, one shouldn't go. That was enough for me right there. The only sand I walked on was the 100 feet from the strand to the edge of the Pacific to place my folding chair every day at sunset. I would guess in the eighteen years that I lived along the Pacific ocean, I missed the sunset just about that many times. The sunset was the central nexus of my life. Ten miles sounded impossible and, at the very least, potentially humiliating.

The second reason was most likely the more honest "excuse" that kept me from going. I knew, somewhere deep inside, that trips to the desert with Rama would change a person's life forever. I had heard many stories of miracles, Rama moving the stars, Rama disappearing, Rama growing hundreds of feet in the air and back again, but that was not the issue. In his book, *The Last Incarnation*, students wrote stores about what they had seen in the desert; great beams of light pouring out of Rama, illumining the night sky, Guardians, Allies and "doorways" to other worlds appearing. But those were not what held me from going.

There was a magic that happened in the desert. It wasn't the magic of seeing other dimensions or feeling an inexplicable warm wind blow through your hair when the temperature was ten degrees above zero. The desert was Rama's true home. It was his world. As one walked into the desert, away from the city and all the people, it was impossible to hold on to the structures that made you you. There were no ads saying what a woman was or was not. There were no buildings holding in the people as they worked or made dinner. There were no streets filled with cars and familiar stop lights. There were no relationships or relations dictating expectations and dis-appointments. You couldn't be sister, daughter, wife, friend, bookseller, etc.

Something in me did not want to let go of the world as I had come to know it, as I had insisted that it should be. I knew that if I went to the desert, I would never be able to hold my little world together, that world I call Zoe. I wanted to remain important, political, social, labeled, solid for a bit longer. Rama's magic interested me, enticed me, but I wasn't ready just yet.

Patty went. Patty is a Sagittarius. No adventure was ever held in check. I admire her. I love her. There are people along the way who leap out of the morass and enter another person's life with full force. They pop up and claim a place that goes beyond family or friends. Believing in reincarnation, we both knew that this was a relationship that had gone on for many lifetimes.

I met Patty while teaching World Religions at a coed Catholic high school in Southern California. I was twenty-two. On the first day of class I handed out a very precise and comprehensive document that explained what the entire course would cover and the requirements for an A, B, C, or D. On the bottom of the page was a simple statement that a student could receive an automatic A, any time throughout the semester, if they read the book *Siddhartha*, by Hesse and could intelligently discuss it with me. I thought it was a fairly difficult task and certainly revolutionary for a Catholic high school junior.

Third period, sitting by the window, was Patty. I noticed her immediately and could not stop looking her way. She was not like the others. She had not been beaten down by the years of Catholic school. She was not driven by the desire to attain grace and to avoid sin. She looked wise at fifteen. Oh, she looked fifteen. She was very pretty, with long straight black hair. She deviated from the school's brainless uniform code as much as the law would allow. Her plaid pleated skirt was not rolled up, like the Pep Club girls. She was clearly not interested in "cute" or "in." She had a mind of her own and she had no trouble making clear what was on it.

When the bell rang and class was over, Patty walked right up to my desk and said, "I've read *Siddhartha* three times, what would you like to know?" That was it. That was enough.

The Passionate Heart

What more was there to say? We were sisters. We were inseparable. She came over to my beach apartment that very day and seldom went home. People actually thought we were sisters which was particularly fun because her real brother was a Franciscan priest who also taught religion at the very same high school. It was all so instant. It was all so easy. We knew each other.

Patty was an athlete. She played volleyball. Patty was a poet. She was always either writing in her journal or reading some book she had heard about. I found her writing almost incomprehensible, in that it was so deeply poetic. The letters she wrote to me during the year of college she spent in Europe are still a mystery to me. We were as different as two people could be, and yet we knew each other.

We both had husbands for a while. Then we were single. She loved beer and felt natural in a bikini. I hated beer and never felt natural. We changed careers. We changed cities. We had two entirely different circles of friends. But we always came back to one another, like the swallows to Capistrano. At the core of things, the essence of our lives, we were the ones who understood what mattered to the other.

I couldn't wait to hear what had happened in the desert. We were going to meet before the weekly meeting, as always, at our favorite restaurant on Melrose Blvd. It was the most amazing thing that each week we would meet for dinner and no matter what we talked about, Rama would address the very same subject that night. It was never a conscious thing. We never tried to guess what he was going to talk about or pick a topic in hopes that he would discuss it. It was always a shock, always a surprise. We would glance at each other in the hall in utter amazement that somehow he must have been eaves dropping on our pasta dinner conversation.

One evening we had been blathering about one thing or another, and I said that I wondered if Rama would allow me to sell his tapes in my bookstore. Rama had an entire series of tapes that were sold at the weekly meditation meetings. They were on specific topics such as *Purity*, *Humility*, and *How to Know God*. They were not available to the public except through a seminar series. After dinner we stopped at a florist shop to buy flowers to bring to the meeting, as was the custom. I always bought pink roses. Upon walking in the door of Unity by the Sea, the Unitarian church, I turned to the right to set my roses down. I looked up and saw Rama sitting just on the other side of a huge mountain of flowers. He smiled and said to me, "You know, it would be okay to sell my tapes in your bookstore."

Patty arrived at the restaurant and began to tell me about her trip to the desert. She had seen miracles. She had seen Rama leap to the moon and back. She had seen him grow a hundred feet in the air and return to his physical size of six feet. I believed her. She wouldn't make it up. She went on to explain that at first she wasn't at all sure of what had gone on. She tried everything she could think of to dismiss it, discredit it. She figured that she was just imagining things. Maybe something was in her eyes. Rama had told everyone to meditate and watch what he was doing. After about thirty minutes, he asked the group to describe what they had seen. A woman said that she saw him leap to the moon and back, as if on a spring. Rama said, "Like this?" He did it again. He was doing an instant replay confirming each and every movement. Another student said that they had seen him disappear. "Like this?" He disappeared again. Example after example, Rama repeated each miracle as the student told him what they had seen. Any doubts Patty had about what she had seen or not seen vanished.

I wondered what really happened to Patty on the inside. She looked the same although much brighter and clearer. Had she been transformed in the desert? What had happened to her inner being, her soul? She said that she felt very different but couldn't describe how. She told me that on the drive out to the desert she saw a billboard that she thought had said, "Dissolve Yourself." On the way back she read it again and realized it said, "Discover Yourself." Either way, it was the proper road sign.

We sat in a restaurant on Melrose Blvd. We ate our dinner. We went on with our lives. But Patty had seen miracles. It must be like losing one's virginity. Before it happens, one can only guess what it will be like and once it is over, it lasts forever. I believed in miracles. I had been to Lourdes and read the Bible. I just hadn't seen one yet. I knew I would one day.

The Passionate Heart

Now it was just fun to sit and gasp, "No!" or "Wow!' between the linguini and the ice cream.

Rama told us that a Teacher performs miracles so that students can believe in the power of the Infinite. All of life is a miracle, but to watch a Teacher move the moon and stars across the night sky from the East to the West serves a certain purpose. It helps a student realize the transience of this world and the possibilities that lie beyond it. It gives a student faith in their Teacher and the process of Self-Discovery. Besides, not the least of which, it is fun.

I had been attending Rama's classes for five months and had not seen a thing. According to Rama, there are several reasons someone might not "see." One is that a person is just too clogged up with psychic impressions from the world that will melt away in time through meditation. Another is that they haven't developed their psychic vision yet and with patience it will evolve naturally. Finally, it is because they simply can't let go of their definitions of the world that exclude such possibilities. I was sure that I fit all three categories.

One night, at a meeting at Santa Monica high school, while sitting in the second row center watching Rama meditate, I suddenly realized that Rama was floating in the middle of the night sky. The stage had completely disappeared. The couch was gone. The curtain behind him had evaporated. The entire back of the building had dissolved. Not only had the building vanished, but it didn't lead to some street in West LA, but to the heavens, filled with the constellations and the moon. Rama was suspended in the twinkling star-studded sky meditating with his eyes closed. I could see it clearly. I could see it perfectly. I wanted to jump up on my chair, point straight ahead and shout to everyone, "Wow, can you see that?" No matter how I blinked or twisted in my seat, there he was sitting in thin air, like a painting on a chapel ceiling from the Renaissance. But this was no painting. This was 1983. This was LA. This was the USA. This was *my* life and I had seen a miracle.

Chapter 6

If I had to choose just one talisman, one symbol for Rama, it would be his briefcase. Over the years, he has had so many different briefcases that I couldn't possibly remember them all. Certain ones do stand out, like the rosewood and Velcro. He used to hold his microphone next to the straps, rip one away, and joke about the sound of "fresh Velcro." At one meeting, he walked on stage, took a portable telephone out of his briefcase, and made a call. The music drowned out the conversation, but it was so ridiculous, joyous, and oxymoronic to see my Enlightened Teacher sitting on stage, dialing a phone, and chatting away.

It took me a long time to realize that every gesture, every movement that Rama does in front of his students has a meaning. They are koans; puzzles that befuddle the mind until the mind reaches enough clarity to grasp its meaning. The classic Zen koan is, "What is the sound of one hand clapping?" Rama would never resort to something so cliché. His koans involve modern day advertising, Monty Python, or a delicate subtlety that could take years to interpret. Part of the magic of watching Rama on stage is knowing that there are always layers upon layers of meaning, waiting to be seen, to be uncovered.

What was his gait? What was his intention? What did he want us to learn that night? In the beginning, I found it almost irritating how the senior students watched his every move with total focus and total intensity. Then I realized that there was much to be learned in just these first few minutes when he entered a room and I couldn't take my eyes off of him either.

His posture is fit for royalty. All six feet stand perfectly straight, and yet there is a kindness, as opposed to any iota of arrogance. He is completely at home in his body, even though he often travels very far away from it. We are physically the same height, I am six feet myself, but there is a special feeling when talking with him. I have watched him talk with women and men who are taller or shorter, and Rama always has a way about him that says, "Welcome, I am interested in you."

The Passionate Heart

Maybe it is a presence that permeates every part of his being; nothing about him is unconscious.

Having risen above the planes of desire and repulsion, Rama doesn't dress for himself, but for those who are going to be in attendance. There is no vanity or false humility, so his outfit is chosen most carefully to express something specific to the viewers. He may wear all leathers with dozens of zippers, a tuxedo that defies description in class and taste, a sweat suit that has more colors than one thought possible, or a double breasted suit, impeccably tailored; but he always looks completely natural and comfortable with himself. Imagine if you knew that your date was dressing exclusively to tell you something, the action would take on a whole new meaning. Certainly you would be compelled to pay particular attention. Waiting to see and carefully observing what Rama was wearing was never a disappointment.

Once he reached the couch or chair, Rama would usually sit down and take off his shoes - sometimes they were boots. They would be placed perfectly either under his chair or next to the couch as if the motion were deeply important. Never have I seen him do anything as if to say that it was trivial. Then he would take off his watch and his ring and place them discreetly on the table. All the time, he was teaching us grace, mindfulness, and most of all respect for life through his example. He was continually showing us that every aspect of life deserves attention, perfection, intention, and has a precise etiquette.

Always, there was something in his briefcase that would change our lives. It could have been a magazine article, an advertisement, a new song on cassette, a study from the Wall Street Journal, a letter from a student. But, mostly I remember Rama's yellow pad. Sometimes during the week, I would imagine Rama sitting in his backyard or in his living room writing on his yellow pad. I would picture him concocting the latest and most revolutionary scheme he could come up with to encourage us to change. He would be relentless in the search until he found the most simple, pure and radical suggestion to direct our Self-Discovery. He would make scads of lists. Rama loves lists. Nothing or no one escaped finding a place on one of Rama's lists; lists of what gives you energy, lists of what robs you of energy, lists of things to do, lists of what to throw away, lists of people who aid you, lists of people who hinder you, lists of thoughts that enhance your life, lists of thoughts that need to be weeded out, lists of lists.

The goal of all of these lists is the practice of Self-Discovery. It is the essential core of all of Rama's teaching. He has taught Zen Buddhism, Hinduism, Confucianism, Taoism, Tantric Buddhism, Astrology, Transcendentalism, Native American Spirituality, and Mysticism, but Self-Discovery remains at the center of it all. The principle is simple; that inside of each woman and man is the Self, Nirvana, Eternity. It has been covered with layers of conditioning, lifetimes of tendencies, and fear of the unknown. Through the practice of Self-Discovery all these layers are peeled back eventually revealing one's true nature: perfect pure light.

Meditation is the primary way to peel back these layers. Through meditation, the mind becomes clear and sheds old "selves." One time a woman asked Rama what she could do about a terrible addiction she had to chocolate (she was inhaling quarts of chocolate ice cream on a daily basis). I shuddered at the question because I didn't want to hear him tell her to simply give it up and walk away. I love chocolate too much myself. He said that she should not obsess about it anymore. Instead she should meditate and become someone else, someone who doesn't even like chocolate. The desire would fall away naturally through the practice of Self-Discovery and meditation.

Besides meditation, there are many things that a person can do to practice Self-Discovery. They are all on one or another of Rama's lists. First and foremost is the list of things to do to "collect personal power." Personal power is a term I had first heard in reading books by Carlos Castaneda. His Teacher is a Yaqui Indian, don Juan, who took him through many adventures that fill a dozen books. I read each one as they were first published, impatiently waiting to see where the stories were going to take him next. Carlos was a constant source of amazement and disgust to me. He seemed to always be holding back, complaining ceaselessly, giving into fear, and missing his Teacher's points entirely. One time, upon finishing the very last line in one of his books, I slammed it shut, threw it at the wall, and swore I would never suffer through another one of his sloppy, half-assed journeys again. Of course, my sentiments diminished long before the next one was published.

Don Juan taught Carlos about collecting personal power. Personal Power is energy. It is the energy that gives one the ability to change, to move out of a particular state of mind. The Buddhists teach that there are ten thousand states of mind and each one of them has to be experienced before reaching Nirvana, the stateless state in which there is no thought. Everything in a person's life is dependent on the amount of personal power they have; their health: their perceptions, their finances, their success, the states of mind that they live in every moment. The student of Self-Discovery is trying to collect enough personal power to not get caught in just one state of mind and to move easily through many more. Mostly the Teacher helps the student collect personal power by giving them tasks. Carlos' tasks were very specific to the Yaqui teachings, the Sonora desert, his life, and his karma. Rama used tasks that had direct relevance to his students' lives: the '80s, California, their karma.

Number one was our closets. It was the place where it all began. In early 1983, Rama spent hours talking about our closets. It drove my friend Nancy crazy. Actually, it finally drove her out of the program. Nancy had the worst closet in recorded history. It wasn't just her closet. It was her purse, her briefcase, her cupboards, under her bed, her endless bookshelves, her file cabinets, her coffee table, her entire apartment. Everything was always in complete chaos. It seemed that somewhere in her tiny two-room duplex, she had every article, book, photo and knick-knack from as far back as kindergarten. Her two lumpy adorable cats just picked a place, on whatever happened to be piled up, to take their daily naps.

I loved Nancy. I met her in 1978. I certainly did not love her at first. She walked into the bookstore wearing high heels and dyed blond hair. She appeared to be a classic scatter-brain. She bought bags full of books and never seemed to read them. Nancy was studying to be a Marriage and Family Therapist.

She was trying to do entirely too many things at once and never finished most of them. Why was this male-identified woman buying the most astute and advanced feminist books? I couldn't figure it out. Week after week, she would come in and drop fifty dollars on Mary Daly, Virginia Woolf, Charlotte Perkins Gilman, Andrea Dworkin, Germaine Greer, Lillian Hellman. What was she doing with these books?

And there I was, in my pleated trousers, polo shirt, and pocket watch, or overalls, with my graying hair in a three-foot long braid down my back. Nancy didn't seem to mind that the difference between us was incalculable. She was so steadfast in her acceptance of me, and the choices I had made with my life, that I began to wonder why I was so very disturbed with the ones she had made about hers.

Nancy invited me to a NOW meeting. Even though I thought NOW was just a quarter of an inch to the left of Nixon, I went. Here were all of these women caring about other women. They weren't lesbian, at least not overtly. Some even brought their husbands. Here was a room filled with women and men discussing legislation that would affect women. They were working on the ratification of the Equal Rights Amendment, the Freedom of Choice Movement, and the election of women to public office. There was even a Lesbian Rights Action Committee. On top of all of these surprises, they invited me to speak and my angry leftist talk was well received. In just a matter of months, I was Vice President of the NOW chapter and up to my elbows in flyers, mailers, phone-trees and politics.

Through it all, there was Nancy. She was always beautiful, wearing a lovely outfit, high heels, and smelling of some expensive perfume. She was the last to arrive, but would always show up. She would have a hundred things to do but made sure that the labels were run, envelopes were sealed, and news was out that Ms. So-n-So was running in the 9th district. Nancy opened an entire world for me. Suddenly I saw that all women were sisters, even the pretty, high heeled, sweet smelling, red nailed ones. It brought millions of women into the fold for me.

The Passionate Heart

When I met Rama, I couldn't wait to tell Nancy. I knew that she would love him instantly. She walked into the meditation hall and gasped. She had been dreaming recently about a tall man with curly hair. It must have been Rama. She loved his tapes, his books, his talks. She applied to be a student and was accepted. Somehow in the midst of her already jam-packed daily planner, she made time to go to meetings. Nancy began to shine. Although she didn't have time to meditate every day, she did the best she could. She would often call me in the bookstore, swoon on and on about how her life was changing, and how much she loved meditation.

But then Rama began his militant discourses on closets. "To collect personal power you have to go through every aspect of your life and put them in order, one at a time," he explained. It was to be done in baby steps. Everything should be organized, taxes paid, health insurance in place, cars immaculately clean, cupboards in order, refrigerators arranged perfectly, but one thing at a time. Closets were first. "If you haven't used it in six months, you don't need it." "When in doubt, throw it out." "Get rid of the wire hangers and put everything on colorful plastic hangers facing the same direction." Rama went over the entire operation as if it was the most important thing in one's life, to bring order to the material plane; patiently, calmly, but ruthlessly.

At first, Nancy saw the wisdom in Rama's plan. She knew that all of the sentimentality, nostalgia, clutter, and chaos of her closet was a direct reflection of her mind. She was fully motivated to clean it up. Each week, the task dragged on. Each week, Nancy had not even approached her closet. Each week, Rama continued. He was definitely enjoying watching his students clean up their closets and clean up their minds. Nancy was spinning down in a sea of frustration knowing the significance of her avoidance. Finally, she left.

We remained friends. I wished her well in all of her work, and she in mine. Women all over the country would benefit from her counseling, her politics, her openness, her love for women. I moved on in my direction, with a perfect closet and a small start on ordering my mind. Rama went to the store and bought more yellow pads.

Chapter 7

In late winter, Rama invited his students to go to Fonts Point in the Anza-Borrego Desert in small groups divided by age. This was my chance to go without the concern that I would be unable to make the trek in. There would be no sprinting nineteen year olds leaping their way miles ahead of everyone else. My group would all be between the ages of thirty and forty-two. Naturally, I had several reservations, none of which deserved recognition. I arranged to drive with Janet and Penny. They were a few years older than myself and had a very nice car. It was going to be a long drive, five or six hours, and driving alone was discouraged.

For several months now, I had been experiencing the most peculiar condition with my back. Everyone had an opinion. Some said it was stress. One woman said it was my shampoo. The doctor said that it must be an allergy. After getting through thirty-four years of my life without a pimple or skin condition of any type, my back had broken out very severely. It had gone on for about two months before I found the humility to ask for help. Just the lightest shirt was painful to the touch.

One person I asked was a therapist whom I had been seeing from September to March. Going to a therapist was not something I would have done on my own, but upon my return from Illinois and the defeat of the ERA, many of the women in the community were worried about me. My plane hadn't been on the ground for three hours when my lover told me that, in my absence, she had been having an affair and would be leaving shortly. She also announced that since she had worked those seven weeks by herself, she was never going to step foot in the bookstore again. And so, on the very first morning back, after losing thirty-five pounds in just as many days, it was business as usual. In my imagination, I had thought I would be spending at least a week getting my strength together, both emotional and physical. No such luck.

Because things were not exactly picking up, a friend suggested that I see a particular therapist, Jane. I thought the entire idea was moronic. Therapists were people who had nothing better to do with their lives than play games with other peoples' lives, possibly more interesting lives at that. I was not crazy, I was not coo-coo; moreover, all I needed was equal rights for women, a couple of weeks of sensible eating, and I would be fine. The only significant thing I lacked was the energy to refuse going, oh yes, and the money to pay for such a service. My friend telephoned Jane, explained who I was, and my current financial situation. Jane offered to see me for free. There was nothing I could do now - but go.

Jane was the cutest woman I had ever seen. She was petite, funny, strong, fashionable, and a lesbian feminist. Her entire wardrobe was composed of complete Liz Claiborne outfits, down to the shoes and socks. If that wasn't enough, her specialty was developing methods to help sexually abused children talk about their most painful experiences. She had been called upon many times by the Orange and LA counties court systems to assist sexually abused children testify. I hated being the center of attention in her office, but loved seeing Jane.

Jane asked me why I disliked the idea of therapy so much. I admitted that I couldn't stand the notion of being so simple, so predictable as to be understood by some counselor. But Jane was not just some counselor. She was a feminist. She was political. She was articulate. She was complex and interesting. I liked her. I imagined that she liked me too. During the last fifteen minutes, Jane explained that I had every right to feel deeply defeated and that she would consider it a privilege to help me piece my life together. She would not think of me as a patient, but as a woman and a feminist whom she wanted to help. Jane waived her normal $75 an hour fee, set my appointment at the end of the day and asked only for the amount it cost to lease her office for an hour.

As the weeks progressed, never in my life had I known such an hour. It was an hour that was mine. I eventually stopped apologizing for talking about myself and accepted that it was okay to focus on me. Together we sifted and sorted through my life with respect, not judgment. Usually I had been afraid to tell someone about the circumstances of my life, believing them to be lofty, philosophical, intricate, and privileged. It was different with Jane. For several weeks, we dissected my obsessive dislike for my mother. I hated her. She was everything that I hated about upper-class women. She had a college degree and never worked outside her home a day in her life. Widowed at forty-five and a staunch Catholic, she felt she could not remarry. She was an alcoholic - possibly the only thing she ever did with total dedication. At age nine, I was a co-dependent.

Eventually, Jane said to me that I should squarely face that I was a victim of child neglect. Basically my parents had not participated in my life. She asked me if there was anyone in my childhood whom I had loved or who had loved me. It was good thing it was at the end of the hour because I was pissed. Never had I considered, nor would I consider that I would be so stereotypical, so cliché. I wanted to be eccentric, exceptional, much too complicated to fit into some national mental health category. The twenty minute drive home that night was painfully long. Jane was right. I grew up at eight years old. I was my Mom and Dad. Sometimes I was my Mom's mother.

I arrived at my apartment, parked the van, walked up the stairs and opened the door. Upon scanning my living room, I burst into tears. My apartment was a replica of Mary's tiny humble apartment. Mary was the housekeeper. Mary was tall, kind, and loved me. She made breakfast for me and when my dad sent me to bed without any dinner, Mary would sneak up the back stairs with a bowl of frosted flakes. Mary could sew. She had hand-made quilts and a collection of dolls. I thought of her as a single woman, although she had been divorced many years before she moved into my house. She took me to the Zoo, met me at the bus stop, ogled over my school work. She ironed perfectly and worked harder than anyone else I knew. She was poor and had tremendous heart. She was the first woman I loved. All of these years, I had unknowingly been fashioning my life after hers.

When I was fourteen, living at boarding school, my mother casually remarked over the phone, "Oh yes, I forgot to tell you, Mary died a couple of weeks ago." Of course, Mother was drunk, but regardless, she never cared how I felt about Mary. Mother never cared how I felt about many things. At the start of my sophomore year in college, my mother dropped me off and after she saw me hugging a black friend, she took me aside to tell me that I should never be friends with black people. I broke out laughing in her face and said that it was much too late for such a prescription. "You have to teach that before age five or six, Mom," I told her and walked away.

Week after week, Jane and I would stitch the patchwork of my life together. It was a search for truth and I liked that. In many ways it did set me free, free from shallowness and bullshit, both of which I detested fully.

Jane knew that I had applied and been accepted as a student of a spiritual Teacher. Sometimes I would tell her about the meetings or learning to meditate. She thought it was great. She could see that it was making me happy and supported my choice. Jane was raised Jewish, but had long since sorted out the wheat from the chaff. Being Jewish and a feminist aren't necessarily mutually exclusive, but it calls for a very compartmentalized mind. Better to pick one and go with it.

It had all been fitting together perfectly until March. I began to realize that to practice Self-Discovery meant to dissolve the self, and it appeared that on Tuesday evenings with Jane, I was gluing myself back together. I would see Rama, learn new ways to erase the past, and then spend an hour with Jane dredging it up again. Meditation was going into the light, to diminish the layers of conditioning, and therapy was beginning to look counter productive. Besides, the goal was to be happy, and Self-Discovery was clearly working for me. The only glitch in the system was that Rama was a man and, for some reason I had yet to figure out, it didn't seem to matter. I had to tell her.

Jane understood immediately. She said that she was about to suggest ending our Tuesday sessions. To my wild amazement, she then told me three things. One, she could not be friends with a client, but now that I was not her patient, could we be friends. Two, she never felt that I was really clinically ill and so she never kept any records of our visits. And three, would I take her to see Rama some time. Jane certainly understood. And so, when my back broke out so terribly, Jane was the first person I asked what it possibly could be. She sent me to a doctor who also was stumped. The desert trip was too important to miss so I wore a tee-shirt next to my skin and went anyway.

The drive was spectacular. Not being outdoorsy in any way, I had no idea what beautiful terrain was just a matter of hours outside of Orange County. We were to meet at Joshua Tree Park at 4:00 P.M. We left around 10:00 A.M. During those six hours there was a sense of actually leaving the city behind. All the people, the demands, the stress, the phones, the politics, even my city-self was left behind. Maybe it was like driving through a machine that peels away all the husk, the shell of a city-self. Upon arriving, the only thing left was an essential self who had fewer things in mind, fewer thoughts. Family, friends, worries, bills, responsibilities seemed to have stopped shouting and competing for attention. They were all very far away, much further than 250 miles.

Fifty or so people assembled in the parking lot. The sun was about an hour from setting. It was in the '40s, but it would certainly get colder as the night progressed. We brought sandwiches, flashlights, and drinks in our daypacks for a short hike in. Rama drove up around five o'clock. He parked the car and motioned for us to cross over the small fence surrounding the parking lot. We walked only a few yards when he directed us to sit on the rocks. He offered to answer questions. People asked about their lives in the city. They wanted to know about their jobs, relationships, personal power, etc.

Then, almost without my permission, my hand went up. He called on me with a nod. "Can we pretend that we are alone out here?" I asked. "Sure," he said. I told him that something terrible was happening to my back. I had seen several professionals about it and no one could offer me any help. I told him that the condition was so severe that most of the time it was open and bleeding. Rama began to explain. This was not unusual for someone who was just starting to meditate. It was the Kundalini. The energy that had been dormant in the base of my spine was now beginning to awaken. All the activity from the energy rising up my shashumna was significant enough to cause my back to break out. Rama then said not to worry about it, he would take care of it, and that it would be healed in a matter of a few days.

Rama talked for quite a while about what can happen when the Kundalini begins to rise. He joked about the strange siddha of being able to make women begin menstruating. Many times while meditating with Rama, women found that they started their period days before their cycle. When meditating in the presence of an Enlightened being, the force of the Kundalini is so strong that it can create a tangible physical effect. Sometimes people feel energy shooting right up their spine. They might find themselves involuntarily sitting up straighter, forced by the Kundalini itself. There may be a phase in which there is some discomfort. He advised that it was something that would pass and to try to sit very still and straight regardless of any minor physical aggravation. One of many reasons that Rama recommends martial arts to his students is to aid them in developing a strong body so that while going through the different states of meditation and beyond, they can sustain any physical changes that might occur.

Many other things happened to me on that, my first trip to the desert with Rama. Mostly I remember my embarrassment about asking such a personal question, Rama being so very kind in his answer, the affirmation that the Kundalini was beginning to awaken in me, and that in just one week, my back had begun to heal.

Chapter 8

The Beverly Theater, on Wilshire Boulevard, is a big, beautiful, velvety building where we met with Rama for several years. There were lots of performances each week: singers, bands, and virtuosos. Sometimes we could feel the residue of their vibrations when we first arrived. If there had been a hard rock group or some oldies group from the sixties, like the Temptations, performing the night before, it would leave a completely different feeling. But, mostly, we felt Rama.

Weekly meetings were scheduled for 7:30. Some students would be there early to get a seat in the front and others would filter in by 8:00 P.M. Rama would arrive as late as 9:00. At first, I wondered why he was coming so late. I wanted him to come earlier so the meeting could be longer. As my ability to see developed, I began to understand that Rama got there right on time, 7:30. His aura would fill the room long before his body arrived. It was a wave of clarity that would billow through the entire theater, clearing away all that had come before. We would sit quietly, reading or meditating, for an hour or so, just soaking in the clear light that Rama had sent in advance of his physical arrival. Eventually, it became visible to me. It was a brightness that had a current to it, like currents in the ocean. One time a woman in a San Francisco meeting said that she wished whoever was fooling around with lights would please stop. She complained that it was distracting her concentration. Of course, no one was "fooling" around with the lights, except Rama.

The registration process was simple. We have always gone by our first names. We would check in at a table, with our first names in alphabetical order, and that was that. It was particularly easy for me, for I have always been last on the list. There is something remarkable about finding your name on a list of students of an Enlightened Teacher. It is like being a student at a university and marveling at the alumni, only mine is the Tibetan lineage; Milarepa, Marpa, Naropa and Tilopa, as well as Yeshas and Vivekananda; better than *Who's Who in American Universities.* As Chuck said to me, "Any day your name is on the list is a good day." The staff was volunteer with the exception of one woman who took care of a tremendous amount of administrative duties and correspondence for

The Passionate Heart

Rama. Many of the tasks were done by students in rotation, to avoid any special attention.

Students brought flowers. There were dozens and dozens of flowers. We left them at the table upon our arrival. They were taken back stage and arranged by a woman who placed each and every vase in just the right configuration around Rama's couch, a six foot long dark blue floral couch. Much to my delight, Rama began playing classical music at the meetings: Vivaldi, Beethoven, Pachelbel, etc. There was lots of room at the Beverly, so we could take up as many seats as we wanted. The front row was always reserved for students who had birthdays that week. In the course of each meeting, Rama would give a special Darshan to those in the first row.

Week after week, I would get in my VW van and drive up the coast to the Beverly Theater knowing that I would change that night. Something would happen, something would be said, something would be discussed, and somehow I would change. Did it happen during the meditations? Was it a certain series of words that were spoken? I am not sure. The only sure thing was that I would change and I couldn't wait to see what the next change would be. It wasn't necessarily external, although there were many external changes taking place in my life. My clothes were becoming more graceful. I threw out my overalls and butchie stuff, and felt more comfortable in clothes that had more of an aesthetic. My language has always rivaled any truck driver, but I found that my vocabulary was noticeably expanding. Four letter words were not suffering the usual overuse. Housekeeping has always been natural to me, but I found myself wanting to make things more simple, more refined. The peripheral junk was either tossed or put away in a new preference for open, uncluttered spaces.

The internal changes were far more reaching. The anger was diminishing and there had been a lot of anger. I was carrying anger for every woman who had her feet bound, been infibulated, raped, beaten, enslaved, held in ignorance, or thrown herself in suttee. I had been a stick of dynamite, waiting for some unsuspecting man to say or do just one wrong thing to start me off, and ignite with my hate. But now I was finding that it wasn't hurting quite so much to be a woman. Rama loved women. Rama wanted every woman to succeed, not just to become better waitresses and nurses, but to become powerful, wealthy, respected people. Rama teaches that women are more powerful than men. They have an energy and a capacity for power that has been completely buried in centuries of conditioning and being beaten down. Rama is dedicated to the Enlightenment of women. He has a focus that no other Teacher has taken on, to see that more women attain Enlightenment. Some kind of magic was happening to me at the Beverly Theater and I just couldn't get enough. I was being healed, transformed, informed, educated, and most of all respected.

When Rama arrived, he always had something special to tell us. He had some wonderful idea that would enhance our lives, improve our meditation, or just lead to greater happiness. He was always optimistic, even, and joyous. He would make us laugh at ourselves, mimicking our self-pity in a ridiculous voice, "Awe, honey, life got ya down?" Or take off in an Irish brogue, as Father Murphy, telling us hilarious stories. One night he even sang a lullaby to us that he had learned from a yoga teacher. Walking down the aisle, finding the perfect seat for the evening, I never knew what mysterious and lovely thing was going to unfold. It was a secret world, a happy world, a beautiful world, a world of magic. There was so much to learn, to see, to marvel at.

During most meetings Rama would spend hours answering our questions. He was patient. He was funny. He was stern. He was always crystal clear and complete. Early in his life, he had been an English professor and his skill with the language and structures are articulate and exquisite. Sometimes one answer would fill an entire evening. It was always fascinating and as the weeks passed by, I began to realize that there was much more going on than some Socratic dialog of question and answer between teacher and student.

To raise a hand and ask a question may seem like a simple action, but to ask Rama a question and receive an answer is as complex as any interaction in the universe could ever be. Both parties have spent lifetimes preparing for that one moment. The questioner has worked hard to reach the point in their life when they can absorb the answer, or they would not be finding themselves asking the question at all. Many students would say that they have had a particular question brewing inside for months before actually putting up their hand. It may seem as if they are trying to form words or find the perfect way to say something, but really they are waiting until they can accept or incorporate the answer into their life. That is the way that an esoteric Teacher teaches their students. It is not simply words, but a transferring of knowledge. The student prepares and when they are ready, the Teacher gives them more than a verbal answer; he gives them an understanding.

Asking a psychic person a question can lead to some surprises! A student may believe that they are asking one thing, when in fact, what they really want to know is something quite different. Even though they have taken great care to cover the underlying truth of their inquiry, Rama has no trouble seeing directly to the essence of their question. They may use certain words, but whatever it is that they are really wondering about, Rama can see it immediately. Rama may choose to not address it at all or he may go straight to the center, depending on the specific situation. Either way, it is the outcome of his psychic vision, his ability to "see." Even in deciding which student to call on, Rama can look and determine who is the correct one at that very moment. Many times I have put up my hand and not been called on. And yet, one time I got called on when I hadn't put up my hand at all. He knew that I had something to say that was appropriate for that split second, even if I didn't.

Many times I have heard the identical question asked by two different students and heard Rama answer in two entirely different ways. It is because of the attention and attitude of the students. If a student is being snide or curt, Rama will answer in such a way to reflect it back. If the student is sincere, no matter how silly the question may sound, Rama is respectful. It was always fun to listen to the tone of Rama's answer and get a glimpse of the attention level of the student. Once I heard a student ask how to get to the desert for a certain trip. Rama said, "Go to San Diego and turn left." Obviously the student knew exactly how to get there; they simply wanted attention from Rama.

There are so many components worth noticing; the person called on, their question, the tone of their question, the content of Rama's answer, the way in which he answers it. Nothing is insignificant. Why am I there? Why am I hearing this question and answer? How does this relate to my life? Many times when I put up my hand and not gotten called on, another person would ask the very same question I had. As much as we each struggled to be unique, many of us were going through similar lessons at the same time - passages on the path of Self-Discovery.

One very special night, Rama had been discussing the intrinsic natures of men and women. "It is the Kali Yuga and everything is reversed," he told us. "The roles we find ourselves in now are actually the opposite of our true natures. The truth is that women are more powerful by nature and men are the ones who are gentle and inclined towards service." A student asked Rama who would be appropriate role models for men and for women. Rama thought about it for an unusually long time. First he answered about men, "The proper role model for men is Mahatma Gandhi." Gandhi changed an entire nation of millions of people through peaceful non-cooperation. He was not violent. He used patience and wisdom to create change for all of India. Men, he explained, could look to Gandhi as an example of their true nature.

Gandhi had been my primary, my principle inspiration for the previous ten years. At one point in my life, I attempted to read every word published in English about my beloved Gandhiji. I wrote to the library of Congress to get copies of the newspaper that were published at his ashram. I studied everything I could about ahimsa, the adherence to truth. He died on January 28, 1948, just eight months before I was born, and I fantasized that maybe I had known him in my most recent incarnation. I loved him.

He was the inspiration for my fast. He was my political hero. He was warm, human, and yet, completely effective in bringing his principles of satyagraha to millions of people regardless of their religious preferences or gender. Although it was thought to be scandalous for simple village women to partake in politics, Gandhi insisted that they should be able to participate in the anti-British protests. There are stories that

The Passionate Heart

at Gandhi's request, older women, who had never left their homes before, would be taken to sit outside shops, holding placards, to protest the selling of British goods. Gandhi was effective because he loved God and loved both Muslim and Hindu alike. He simply refused to participate in bigotry and discrimination. His determination, patience, and faith in the truth were felt by all of India. His spinning wheel, his dodhi, his pocket watch, I studied them all. I loved him.

Kastarbai, Miraban, Patel, Nehru were like family members to me. I think my Wisconsin family must have found it most peculiar that I could flip into an East Indian accent and speak almost more easily than with their mid-western twang. I found it odd too. It was as if I knew him. Gandhi was a complicated man. He was not without contradictions. I can't forgive him for teaching that rape is a woman's karma. But somehow, his zeal to have women learn to read, to abolish suttee, and his respect for women in politics is too much to dismiss. *My Experiments with Truth* was his apology and I thank him for being so humble as to share his internal struggles with all the world.

The most wonderful part about Gandhi is all the contradictions that surround him. Although British educated and a barrister, he lived like an Indian villager. He was a strict dietitian, but allowed others in his ashram to indulge in their own culinary customs. He was militantly gentle. He let the whole world inside his conscience, regardless of any loss of face to himself. One hundred years after his arrest in South Africa, apartheid continues. In Pakistan and India there is still bloodshed. But Gandhi changed. He let all of us scrutinize his heart, his internal struggle, so that we could learn. He taught me that one does what they can for the world through politics, but the real revolution is always internal.

What an amazing world it would be if all men were like Mahatma Gandhi! I simply could not imagine how it would feel to walk safely through American streets. We would have no women's shelters. There would be no need for a women's movement. To hear my Teacher say that Gandhi was the appropriate role model for men's true nature made my heart want to burst.

Then it came time for Rama to say who the correct role model is for women. I held my breath. Who could it possibly be? I have searched everywhere that I could think of. There is no one. St. Joan is hardly Everywoman. Cleopatra is too lofty for anyone I know. Grace Kelly is a fantasy. Cher is not embracing menopause as a symbol of personal power. Mother Theresa is setting birth control back two hundred years for the women of India. Whom are we given to pick from? Betty Crocker, Margaret Anderson, Madonna? We are either sluts or saints, moms or failures, or at best exceptions. There is no woman to look at who is her own source of power.

Rama took an extraordinarily long time to answer. He closed his eyes and went very far away. It felt as if he was scanning through the last few centuries, the ones his students could consciously reference, as if they were pages in a book. As long as I live, I will never forget his answer. He paused, opened his eyes, and said, "I know that some of you will find this very hard to accept, but there is no one. There is no woman you can reference this way, as the men can Gandhi." He went on, "The only person you can use to exemplify a being accessing power, as fully as women are meant to, is me."

The Passionate Heart

Chapter 9

It had been five months since I walked in to that first Lakshmi meeting. What was happening to me? Looking in the mirror, there was no resemblance to the Zoe who first sat at the Sheraton Miramar. I began wearing dresses almost everyday. I shaved my legs. My duck shoes had been retired. Most of all, there was a smile on my face and I wasn't searching for the next, nearest reason to be angry. Everyday I sat and meditated for twenty minutes. Everyday I was becoming someone else.

The women in my social and political circles were confused about what was happening to me. They couldn't equate my newly acquired calm with anything external. I believe that in some ways they were relieved to find that I was easier to be with, less argumentative, but there were a few who thought that I was selling out. They didn't have the nerve to confront me, but I felt their disappointment. My guess is that they were allowing me whatever latitude I needed to recover from the fast and the defeat of the ERA. 1983 was a very difficult year for American political feminists. Burnout was wide-spread. Although during the campaign we had warned politicians that we would not forget their opposition on election day, the reality was that many women had already forgotten. We had to go on with our lives, regardless of unequal pay, unjust insurance regulations, inadequate child care, and diminishing public health programs. Maybe it was just best to let it go for a while.

Internally, I was going through a new struggle. Was it okay that I was getting happier and more at peace with life? Was meditation taking me anywhere in which I could be of some service to my sisters or was it just for me? I vacillated on an hourly basis from the feeling that this was all very selfish, to loving it so much that I simply didn't care. No matter what I heard in the news or read in the paper, all I really knew was that I couldn't wait to see Rama again.

Most of what Rama had to say felt like home to me. I would hear his words and within me there was a simple, quiet internal nod. He was right. It was not an issue. "There is no sin. There is only smart and stupid." I felt that when I was seven and forced into line at the confessional. "Life is eternal and there is no death." I remembered other places, other times as if they were part of one single multi-life expression. Rama brought together all the religions, all the gods and goddesses, all the customs and rites I had been sorting and sifting through for years, and offered one resounding "yes" to them all.

What could I do that he was a man? No matter how much I disliked the situation, it was something I could not change. He had information. He had power. He had access to worlds that I had to find. Even though Rama was male, he was not withholding because I was a woman. On the contrary, he was very forthright that his primary focus, in the current incarnation, was the Enlightenment of women. I often wondered if the men in the group resented Rama's position. Being humans, I would venture that some of them did, but the directive was very clear, very precise; there would be no sexism in the group and if Rama detected sexism coming from any of his students, they would immediately be shown the door. "Now, you can't ask for more than that," I told myself.

Still, this was a twist I had never anticipated. I had not been looking for a teacher. I was not looking for someone to appear with the answers. I had insisted that the answers were buried inside and through self-will, hit-or-miss, and refusal to assimilate, something would eventually happen. Since reincarnation was a given, all one had to do was keep growing. That was the essence of my lectures over the last few years. It was mathematical: grow up, toward the light, and evolution was unavoidable. Of course the talks were heavily peppered with pointed statements that since the oppressors were pushing down, away from the light, they were devolving.

As my luck would have it, I stumbled on to a Teacher who has what I need and who happens to be male. God must have a sense of humor that breaks all boundaries. But, Rama was not without compassion about this mind-boggling conundrum for his feminist students. I had heard that sometimes students would see different manifestations of Rama sitting on the couch in the front of the theater. One night, in the meditation hall, I looked up and there sitting on the couch was a woman. She was from another time, maybe even another world. But clearly this manifestation of my Enlightened

The Passionate Heart

Teacher was a woman. She had dark brown hair and some type of hat that I had never seen before. She was young and radiant with ruby red lips. I saw her off and on for two years. Over time I heard many of the other feminist students describe this female figure and we were all seeing the same person.

Rama had spent thousands of lifetimes learning to meditate, dissolving the self, and going through the Enlightenment process. The different figures we would see on the stage or in the desert were actually previous incarnations of Rama. This woman we were seeing was a manifestation of one of his lifetimes as a woman. Rama had spent so many lifetimes meditating and practicing Self-Discovery; he was no longer held within the boundaries of gender. He was neither male nor female. In Taoist terms he was both. I remember a black student once commented in a meeting that through meditation, he had found a state that was beyond the confines of race. He said that he found a place inside that wasn't held down by the definitions of being black. He had discovered a self that had no race. He was definitely practicing Self-Discovery.

Even in the world of Buddhism, Rama's dedication to the Enlightenment of women is unprecedented. Buddha did initiate his mother, but it was not without extenuating circumstances. She, and her sister nuns, had to remain in a diminished position. They were not allowed full access to the teachings nor to the men's meditation hall. The only fully Enlightened woman I could find anything written about was Yeshas. She was a student of Padmasambhava, the great Tibetan Master. Ramakrishna, a famous Enlightened Hindu Teacher, married. His wife, Sarada Devi, was honored as an advanced soul, but she too was separated from the monks. She lived in an adjacent building, cooked for her husband, and saw him primarily when serving him meals.

Rama had something entirely different in mind for his students. He wanted to change things at the very core. He insisted that all of his female students advance as far as possible: find their own power, become physically self-sufficient, learn martial arts reducing the chances of victimization and abuse, destroy all oppressive conditioning, and realize their intrinsic natural power. He was not going to be satisfied with mere economic solvency. He wanted these women to become corporate leaders, business owners, brilliant minds, and take their Enlightenment as far as possible. Rama wanted this for all of his students, but to want it for women was, and is, revolutionary. He was totally candid about it and if anyone stood in the way, they would be removed. As I heard him say, "I am right and the world is wrong."

Rama explained that the primary way women lose power is through relationships. Men had been wise to the system for centuries. A man finds a woman with energy and simply uses her up. She dedicates her life to a man, bears children, raises a family, and by the time she is thirty, her subtle body is so damaged that she is unable to reach clear or meditative states of mind. Then, when she loses her beauty and vitality, the man discards her for another woman with more energy. Men actually stay younger and more powerful through siphoning energy from women. It made perfect sense to me. I always wondered why men didn't seem to age as quickly as women, or why older men could be with significantly younger women in this culture, while for women the reverse was not acceptable. Many men in their sixties, with successful careers, mated with a consecutive series of women of decreasing age. Often these men started a second family when their children, by a previous wife, were adults themselves. I had noticed that some men seemed to find a new young wife just as they were making a significant career jump or winning a financial victory. The fact is that women were not using their own power for their own advancement, but rather for the advancement of men.

It was never suggested to us that we should stop having relationships. It was made clear that men and women alike should be aware of the exchange that happens in a relationship. When two people meet, someone leaves with more energy and someone leaves with less. It is true of all transactions: families, lovers, friends, teachers, even passing ones in the subway or grocery store. It is the way that all creatures on earth interact. It is natural and nothing to be afraid of, but it should be understood and dealt with intelligently. A relationship should be a conscious choice. Most people don't even consider it an option. Like office Christmas presents, most relationships are obligations.

The Passionate Heart

Rama wanted us to realize that, in the practice of Self-Discovery, understanding the mechanics of energy is essential because the amount of energy a person has affects every aspect of their life. As teenagers, we may feel that there is an unlimited supply, but that feeling doesn't last long. Somewhere in their twenties, women know things have radically changed. Their bodies have lost the battle against aging before they even know that it began. Somewhere between the Prom and the daycare carpool, life took an unexpected and irreversible turn. Cosmetic companies and plastic surgeons may be making a fortune on it, but by thirty-five, Victoria's secret is not a mystery anymore. Garter belts and push-up bras cannot compete with youth.

For the most part women spend their energy simply trying to go along with the program. They use it to attract and sustain a relationship. Had the exchange rate been on equal terms, both parties would not have ended up so out of balance with one another. Who is to blame when a younger and more energetic woman catches a man's eye? She too was only acting out what she had been taught since preschool, that the quality of a woman's survival is in direct ratio to the power level of the men in her life. Ask any First Lady.

Rama began teaching us about a world that goes beyond the physical. He described it as the subtle physical world. Besides our physical bodies, each of us has a subtle physical body. It is an intricate network of vibrating light that is just a little bit larger than, and extends a bit beyond, the physical body. There is light flowing throughout this subtle physical body known as kundalini. When a healthy baby is born, their subtle body is in perfect condition. Kundalini is circulating freely throughout their entire subtle body without any obstructions, the network is intact, and they literally glow. It is similar to having healthy blood and clear, strong arteries. Just as the physical body can be hurt, the subtle body can be damaged. When it is hurt, kundalini cannot flow evenly. An obstruction or a "hole," in the subtle body inhibits the flow of kundalini and often manifests in the physical. In other words, the condition of a subtle body dictates the condition of the physical body. Disease, cancer, old age, even beauty or vitality are reflections of the subtle body's condition. An amputee's subtle body can be completely intact. He or she may speak of being able to still feel their missing limb, but damage to a subtle body will eventually show up in the physical.

Subtle bodies are affected by vibrations. It could be vibrations in the land, vibrations of other subtle bodies, vibrations of thoughts. The quality of the vibration, as it meets a subtle body, can be neutral, constructive, or destructive. Thoughts of encouragement or respect can aid a person, actually lift them up. Driving through a depressed area can make the driver feel despair. After talking with someone who is toxic, a person can feel out of balance. If a subtle body is constantly pelted with negativity, it will eventually wear down. A person with a damaged subtle body will not be able to collect or store the kundalini necessary to advance or even sustain their life. That is what eventually brings death; the subtle body is unable to conduct kundalini. Kundalini is life.

In this culture and age, we are continually living in vibrations of aggression, violence, and hate. All of us are battling for our lives in this sea of negativity. The distinct advantage men have is that they have developed a system, a culture that provides them with a renewed source of kundalini, the oppression and ownership of women. Women are held down, held away, held from their own advancement. Through the learned skills of service and subservience, women give their very life force away. Women are taught to believe that they will be loved and valued if they devalue their own life.

As a boy or girl travels along, they are bombarded with the thoughts and impressions of everyone they meet. Even before being able to speak, so much is understood and *felt*. Boys should go play and not come back until the game is won. Girls should stay near the backdoor, within mom or dad's view and, most of all, come right home if there is any trouble. As Barbie said, "Math class is hard." Toy stores are filled with dolls who eat, spit-up, dirty their diapers, require potty training, cry, have their own babies, and whose sole purpose is to make abundantly clear what girls are for. Rama wanted us to know that all of this could be changed. Our conditioning, no matter how ingrained, could be uprooted through meditation. By stopping thought and going into the light everyday, a woman can shed the layers upon layers of lies that shroud her advancement.

The Passionate Heart

Rama talked for weeks, for hundreds of hours, teaching us that no one was going to win in this familiar and culturally accepted cycle of men oppressing women. Rama was not going to participate in any tradition of teaching men to meditate and confining women to the ashram kitchen. He wanted success for all of his students. It was going to take a lot energy for each of us to meditate well, to still the mind, and to move into progressive levels of attention. If we want to stop our thoughts, we would have to reject everything society taught us about men and women. We would have to interact with each other with awareness and equanimity. Oppressing anyone would extinguish the entire process. Men and women would be equal in his community. They would have equal chances to advance. They would be treated equally in all tasks. Women and men would learn martial arts, mysticism, occultism, and to meditate. Enlightenment equally beckons us all.

Chapter 10

A two foot long braid was not politically correct in the '70s. Some lesbians made fun of mine occasionally, saying that I was a "femme." There may have been a few couples playing out the stereotypic roles of butch and femme but, by the mid-'60s, those terms were said mostly in jest. I did look different from the majority of women-identified-women though. I never liked the barber shop haircuts that some women wore. They looked like men's haircuts to me. As Gandhi told the young men of India, it is wrong to adopt the worst of the oppressors; such as British suits, affectations and classicism. Likewise, women looking like men seemed a contradiction to me. I hated short hair on my lovers and on myself.

I usually wore my exceptionally long braid with a bow. This was not a rebellion against mimicking men. It was because I hated the idea of having someone wash and cut my hair. Nothing could make me more uncomfortable than being fussed over. I shuddered when anyone said, "Oh, let me see; turn around." With the exception of a lover, I couldn't stand being touched so I never had my nails done, my hair professionally cut, or anything that required being touched by strangers. This phenomenon was not a mystery to me. It was the outcome of two very specific incidents. When I was three years old, my sixteen-year-old sister died of Lupus. It must have deeply affected my father because from that time on he never touched me: no more hugs, no more kisses, no more piggy-back rides. Second was the horror of unwrapping a dozen Christmas presents every year with my mother insisting that they will fit. I knew that they wouldn't fit before I opened the box, let alone after seeing the size on the label. But, nonetheless, mother would demand that I try each item on. As I crawled from the bathroom, unable to button or zip, my mother started with tears and shortly moved to yelling that she couldn't believe I was so fat. The conclusion was clear - anyone who touched me would have to be significantly repulsed.

For some unknown reason my braid and long hair had begun to bother me. It could have been because Rama was teaching us that to break through ideas of who we are, it is essential to change things around. Habits and routines hold us in a single point of view, he explained. Meditation would make it easier to change, but we had to let go of the images of who we are and who we are not. The goal was not to become someone else, but to become fluid. Rama wanted us to be able to traverse our lives without being stuck on one "self." We should always be polite, with impeccable etiquette, but let go of any notion or script about who we should be. If we were going to rise above our conditioning and realize our intrinsic power, we would have to discard the definitions our parents and teachers so vehemently and relentlessly pushed on us.

Rama taught that both men and women have been convinced that they are certain specific people. Even if a man or woman has escaped the strangle-hold of parental or social expectation by becoming a rebel, it is still a reaction to another person or persons. The result is that an individual gets caught in a web of belief designed by others that dictates who they should be or have to be. Then, when life presents circumstances that require some different type of person, they are immediately disqualified. If a girl has been taught that she cannot and will not ever understand accounting, she will be lost in banking, business, and taxes. If a man has been taught that he must be aggressive to succeed, he will be missing the skills of diplomacy, tact, and patience. If a man or a woman is taught that women should not reach top executive positions, both genders carry out the lie. Rama wanted us to break through the confining boundaries of social, parental, and peer pressure so we would have a complete array of possibilities and skills. He wanted us to live our lives with confidence, ease, and control, no matter what circumstances life should present to us. Since Rama always recommended that things be done in baby steps, he suggested we begin unraveling our ideas of who we are by examining simple things like preferences about appearances, tastes in colors, or beliefs in personal limitations. Rama explained that we should buy something we thought we would never wear. Rearrange our furniture. Conquer a subject that we were convinced we could never do. Shake it up.

After surveying my life, I felt that one thing that would radically change my self image would be to cut and perm my hair, but how would I ever be able to do such a thing? I had been wearing it that way since I walked out of my parents home fourteen years ago. Everyone knew Zoe had a braid. It was *me*. Furthermore, how could I let someone cut my hair? They would have to do a lot more than just touch me. There was a man whom I had met in the bookstore, Adam. He was a nice guy who didn't seem to be on a macho jag. He was a hair stylist, a Cancer, and very gentle, so I decided to broach the subject with him. I had many conditions. First, it had to be off-hours so no one else would be around. Second, if I freaked out, he would stop and let me regroup. Third, we would agree on what was to be done. The day and time were set.

Friday night I went to his shop. We played music and plotted my new do. I closed my eyes and said, okay, let's go. In one fell swoop Adam took hold of my braid and gave it a samurai whack. No longer attached to my head, he placed it in my hands. There was no turning back. I squirmed inside, yet held as still as possible, while he wrapped little swatches of my hair in papers and turned them around plastic pink curlers. Occasionally, accidentally, I caught glimpses of myself in the huge mirrors and thought I looked ridiculous. As Adam saturated each and every wand with some magic potion, it was cold and ran down my neck. I didn't move. I hated it. It began to burn. I hated it. Thank God, in twenty minutes, it was time to wash the potion out.

Who was this woman in the mirror? Who was this person with layered curly hair? I had no idea. I would have to meet her from scratch. I didn't know how the world would treat her. Would they laugh? Would they gasp? I giggled. I blushed. I felt as if my insides and my outsides would have to get used to each other all over again. I looked softer. I looked different. Did I look silly? Without seeing anyone else, I drove home and went to bed. In the morning I got up, took a shower, and washed this strange new hair that was living on my head. Later that day I needed to go to a department store for a few things. It was spring and warm out. So, for the first time in fourteen years, I left the car window open without concern for unraveling my braid. My hair was blowing around. The sensation was totally foreign to me. There was no braid, no barrette, no bow holding it all in place. It wasn't plastered against my head. It was flying in the wind. It was tickling my face and swept across my eyes. I was enjoying even the tiniest movement. When I walked into this very upscale department store, breezing past the counters as usual, I heard a woman from the cosmetic department call out, "Can I help you with anything?" I couldn't believe my ears. Never before in my thirty-four years had a woman from a cosmetic counter asked if I wanted help. Much to my surprise I liked it.

I had changed. My outsides had been changed and, in doing so, my insides were finding themselves on an entirely new adventure. People, who in the past had nothing to say to me, were suddenly engaging me. It went beyond the woman at the cosmetic counter. Customers, salespeople, just people on the street were sending me entirely different thoughts. It wasn't that the "vibes" were of one nature or another. It wasn't that they thought well or poorly of me. It was that I was having a totally different life experience. I may still have been Zoe, but now I wasn't so sure that the Zoe I had been defining was quite so solid. Maybe someone thought I looked more feminine or more approachable or less socially rebellious, but none of that was the point. It was that there had been a deep and significant change that was requiring me to completely reevaluate my relationship with the world and myself. Until that time I had been convinced that I was someone in particular and the maintenance of that someone was my responsibility. Now it was dawning on me that this had all been an option, either conscious or unconscious. As a person seeking self-determination and liberation, I wanted all of my choices to be conscious. So, scary as it would be, I now would have to discard and acquire, adopt and reject everything in my life, in one big experiment, until I could discover who ultimately would be left.

On the heels of this astounding revelation, how could I resist going on the next desert trip? Rama announced that all of his students were invited to a trip to the Anza Borrego desert. It would be a hike, as always, and if one could not easily make the distance they should not go. I didn't care this time. I would have to force myself and simply find the endurance. I took my van filled with six girls and drove the five hours winding through the curving canyons. Patty drove part of the time and as I told her, "Those yellow signs with speed limits for the curves actually applied to the van, we could easily slip off the road." She doubted me only once.

I had packed sandwiches and boxed juices. I had my flashlight and waterproof poncho. I carried a backpack and attached a sleeping bag for a comfortable seat. Although I was nervous beyond comprehension, I was on my way. We arrived about 5 P. M. and the sun was close to setting. After parking the car, we checked in with a designated administrator who marked off names on a list. Then we walked a few hundred feet into the area and sat waiting quietly. The great outdoors was never particularly great to me. My idea of a vacation was a cozy hotel in a cute shopping area. Once my husband had taken me camping and after four days drove me straight home because I could not last another instant without a shower. Now I was sitting in the middle of a desert with sand, cactus, hills, and nothing else. It was knocking me out.

In about two hours, Rama arrived. He drove his bronco onto the sand and got out. He had on the most beautiful running outfit. He talked to us for an hour or so before the hike began. It was explained that we would walk for several miles and then sit for a while. We might hike in even further after the rest. People should walk in twos and there was no need to race. Be quiet and talk only if necessary. Use flashlights only when absolutely necessary. This was to be one very long meditation. All of a sudden, with Rama at the helm, eight hundred people got up and took off for the unknown. It felt like a stampede. I was horrified. I would never be able to keep up. The sand was dry and soft. My feet were sliding and slipping with each step requiring total effort.

After a mile, which seemed to be ten, I became obsessed with the situation. I could think of nothing else but how would I make the next step. I fell back to the end of the pack and watched the distance between me and the others begin to grow. A student was driving the bronco at the end of the parade, but it had been made very clear that it was not there to give wimps a lift. There were two students who were doctors and they would help in the case of an emergency, but I did not want to be an emergency. I was panicking and resorted to the only thing I could think of - Broadway musicals. Ridiculous as it was, the only thing I could come up with to still my mind was to sing Broadway musicals to myself. They had to be complete lyrics, no humming, and in the order of the performance. I began with South Pacific, moved to The Sound

of Music, on to Cats, Peter Pan, West Side Story, My Fair
Lady...

I was not speeding up. The others were pulling away. The
bushes were still trying to trip me. But I stopped thinking that
I was going to die. If Rama was reading my mind, he must
have thought that I was coo-coo singing musicals in the
desert, but I didn't care. I was on survival mode. The songs
were occasionally interrupted with emotional prayers asking
God to please place the group just over the next bend. Finally,
after what could have been two hours, I saw Rama's flashlight
signaling students to sit in a semi-circle around him. Thank
you, God.

Much to my great surprise and delight, I was not the last
person to arrive at the circle. There were four or five other
stragglers who helped me avert total shame. I found a place to
nest, way in the back. Before unrolling my sleeping bag, I
checked for snakes with my flashlight, as had been
recommended. People were shuffling and shifting to find the
ideal spot. After a few minutes, Rama said to get settled for he
was going to start soon. The men and women around me took
positions. It was positively amazing. They were sitting
perfectly straight and still. They never seemed to move a
muscle or cause a noise of any kind. Within ten minutes, my
legs were screaming, but it was obvious that to budge would
be a serious breach of etiquette.

Finding my will, I stopped listening to my body with all of its
demands and looked up. Never in my life had I seen such
stars. It wasn't like a string of twinkling lights on a Christmas
tree. It wasn't even like a hundred strings of lights. It was as
if a great paint brush had swept across the black sky a dozen
times leaving streams and streaks of varying light. It was the
sky Van Gogh must have wanted us to see in *Starry Night*. It
was massive and engulfing. I felt minuscule and wondrous. I
felt that the stars were alive and looking at us, amused at how
puny and ignorant we are. They seemed to be creatures of
such grandeur that to stare at them was a privilege. They
didn't merely twinkle; they were bursting with energy. The city
lights that normally drown them from view now seemed to
have been an insult. I felt apologetic.

It was quite chilly out in the middle of the desert regardless of it being April. Even if it was forty degrees, to sit there totally exposed, it felt colder than any city April night. Weather was in control, not glass or concrete or wood. There was no breeze; it was still and crisp. There I sat somewhere between the earth and the stars with weather all around. To a homebody, library-bound, city girl, it was breathtaking. Nothing was familiar, not my posture, not my shoes, not the company, not the terrain, nothing. Rama asked if we were cold. Many answered yes. He said that he would fix it. He lifted his arms high into the sky and made an eerie whistling noise. I listened with total focus. Suddenly I realized that there was a sunny warm wind blowing across my face. It was a sweet gentle wind that carried comfort and tenderness. The more I concentrated on it, the more it enveloped me. Then I noticed that my short hair was sweeping all around my head. There was a seventy degrees breeze combing through my salt and pepper curls. It was tickling my nose and brushing my cheeks. This was a magical wind ruffling my hair, performing at Rama's request. Surely cutting my hair was one of the best ideas I had ever had.

Chapter 11

The distance between Newport Beach and the Anza Borrego desert cannot be measured in miles. I know that I was sitting on sand, surrounded by hills, bathed in starlight, but who was sitting there? Eight hundred people and their Teacher hiked several miles in the dark of night to sit and meditate. I saw people walk in, but who or what had they become? All the imprints, the conditions, the definitions of civilization were very far away. We had left the man-made earth and were a community of beings floating outside words, structures, or references. It felt as if all the forms that I had adopted, melted away. No one had control over who I was, not even me.

The semi-circle around Rama was quite big and four or five people deep. For several hours, Rama told us to watch him and then he would call on us to describe what we had seen. Rama stopped every twenty feet and said, "Now, watch." I could hear the sand beneath his feet as he moved to the front of each section. It may have taken him an hour to make it once around the entire area. Students would call out, "Rama?" Upon hearing him say yes, they would explain in detail what they had seen. I could easily hear the responses coming from my immediate right or left. When he was further around the circle, I could not make out what the students were saying at all.

When Rama stood in front of my section I could see him spin and turn. He would lift his arms over his head, direct his hands up to the sky, and sweep his palms from one side to another. He slowly walked back and forth, fifteen feet in either direction. Every now and then he would make great whooshing noises or strange hollow whistling sounds. I watched every move, every motion, hoping to "see" something.

Students said that they saw Rama disappear. He grew hundreds of feet in the air and back again. He opened up other dimensions. We all went to another world. He moved the stars. He leapt to the moon and back. Some saw the stars all swirl around the moon. Others saw the moon move from one side of the sky to the other. Rama would laugh, "Oh you saw that, good." It was obvious that he enjoyed what he was doing. The desert was his favorite place and he was giving us the grand tour. Each person who spoke had seen a miracle. Some had seen them all. Many times students said that they had seen something and not understood it until they heard it described by someone else.

Rama offered to answer some questions. There were long intervals when he was talking on the other side of the circle and I could not hear any of the exchanges. After thirty minutes or so, he worked his way over to my area. Just a few feet on my right, a woman called out, "Rama?" Walking towards her, he answered, "Yes?" She asked him if there really was a man in the moon. Rama stopped everything. He sat down next to her, wrapped his arms around his knees and starred up at the moon with her. He was talking as if they were the only two people in the world and he was sharing a sweet secret. "It isn't exactly a man," he said. "Everything in the universe has a consciousness; the planets, the stars, the earth." He sat and chit-chatted about the moon for almost ten minutes. I couldn't hear all the conversation, but it was clear that Rama and the moon were friends.

As I listened to the fantastic stories about what people were seeing, I was finding it impossible to squash my desire to see. I didn't doubt that every word I heard was true, I just wanted to see too. Rama had given us some reasons why one would not be able to see and I certainly fit into any of the categories. I was filled to the brim with social conditioning. I had only been a student for five months. I did have a lot of trouble letting go. But all the reasons in the world could not stop me from calling out his name, "Rama?"

"Yes?" he replied. "I can't see any of the things the others are talking about," I blurted out. Rama turned and walked straight towards me. "Because you think this is all a movie. You think that you are separate from what is going on here," he said crisply. I wanted to disappear into the sand. I felt that he was not happy with my question. I wished I had never spoken up. He went on, "As long as you are separate from the experience, you will never be able see what is actually happening. It is time you went swimming." He turned and walked away. Looking over his right shoulder he continued, "Laps!"

The Passionate Heart

What could he have meant? No matter what else was going on, all I could think about was what did he mean about swimming -- laps. Did he mean that I should consider all the desert part of one big ocean? Did he mean that I had to "flow" with what was happening around me? The only thing I was sure about was that it was terribly metaphysical and mysterious, a koan. He was much too intense to speak literally. I was much too sincere about wanting to have psychic vision for him to deliver a worldly answer like literally swimming.

The rest of the night and the entire hike out, all I could think about was how sorry I was that I opened my big mouth. If I couldn't see, I should have simply accepted it and waited. I should have not complained to him, particularly in the desert. The hike out was long and I drifted to the rear, away from the crowd, but I had a new obsession to focus on -- swimming. When I reached the road and navigated to the car, it must have been 4 A.M. I met up with the other women who rode in my van and after shaking pounds of sand from our shoes, we drove off for civilization.

All of us were more hungry than ever before in our lives. We ate everything we had packed for the trip and counted the miles to reach a store of any kind. The sun was coming up by the time we got to the freeway and a few San Diegons were already on their way to work. It all looked rather strange. The huge green freeway signs, the billboards, the gas stations, the golden arches, all looked fake and flat. What did these people know of miracles? Would they believe that we had seen and felt miracles? What would they think of us if we told them that we went to the desert and saw stars move, people disappear, and felt a summer wind come right up the center of the gorge? We were different now. We were witnesses of the impossible. Actually, nothing was impossible now.

When I got home, I took out the dog, fed the cat, got into bed, and knew that my whole world had changed. Now there was a deep and nagging conflict between the world of the desert and the world I live in. I was Zoe, the bookstore owner. Everybody in my neighborhood knew me. Hundreds of women knew me. I may have cut my hair and started wearing dresses, but now it wasn't enough. My insides had radically changed and I wanted to reconcile the outside to match. I fell asleep as the noon sun shone brightly on my bed knowing that I had become someone entirely different.

After several hours, I woke up and saw only one course of action. I had to sell the bookstore. If I kept it, I would never change. It had been seven years, almost to the day and I knew exactly what I was going to do every day, every season. In July, I bought Christmas. In August, I bought calendars. In October, I bought valentines. In January, I put everything on half price. I was carrying out the Hallmark dream, just a few months ahead of everybody else. People came in and knew that I would be there, ready to blather about this or that. The Magic Speller and I had become one and the same and one of us had to go.

There was a woman who was very intent on buying the store. She would ooh and ah about how much she wanted a bookstore just like the Magic Speller. I called her and offered to sell it to her for next to nothing. She immediately said yes. So, within twenty-four hours of hiking into the desert, I sold my beloved bookstore and all that it represented. It would be a total revolutionary change for me. I would have to find another kind of work, move to another apartment, and never buy wholesale again.

There was a Lakshmi meeting the following night at the Beverly Theater. I drove to LA in a bad mood. I was irritated about practically everything. I was uncomfortable inside of myself, like wearing clothes that didn't fit. I was agitated about something and not sure what. I got in line outside the theater, waiting for the doors to open, and found myself standing next to Chuck. "How was your desert trip?" he asked. "I hated it. I am angry about everything," I told him. "Oh, it must have been a really good trip," he retorted. Then he looked me in the eyes and asked, "So did you join a health club today?" "What do you mean?" "Well, I was sitting near you and heard Rama tell you to start swimming laps," Chuck offered. "That isn't what he meant at all, Chuck," I assured him. "He was speaking metaphysically. He certainly didn't mean anything so mundane as to actually swim laps." Chuck laughed and said, "Well, you can look at it anyway you like but the fact of the matter is that he told you to start swimming laps and you better get your ass to a health club."

The doors opened up and I made my way into the familiar theater. I was distressed and could hardly sit still. Chuck came over and sat next to me. He wanted me to know that sometimes when Rama sees us over a series of consecutive days, particularly when it includes a desert trip, it may create a sense of internal upheaval. "Rama opens you up, leaves you wide open during those days, and closes you back up on the last night," Chuck told me. "It is like having psychic surgery. He loosens up your bands of attention so that you can change." I did feel as if there was nothing holding me together, all of my comfortable boundaries had disappeared. I just didn't know how long I could survive like that. Chuck said, "Don't worry, he won't leave you that way."

But who was I? I wasn't a bookstore owner anymore. I wasn't a lesbian anymore. I wasn't a political activist anymore. Who the hell was I? Inside everything felt chaotic and I hated it. Rama walked out on stage and began to teach class. We meditated as always. Students talked about their experiences in the desert. It all seemed very normal to me. But I was completely different. As I drove home, I noticed that I wasn't a bundle of disorganization any more. I was happy and more importantly, I felt lighter. I felt as if layers of muck and confusion had been lifted off me. There were fewer thoughts inside my head. It wasn't a feeling of being stupid, dragged down, or drugged, but rather a sense of clarity, as if there was more room in my head. Some of the shouting about whom I should be had stopped. There were fewer do's and don'ts directing my thinking.

When I first began meditating, it seemed as if there was a great torrent of thoughts roaring through my head. I was astounded at all the incessant internal conversations. Rama explained that when you first begin practicing meditation, it may seem as if you are actually thinking more. The reality is that it is simply the first time you have bothered to stop and notice exactly what is going on in there. It isn't that meditation is causing more thinking, it is opening up a window to see what is going on in your mind. My mind was one giant conversation with people, with things, with myself. It never shut off. Now the conversations had slowed down a bit. I was concentrating on what I was doing at the time instead of doing one thing and thinking about another. In the shower, I would try to only think about the shower: the water, the soap, the shampoo. Much to my disgust, I could hardly do it for more than a few seconds before I would find myself thinking about a dozen other things. I began to realize that I was barely present in anything I was doing because the thoughts in my mind were controlling everything. The recognition of this oppression was just as sickening as my first understanding of misogyny. I wanted to have control over my mind and my life.

The next morning during meditation, it became abundantly clear that I had to go swimming. I fought it with everything that I had, and there was a lot of ammunition. When I was eleven, my Mom made me go to a spa for workouts. Once a week after school, she dropped me off at the most chic and horrible place. There were all of these fat middle age women, sitting around in leotards, who inevitably told me that if they were my age, they would certainly lose weight. In addition, I did not own a bathing suit and had no idea what I would wear to go swimming. Third, I was not about to change clothes in a locker room with other people around. Lastly, I would not go to any club that was co-ed.

With all of those conditions, limitations, and concerns, I was still not able to dismiss the feeling that I had to go swimming. I made one phone call, to a health club in Costa Mesa. They had an indoor pool. It was women only on Monday, Wednesday, Friday, and Sunday. The locker room had private dressing rooms. I made an appointment to see the place. A woman walked me around and showed me all the facilities. There was a sauna, a Jacuzzi, a workout room, a machine room, and a lane pool. To make matters worse, there were many young women enjoying themselves. No one stared or laughed or stood up to point at me. I filled out the membership papers and could start that very day.

After a trip to the mall, I had a swim suit. It was ugly but functional. And, by 2 P.M. I was dipping my big toe in the water testing my tolerance for change.

The Passionate Heart

Chapter 12

On Sunday I checked the ads for rentals. Highlighting four, Jane, my next door neighbor, and I took off to find my new place. The first was the only one we looked at. It was the cutest house imaginable. There was a fenced-in back yard for Lickie, lots of windows for Alice, and a front yard begging for flowers. After living over the bookstore, planting vincas and impatiens sounded heavenly. Leaving the Magic Speller was not going to be easy, but the charm of this house and all the little amenities made it seem okay. I could have a garden, Lickie could go out by herself, and I would have enough money to not work for a while and write my book about the fast.

On Memorial Day, we all moved in. Laura Ashley would have loved this little house. Every room was adorable, even the bathroom. It was tiny and easy to keep immaculate. Vacuuming took a few minutes, back to front. The best part was that it was all mine. No one else had ever lived there with me. It was my power spot; mine to do with as I pleased. There was no lover to complain that things were too high on the shelves or that pictures were hung too low. I would be able to dream my own dreams in this little Shangri-La.

My desk faced a window towards the street with a flowering tree in full view. I planted a hundred pink and white annuals inside a white wire fence that circled the tree. My bedroom was in the back, out of any visitor's view. It was the perfect arrangement for a real puja, a special place for private prayer and meditation. I bought a small, square, white plastic table at Builder's Emporium and covered it with a starched white cloth.

I put some special things on my table to remind me what meditation was about. There was a yantra that Rama had given us. It was the Sri Yantra which was blue and white with a yellow border. There was a small pink candle, some incense and a special white pitcher filled with flowers. Although it was discouraged, I kept a picture of Rama on my puja. He had told us not to focus on his picture because he did not want us to become devotional or emotional about our relationship with him, but I simply could not resist. Finally, I sewed a blue zafu, a traditional meditation cushion for sitting. Now there would be no excuses; meditation would have to be perfect.

Placing myself on the zafu in front of my puja, I closed my eyes and readied myself for silence. Blaring out of the night, just outside my window, was a gaggle of men's voices incessantly chattering. I couldn't believe it. It was 11:00 p.m. Why didn't they go inside? Why were they all congregating twenty feet from my window? What could I do? Well, I could try to rise above it all and focus on my yantra. I could stare at a pink rose in my little white pitcher. But why should I be intimidated by these people? It was late and they should go in their house. Besides, the fact that they were all men made me feel even more insistent that I should not relinquish my rights to peace and quiet in my own house. They were ruining my picturesque plan. So, I put my coat on over my nightgown and charged out the front door. "It is very late and you should continue your conversation inside," I advised them. They just stood there, looking at me. "I am sorry to get off on the wrong foot like this, but you are making a lot of noise and I can hear every word inside my house." Nothing. They didn't move. In desperation, I turned, walked away, and went in my house. After five minutes or so, just long enough to claim themselves as more powerful, they dispersed.

I was devastated. What would this mean in the future? Was my perfect cottage going to be poisoned by six macho types insisting that they could make all the noise they wanted, any time they elected? I fell asleep in a bundle of irritation, feminist indignation, and exhaustion. In the morning I went next door to settle all accounts. I rang the bell. A young woman came to the door. I started detailing my feelings. She motioned to wait a moment. A young man came out of the kitchen and asked what I wanted. I gave him a blow by blow description of the events of the previous night. "Yes, you are the woman they talked about this morning," he said. "They were very concerned that a neighbor came over and wanted something. But you see, none of them speak any English and they didn't know what you were talking about." I felt like the ass-hole of the universe. In all of my self-appointed, publicized liberalism, I hadn't stopped for one minute to consider that they didn't understand me. I apologized profusely, as did he. He said that last night was unusual and most nights everyone was asleep by that hour. The six men who lived in the garage were very hard working, got up early in the morning, and seldom stayed up that late. I limped back to my perfect little house, white and uptight. In the months that followed, they proved to be wonderful and protective neighbors, shaming me even further.

Now the only problem I had was what to do with myself all day. I had worked in the bookstore six days a week. I was not used to all of this free time. Meditation was a half hour in the morning and a half hour at night. That left a lot of time in the middle. I had been thinking about writing a book about my trip to Illinois and the fast for the ERA. I had boxes of press releases, flyers, letters, cards, telegrams, and hundreds of photos. I wanted to write about it while it was still somewhat fresh in my mind. I organized all the paper, pictures, and memorabilia in a giant scrapbook arranged by day. I decided to write it as if it were a diary I had written at the time. Between the letters and clippings, it would be easy to reconstruct events down to the last detail.

Tuesday nights, I got to see my Teacher. Weeks completely revolved around Tuesday nights, three days before to get ready and three days after to reflect. Patty met me at our usual restaurant on Melrose Blvd. We went to the Beverly Theater together and afterwards we always went to Larry Parker's All Night Diner. We ate pecan pie and gloated about how lucky we were. We went over every detail Rama had said that night and marveled at his wisdom, humor, and humility. Larry Parker's was a lot of fun at that time of night. Celebrities often drove up in their Benz's or Rolls. Stevie Wonder came in several times with his entire entourage arriving in a huge Bentley.

Rama had been teaching us about the relationship between power, energy, and money. He wanted us to see that they were interchangeable and that none of them were inherently good or bad. For months he had been telling us that we would have to greatly improve our living conditions to reach higher states of attention, but he was always met with opposition. We were stuck on an idea that money and spirituality were in conflict. Rama explained that since this was his first incarnation in the West, it had taken some time to figure out why Westerners seeking light were so confused on the issues of money and power. He was accustomed to teaching in the East, where people understood that spiritual evolution required power. Why was this such a difficult concept for people in the West? What were power and energy to people in the West? Why were Americans so confused about power and its relationship to spirituality?

The answer had been obscured, particularly growing up in the '60s. After experimentation and observation, Rama began to understand that Westerners could not build a positive association of money (power) with spirituality. In fact, the accepted concept was that a person could not be wealthy and spiritual at the same time. It was a conclusion that did not reference any of his past lives. If anything, it would have been just the opposite. In the East, it was thought to be a privilege to care for the people who dedicated their lives to seeking light, so that they would be free to focus on spiritual evolution. But to Americans, power is money and money is power and they both exclude being spiritual.

This was an interesting conflict to me. On the one hand, I was a child of the '60s and rejected that money was a god. The revolution was against the corporate establishment and all that fueled the corporate combine. We sang songs and marched to say that we would not succumb to economic greed. We would not worship money. We rejected the Vatican's brand of religion. Like Martin Luther, we would not try to buy our way into the gates of heaven. We wanted peace and love, and if that meant we would have to be poor, so be it. Our god and money had nothing in common. We made the higher choice. It is almost as if we sought being powerless for the sake of purity and as a form of spirituality.

On the other hand, I was a feminist, an educated feminist. I was a daughter of the privileged class and oppressed because of my gender. I had seen first hand what money and power could mean in a person's life. I also knew that being female, I had no direct access to power. Although I had gone to one of the finest French boarding schools and sat in class with the daughters of the wealthiest families in the country, we still knew that in spite of family wealth and unlimited educational opportunities, we were meant to be wives and mothers. A few might deviate and make their own claim; they would be the exceptions. The majority, if not all *good* girls, would have to attach to a man. Men had the power. Men had the money. It was not ladylike or womanly to have money and power.

But it would take power and money to change the political system. The ERA lost because of the rich insurance industry lobby. The right to vote was stalled a hundred years because women did not have power (translated -- money). Abigail Adams reminding John to "remember the ladies," would have never been necessary if women had their own money. Katherine Graham and Queen Beatrice did not invent their fortunes. CoCo Chanel and Elizabeth Arden were not the rule. The reality is that women are powerless unless they can compete with men on their game board, regardless of who gets there first. All the complaining that it is the boys' game board is just a waste of time. To date, it is the only game board in town.

So there was the rub: money is power, and for some unknown ethereal reason, it was thought to be in direct conflict with spirituality. This is not just a catch 22; it is a form of oppression that defies exposure because to openly investigate its meaning borders on blasphemy. In the West, a woman, and a man for that matter, is judged as not being truly spiritual if they seek money and the things it affords.

Rama wanted to blow the whistle on the whole lie. He wanted us to take a chance and truly examine the meaning and consequences of this intricate parlor game that was making such an impact on our lives. Why were we disgusted with the acquisition of wealth? Why did we believe that wealth and spirituality were mutually exclusive? Whose design was this that kept us from freely traversing the earth? We had embraced economic slavery as being spiritual, while it was stopping our ability to increase auric purity. We needed to have a nice place, remove ourselves from over-crowded areas, and live on land that helped us find the stillness we sought. But without money, it would be impossible.

An Easterner knows that higher states of mind require distance from the masses and a vibrationally refined environment. It might have been high in the Himalayas or sequestered in a monastery, but to achieve total stillness, one would have to establish a power base of purity. Therefore, everyone understood that the monasteries needed to be places of incredible beauty and refinement. The gardens, the temples, and the living quarters were lovely so that the monks and nuns could achieve stillness and, in doing so, the entire society would benefit. The people outside financed the local monastery as part of their karmic duty and privilege. They did not think that it was more spiritual to be poor and underprivileged. They understood that if the monastery or temple was beautiful and refined, the dwellers would be able to meditate better and it would bring the contributors honor and boons as well. Spiritual seekers were supported through the generosity and understanding of others, who often provided lives for the monks and nuns that surpassed the luxury of their own. In the West, no one would think of supporting spiritual seekers, certainly not in such a manner that surpassed their own lifestyle. For Americans, the general notion is that meditators are flaky and not capable of making a good living for themselves, and we were believing it too.

So Rama was left with the difficult task of not only teaching seekers to meditate and stop their thoughts, but how to do it without the help and understanding of the surrounding society. Instead of having the support of our families and commerce, we would have the responsibility to create circumstances that would enhance our ability to still our minds and refine our lives. It would take economic mobility to live apart from the crowded areas and in a pure place. We would have to break through the illusion that one could find stillness in voluntarily embracing poverty in the name of spirituality. Many people said that they made a choice "to get by on as little as possible" but it really meant that they would be held economically captive. The laws and traditions of our society would be inescapable. For women it was even more complicated; economic independence was not an easy option.

Rama was telling me something I had fought for fifteen years, money was power and without it I was powerless. I had fought it because I bought into the inverted thinking of the West. I had made a choice to be spiritual, not financially successful. The result of this insidiously oppressive lie was that I could not travel freely. I could not lobby effectively. I could not influence the law-making process. I was lost in a sea of powerlessness and I validated it by calling it spiritual.

Chapter 13

Rama had devised a plan. It was simple. It was fool-proof. It could be done in baby steps. If we did it impeccably, we would be economically independent in a couple of years. Like all plans devised by Rama, it was ingenious. As the Graduate was told the word, "plastics," Rama told us, "computers." Rama has studied the possibilities and told us why he was pointing the way towards careers in computer science.

One, it was the one career in which the demand would always be greater than the supply. If we learned a programming language, such as COBOL, and learned it well, we would always be able to find work for the rest of our lives, regardless of where we lived on the entire earth. Excellent computer programmers would always be scarce. Rama suggested that we enroll in a full time professional computer school. Most of them last about six months. It was the best route to take because the education would be complete, pragmatic, and focused on the essentials. A four year university program would require many additional peripheral courses, the focus would be on systems or hardware, and it would mean three and a half more years before we could begin earning a living. The point was to move up a career ladder in a way that would realize the most income in the shortest amount of time. In addition, the outlay of funds was minimal, nothing like medical or law school that left graduates deeply in debt.

Two, computer programming was a career that had no room for racism, ageism, or sexism. The sole deciding factor was whether or not one could effectively program a computer. The industry was wide open, even to severely physically challenged people, such the blind, deaf, or wheel chair bound. The only bigotry in this career would be against sloppy thinking and inefficient code. Women could be on equal footing with men. Gender did not matter while sitting in front of a computer. There may be a few sexist managers, but the majority of people in the computer industry were young and socially liberal. The industry itself was relatively young and did not have the chance to get deeply entrenched in old boy traditions, yet. The glass ceiling limited women who were seeking career advancement in management, but in programming, it did not apply.

Three, computer programming was a career that required a minimum of human interaction. We would be able to work at our desks, be judged on the performance of our code, and mind our own business. It was clear that we had to live and work in the world, but we wanted to move through it with the least amount of auric interface. We had made the choice to make meditation our principle priority and find the integrity of our own minds. To do this meant that we had to minimize our interactions both in number and intensity. Although this one part of our lives would often be misunderstood, it did not change the reality that the more people we interacted with during a day, the harder it was to meditate. We didn't have to take Rama's word for it. Everyday we proved it to ourselves again and again. It wasn't even necessarily our preference; it was simple mathematics.

Four, computer programming would give us a fast path to economic independence. Now many of us were working for minimum wage or, even worse, in food services, dependent on tips. After we graduated from a professional computer programming school, we could land a job starting at twenty to thirty thousand dollars a year. It would mean that we could live in safer neighborhoods, have more reliable cars, rent nicer places to live and meditate in, wear new clothes, and travel. It would significantly change our self-image from dropouts, losers and flaky spiritual types to responsible adults. Rama had actually investigated various careers and computer science required the least amount of formal education with the lowest investment for the highest, fastest return.

Five, computer programming would clarify our minds. Clean code and efficient programs would serve the same purpose as transcribing the holy texts did for the Benedictines. Tibetan monks spent lifetimes memorizing intricate mandalas and recreated them with colored sand. Afterwards, they would let them blow away to remind them of the transience of life. Spiritual seekers had been learning long and complicated discourses for centuries to order and discipline their minds. Similarly, conquering a programming language would organize our minds, discipline our thinking, and give us something clean to focus on while earning a living.

Six, work was the most time consuming part of our lives. With commute time, preparation time, and working eight hours a day, what we did for a living would take up half of our lives. Had we joined a monastery or convent, the entire day would be dedicated to our spiritual evolution. Rama wanted to offer a way that our careers could be part of our practice as meditators, as seekers. Our work had to compliment our studies, not detract from them.

This master plan was even more fantastic. It could be done incrementally. Rama suggested that those students who were not currently working, could start with word-processing. Some offices paid as much as twenty-five dollars an hour for this skill. In addition, it would mean learning to touch type on the job. Others could take courses in C, COBOL, BAL, Pascal, or FORTRAN at a community college or university. For those who could manage it, if they began professional computer school now, in six months they would be ready for their first job. These schools arranged financial aid and some even helped graduates find their first jobs.

Though clear, precise, obviously intelligent, and simple to follow, many of us freaked. Computer programmers were nerds. They were Trekkies. They were boring and wore white shirts with plastic ball-point pen holders. We were artists, political activists, dancers, performers, nurses. We were sensitive and aesthetic. We loved poetry and literature, not sterile, inhuman computers. This was a leap that would require a lot more than common sense and faith. Regardless of the hours Rama had spent explaining the wisdom of this transforming plan, most of us were still convinced that true spirituality has nothing to do with careers, money, and certainly not computers.

Patty and I took off for Larry Parker's All Night Diner. There was a lot to talk about. Patty was a chiropractic student nearing graduation. She was thousands of dollars in debt already. Although I was not currently working, I did not want to begin a career in computer science. I was thirty-four with an MA in ethics and world religions. I was interested in philosophy, metaphysics, astrology, feminism, and spirituality. We resolved the issue with a simple notation that computer science was merely a suggestion that we could select or reject.

The Passionate Heart

Patty would be able to make lots of money as a chiropractor. I was too old and too stuck to even consider such a radical change.

On Wednesday, I began to organize my book. I bought an enormous scrapbook that was designed for holding an entire page of a newspaper. I sorted out everything I had from my trip to Illinois and glued it in. I got several yellow pads and set out to write my biography. By Thursday, I was infinitely bored. I went to a bookstore in Laguna Beach. My intent was to look at what had just been published, what was new, what was happening in the world of books. Quite by chance I found myself wandering through the computer section. I bought three books on computers. One of them was on the history of computers. I took them home, but didn't crack them open.

I got a call from Jane, my friend the therapist. She said that she had met a woman whom she felt I would like very much; we had a lot in common. Would I consider meeting her? Sure, I told her. I had plenty of time. So Jane gave this woman, Pat, my phone number. Pat was a school teacher, an ex-Catholic, a lesbian and divorced. She called me that day. I invited her over. She was blond, intelligent, fun, and seemed like a person I would like to be friends with. We laughed and shared our common secrets. I told her about the book I was trying to write, showing her my huge scrapbook. Pat just couldn't believe that I was writing long hand on legal yellow paper. The fact was that I was not getting very far. Pat noticed the three computer books and asked if I was interested in computers. "No," I told her, "I just thought those books were interesting."

Friday afternoon, Pat called and asked if I was going to be home all day. She wanted to drop by. It was fine with me. Around 4:00 p.m. I saw Pat drive up and park her car in the driveway. She was taking forever to get to the door. I opened it up just in time for her to say, "I thought you might use this to write your book." She was holding a computer, a box of disks and a word-processing manual. What could I possibly say? It was an Apple IIC. It had two disk drives, a green screen, and came complete with my own private tutor. Pat offered to teach me anything and everything I wanted to know.

I became obsessed. I wanted to know absolutely everything. I turned it on at 9:00 a.m. and turned it off at midnight. I sat in front of it all day, every day. The TV had been abandoned for a monochrome screen. Pat came over almost every day to see how I was doing. If she couldn't come over, we would spend hours on the phone sorting out my incessant questions. As miracles would have it, I went to the next Lakshmi meeting knowing that there was a computer on my desk and mounds of manuals on the floor.

Chapter 14

From time to time students talked about their dreams. Some shared that they had a sense that everything said at a meeting, they heard the night before in a dream. Rama told us that he often used the dream plane for teaching. Buddhists believe that there are three states: the waking, meditative, and dreaming. Advanced teachers use dreams to teach for several reasons: (1) in the dream plane, it is easier to illustrate lessons, (2) it is a way for a teacher and student to have a personal, one-to-one experience, (3) students are more open and receptive to complex or non-traditional lessons, and (4) lessons can include material that reaches beyond the boundaries of the waking state.

I had always thought it strange that the tradition I grew up in dismissed dreams entirely. As a child, I had vivid and wonderful dreams. Nightmares were visceral and created feelings that lasted far into daylight. At five, I thought that they were real. When did I stop believing? Who intervened? Most cultures, religions, even academic disciplines validate the importance, the relevance, even the veracity of dreams. The Aborigine, Native Americans, Moses, and Jung would all support Rama's position. Dreams are real, at least as real as the waking state.

But Rama gave us a warning, dreams are not necessarily as they appear. People, places, experiences could be analogous, metaphorical, or even pure deception. Just because it looks like dad in a dream, it isn't necessarily dad. The rules that govern the waking state do not apply. It could be someone or something appearing as dad, for whatever reason. The dream plane must be observed and traversed with discrimination. It requires practice and mindfulness. Rama told us that in time, we would develop skills in safely navigating our way through the dream state.

Many students relayed dreams in which Rama appeared. He would take them on a journey to another world or another time. He might just sit and talk about their lives, answer their questions, or show them a few of their past lives. Rama advised us to be cautious and be certain it were really him in our dreams. He explained that there are two ways to be sure.

First, when you wake up, everything is beautiful and you feel great. Second, he is very, very funny and you wake up laughing. Should you wake up disoriented or depressed, it was most definitely not Rama.

One morning, early in the summer, I woke up with intense abdominal pains and I was sure I was going to die. The pain was so violent I couldn't stand up. I literally crawled out of my bedroom, pulled the phone off my desk by yanking the wire, and lay on bathroom floor trying to collect the focus and energy to call a friend. I dialed her number and dropped the receiver from sheer exhaustion. With my head on the floor, I asked her to help me. Never actually hanging up, I passed out.

She arrived shortly and drove me to the nearest hospital. The emergency room staff suggested that I had kidney stones and ordered a x-ray. They gave me Demerol to relieve the pain. Finally, I fainted on the x-ray table. An hour later I woke up in ER and was told that I had passed the stones and could go home. I was totally wasted. I got home and fell into bed. With my cat and dog at my feet, I slept for several days.

On the morning of the fourth day, I heard a car drive up and park in front of my house. I peered down the hall, out the living room window and saw a convertible mustang. The top was down. Rama was sitting in the passenger seat and Ganesha, a student, was driving. As they stood up, I could see that they were both wearing gorilla suits: full body, hairy gorilla suits. Carrying the heads to the suits under their arms, they walked to the front door, opened it, came in, and put on the heads.

They walked back to my bedroom. I lay there in absolute amazement. These two enormous gorillas began to dance ridiculously all around my room. Round and round they went until I began to laugh. I laughed so hard I forgot all about the pain. The three of us laughed for almost ten minutes filled with raucous dancing and gorilla noises echoing throughout the house. Then they simply left, got in the car, and drove away. Although I was in bed for several more days recuperating from kidney stones and could not go to the

The Passionate Heart

Lakshmi meeting that week, I knew I had most definitely seen Rama.

Over the next weeks, I continued working on my book, *The Hungry Heart*. Everyday, though I believed I was only writing about my summer in the Illinois legislation, I was simultaneously learning about word-processing and computers. As with most things in my life, I am never satisfied with just a cursory understanding. I began to read about computing. Happily there seemed to be a representative number of women involved with the evolution of the computer, not the least of whom is United States Navy Admiral Grace Hopper, the creator of COBOL, the most widely used programming language on all of planet earth. Computing magazines had many articles by women on all subjects, from artificial intelligence to database design. I knew then Rama must have something very specific in mind for his women students.

All summer long Rama gave discourses on impeccability. It began with closets but soon spread to every facet of our lives. We were to make lists to discover and uncover what was contributing to or detracting from our lives. One of the lists was to carefully watch who was in our minds throughout the day and write down their names. For a Buddhist, it is proper to be completely present for another person when in their company, but when apart, it is incorrect to hold them in our minds. Rama explained to us that since we are very psychic, most of the thoughts, impressions, and attitudes that constantly stream through our minds are actually not our own. They are the thoughts and impressions of those people to whom we are attached. Likewise, if we are thinking about someone, we are polluting their minds by connecting with them psychically. Since the ideal is to have the integrity of one's own mind, own thoughts, and state of attention, it is a breach of Buddhist etiquette to either focus on others or allow others to focus on you.

Rama used the example of answering the phone and finding that the person calling had been on your mind at that very moment. The question is, where did the call actually originate? A simple explanation is that the other person thought of calling and you felt their thoughts. The more complex possibility is that you wanted the other person to call and you sent the message out first, requesting them to give you a ring. On Mother's Day, is it you or mom that actually places that obligatory call?

A classic example is an infatuated teenager. Totally distracted and absorbed in the object of their infatuation, they are unable to eat, sleep, or study. They obsess about Sally or Bob to the point that they lose interest in anything or anyone else. Sally may be in Biology class daydreaming about her dreamboat, Jim, but psychically she is with him in his algebra exam. Not only is she jeopardizing her biology grade and Jim's ability to concentrate on his algebra exam, but her mind is not fully present, not fully her own. In addition, maybe it is Jim who is pulling Sally's heart strings. The end result is a D in biology and Sally's clear understanding that girl's don't do well in science, better to marry a doctor than to be one.

For a week I carried a little notebook with me everywhere and wrote down the names of whoever popped into my head. At first it was overwhelming, embarrassing, and ultimately maddening. There were dozens of people with hundreds of reoccurrences. There were people I hadn't seen in years, people for whom I had only contempt, people whose ideas I found archaic or oppressive. What were they doing wandering around in my head? Whether I was calling on them, or they on me, became a moot point. I only wanted them to leave me alone. There were ex-lovers, grade school teachers, playground bullies, media figures, historical heroes, authors, and, most disturbing, my parents directing me as if they were welcome participants in my life. It became evident that winning liberation in Congress or the Constitution was a small task compared to seeking the liberation of my mind from everyone I had ever known.

I became determined to uncover just who was steering this ship called Zoe. Why had I come to many of the conclusions that were defining my entire world? It wasn't just people; it was Madison Avenue, Hollywood, Cherry Adams (*Student Nurse*), Gidget, and NBC. Naturally, I knew that Helen Gurley Brown and Hugh Hefner had been inventing American female sexuality for decades, but not until I became militant about my thought processes did I really discover the depth of this invasion. I was in a cycle of either rejecting an unacceptable definition or embracing a radical one. Where was my definition? Was I even forming my own definition? What would be left if I scraped away all of the information that had been slathered onto my mind by others?

Rama's prescription was far more simple than the diagnosis: meditation and mindfulness. To sit in stillness every day and go into the light had several immediate benefits. Eventually the thoughts slowed down and became more observable. Thus, it was easier to examine just what was going on in there. It also seemed that meditation was loosening the stranglehold that the thoughts had on my mind. Every time I mediated, it shed a little light, a little fresh air on the overgrown jungle of my mind. I even noticed that the simple action of giving myself this half hour exclusively dedicated to concentrating on my interior life was like planting a flag that said, "This mind is mine and I am going to be its sole owner."

Not having much success with the traditional method of concentration on a yantra or flower, I used any game I could think of to clear my head for those thirty minutes. I pretended that my mind was one of those magic slates with gray cellophane and a wooden pencil. I would lift that cello a thousand times, trying to erase each thought that lodged in my head. I imagined that my mind was a balloon and thoughts were hot air. I would untie the knot and let it blast away. Sometimes I simply sat there holding the notion that I was meditating perfectly regardless of what was marching through. It was a no-holds-barred situation, a battle of wills, and although I was not winning on any consistent basis, I wanted to become a competitor. I wanted to stop the torrent and first I had to believe that it was mine to stop.

The practice of mindfulness was far more complicated and emotional. The more I saw what was happening in my mind, the more I realized that this was not a simple or optional task. It felt as if every person directing my life through my thoughts had a string attached to me and I was not a marionette, but a hostage held in suffocating bondage. This little notebook had become a listing of my jailers, my captors. Even if the people were ones whom I admired, I had never cast a vote on the degree of their intervention. I wanted to invite them into my consciousness; be their hostess, not their slave.

I began to play badminton in my mind, carrying a racket constantly poised for action. "Ping, zing, thwap." I would try to nab them before they could get a sure footing. It was tiring, it was irritating, but mostly it was adventurous, and ultimately revolutionary. More demanding than removing the British from India and more dangerous than escaping from a battering relationship, staking this claim over my mind was becoming my own civil disobedience, my adherence to truth, my act of aggression for liberation. All day long I stood on guard hoping to blow their cover. It didn't take long for me to realize that this was not a game or a sporting event. A badminton racket was not the proper or adequate armament for this battle, not if I wanted to win and not just play.

Several months earlier, Rama had thrown me into quite a stir when he recommended that we see the movies Road Warrior and Blade Runner. At this point in my life I had fourteen years into developing, refining, and deeply embracing active non-violence. It was one of the essential personal definitions I ascribed to myself. Marching in peace parades, demonstrating against the Vietnam War, escorting women to abortion clinics through crowds of rosary swinging morons were simply part of who I believed I was. Carrying it to a purest position, I never went to violent movies. As I sat in that darkened theater on a Wednesday afternoon watching Mel Gibson personify everything I had rejected, I was very disturbed that my Teacher had asked me to see such a movie. Now, in battle for the integrity of my mind, it started coming into focus.

My mind was being violated and the integrity of my mind was more precious than the gasoline the Road Warrior rescued. To win, I would have to become militant, willful, and even violent if necessary. I needed to trade in my badminton racket for an automatic weapon. I would have to set my gun on vaporize, not stun. Upon investigation, I realized that it had been just another uninvited, unexamined thought that kept me from annihilating mental intruders. Dedicated scrutiny within one's mind and justifiable thoughticide would liberate me more than any new legislation. I would become truly dangerous to the social order.

The Passionate Heart

Would we even need women's shelters if women had been able to combat the thought that they could not leave their husbands and survive? Could unwanted pregnancy be significantly reduced if girls didn't believe that they had to have sex to keep their boyfriends? Where did these circumstances originate but in thoughts? Long before Harry actually hit Helen, both of them had thoughts in their minds that created such a possibility. Susie believed that she needed Rick, and so to keep him in her life, she agreed to have unprotected sex. Years before Prom night, Susie psychically picked up that she needed a man to be complete, men should control relationships, and saying no will threaten her femininity. Uproot the thought, blow its cover, and the action, at the very least, becomes an option for Susie. Thoughts, conditioning, traditions, routines, and expectations commit the most violence against women.

It was obvious that I would have to reevaluate my non-violence or consciously accept the position of victim. The battle ground was my mind. It didn't matter that I was white, privileged, educated, and situated such that I could outwardly fight the system. If I was truly going to be a feminist, a radical feminist, even a self-defined woman, first I would have to own my mind and liberate it from all invaders and oppressors. It was clear that meditation and mindfulness are the primary acts of revolution.

Chapter 15

As the summer came to a close, Rama told us about a tradition in Tibetan monasteries. From time to time, the Abbott would ask all of the monks to reapply. It was a chance to reevaluate one's dedication, to look deeply inside, and renew one's direction. The Abbott would examine the applications and possibly release some of the community members, recommending a life in the world. But mostly, it was a process for the applicants to confirm their direction and rededicate their commitments. At the end of August, all eight hundred members of Lakshmi would reapply.

Our last activity as a group would be a trip to Disneyland. I couldn't imagine how eight hundred people could go on an excursion to Disneyland. I hated groups. I hated packs. So far in my journey with Rama, I had only the friends I knew before I met him. I went to meetings only to see Rama, not the others.

My original feelings of judgment and disdain had certainly diminished. Although it appeared that the gender definitions of the student community were contrary to my own, I came to consider that what showed on the outside and the internal struggles of each student did not necessarily match. On the path of Self-Discovery, the high adventure is happening inside. While organizing closets, scrutinizing one's thinking, ordering one's exterior life, everything on the inside is being reordered as well. External balance is part of the practice, and so, even if one's interior life is in the state of disarray or great change, it is correct to maintain outer equanimity. Obviously, internal equanimity is the ultimate goal, but for beginning students, the outside is a good place to start.

I realized that it was not pertinent to judge their politics and their social consciousness. We were a community tied together by our belief in our Teacher and in ourselves. We were seeking Self-Discovery, not social change. Possibly there were women and men in the group who worked in politics or for feminist causes, but that was not the core of *this* association. It would have been inappropriate to bring that part of our lives into the meetings. Like Zen Buddhists, we were seeking emptiness.

The Passionate Heart

Basically, we tried to not draw attention to ourselves. All we really wanted was to be free to practice meditation. Buddhism is a way of life that resides in one's heart and doesn't seek external recognition. On the contrary, it is a very private matter. Unlike the Hari Krishnas, who publicly sing the praises of God, or the Christians who want to "spread the faith," what we wanted was not external. As Buddhists, we were seeking to pass unnoticed, to touch lightly, and to leave no trace. We meditated twice a day, practiced Buddhism, loved our Teacher and quietly sought perfection.

Nonetheless, both Patty and I were somewhat mortified to picture eight hundred people traipsing through the Magic Kingdom. Rama told us the time to arrive and the order of the rides. "Try to have a good time and don't stare." Other than those meager directions, we were on our own.

We began the itinerary with the Pirates of the Caribbean at noon. Patty and I entered the steel maze on a sunny day simply planning on having a happy time by ourselves. Winding through the path, we arrived at the end of the line. Standing immediately in front of us was Rama. He had on a tee shirt, shorts and the most amazing sunglasses. Neither of us had ever been that close to him for such a long time. We tried to keep our composure and chat normally. We began speculating on whether or not the tree in the Swiss Family Robinson house was real or artificial. It seemed real, but how could it be so perfectly sculpted? I finally broke down and asked Rama. He stopped, looked for a significant time, and said that the tree was not real. It was evident that he could see the tree's aura and it was not the aura of a live tree.

I had been enjoying a box of popcorn, and without hesitation, I asked him if he would like some. Instead of digging into the box, he cupped his hands, waiting for me to fill them. I glanced at his hands for just an instant before pouring in the corn. It couldn't have been more than a couple of seconds, but I will never forget what I saw. Although the size was those belonging to a grown man in his thirties, the skin was that of a newborn. Never had I seen anything like it. It was fresh and young, glowing with the look of a tiny baby's. His radiance, his kundalini was beyond description and infinitely unforgettable. The others may have been enjoying the pirates and a chorus of yo-ho-ho, but I was silently lost in reverie.

The next ride on the list was Space Mountain. There was no way on earth I was getting on a roller coaster by any name, in any land. It was not an experience that I had ever had, nor did I long for this particular virgin adventure. I took off in the opposite direction. Suddenly, I felt a strong grip on my right elbow. "Where are you going?" Chuck inquired. "Anywhere but Space Mountain. I don't do roller coasters," I stated clearly. Chuck was not going to let it go. He continued to grip my elbow. "We are going there, now!" he insisted. I was caught between my fear of the ride and my respect for Chuck. Either way, I was walking in the direction of Tomorrow Land.

It is essential to the practice of Self-Discovery to confront and overcome fears. I was doing that on a moment by moment basis in my mind. To my way of thinking, this did not include roller coasters. Chuck felt quite the contrary. He said that it was not an option and he would settle for nothing less than escorting me personally through this one. I stepped on to the escalator knowing that I was now committed. As I progressed through the winding line, there were warning signs for people with weak hearts, for pregnant women, but none for cowards. I gobbled an entire roll of Lifesavers while building my fears to a frenzied pitch. Had it been anyone other than Chuck, I would have been whining and complaining the entire time. But I could not lose that much face in front of him.

The central room of the ride lies deep inside of the mountain. The line wraps back and forth with a full view of the passengers boarding and disembarking the rocket-like cars. Finally, it was our turn to get on board. I stepped into the two-seater, sat down next to Chuck, gripped my safety harness, shut my eyes, and prayed to not barf. Chuck told me that it was most important to open my eyes; I would miss half the fun. Not fully convinced, I opened my eyes half way.

It took off at a snail's pace, jerking its way up a steep incline. Steam was spraying us and lights were spinning at the peak. Once to the top, it cut loose speeding through wild turns. Up and down it tore through the seeming night sky. I screamed. I laughed. I held my breath and screamed some more. In a flash, it was over. The car slowed down and reentered the boarding area. I was flush and elated. Glancing up to the waiting passengers on the left, I saw my Teacher smiling at me. I will never know if he knew what a terrifying and exciting time I had just had. It really didn't matter. I knew.

Although the crowd was mostly low key, both Patty and I felt compelled to break away. We loved seeing Rama's face in the midst of all the people, but we had already had more than our share. We proceeded to go on all of the designated rides, but in a different order. We ate enchanted burgers and drank tikki punch. We saw the parade and watched the fireworks. It just felt better to be off on our own.

By 10 PM, we had done it all, particularly Space Mountain, several times. It was the perfect moment to go. We wandered down Main Street, weaving our way in and out of the shops, knowing that it was possibly the last time our group would ever be together again. There were no guidelines, no guarantees, no assurances that any of us would be readmitted to Lakshmi in September. Somehow it didn't matter at that moment. It had been a glorious year, a miraculous year, a year to last lifetimes.

Carefree and deeply grateful, Patty and I walked out of the main gate to make our way through the sea of parked cars. Suddenly we heard a voice call out, "Hi, girls, did you have fun?" It was Rama. The four or five students who were walking with him stepped aside and let us get closer. "What did you see?" "Did you watch the parade?" "Did you like the new Fantasy Land?" The three of us babbled like grade school friends who had spent the day in the park. When we got to our car, Rama said good night and waved good-bye.

Chapter 16

In September, the woman who bought my bookstore declared bankruptcy, so the promised monthly payments and my dream of not working for a year quickly vanished. With the aid of the computer, I finished my book in just a few months, but I still was not prepared to look for a job. I didn't have traditional work clothes nor a resume; not to mention the many chances I had taken by publicly announcing my politics, my religious beliefs, my sexual preference, and most of all, my intolerance for mainstream corporate America.

I applied for and was offered two jobs: Assistant Director of the California Abortion Rights Action League in L.A. and the Assistant Director of the Orange County Free Clinic. Both were non-profit organizations and paid next to nothing for a great deal of commitment and hard work. I accepted the one in Orange County because it was closer to home and I knew the director. The clinic provided medical, dental and psychological care for economically oppressed people. Funding was meager and doled out by the service performed. A pack of birth control pills for a Native American brought in so much, as opposed to a pack for a Latina. Strange thinking, but those were the only rules in town.

The clinic had only four paid employees. Everyone else was either volunteer or there by a court order requiring community work for a DUI, etc. Paper work was not only monumental, but critical to receiving funding and retaining licenses. Someone in the community had recently donated an IBM PC. I was very enthusiastic about the prospect of moving all of our record keeping and tallying on to a computer. Before I started working there, a volunteer had entered 1,400 charts. On my first day, I sat down at the keyboard and discovered that no one had ever done a backup of any of the records. "This will never do." I announced to everyone gathered around me at the PC. I got out a box of floppy discs and typed in *Format*. The computer read, *press any key to continue*. In a flash of an instant, I realized that I had not entered the required A:! My options were zero. Since *any key* must include the escape key, there was no way to decline the format. I was in that terrifying place of having just enough knowledge to know that I was deep into the danger zone. Thus, on my first day of work, I formatted the hard drive, wiped out the clinic program, erased all 1,400 charts, and had a gruesome computer story for the rest of my life.

In mid-September a letter arrived from Rama stating that I had been re-accepted. I was delighted. I was thrilled. I called Patty. She too had been accepted. Rama had invited four hundred men and women to continue as his students. No matter how many times one goes through such a process, the amazement never diminishes. Why me? Why not so-n-so? What does it mean, or does it mean anything I could comprehend? The questions could go on forever and yet all that seems to matter at such a time is that I will see him again.

In early 1984, Rama began a series of women's only seminars. The posters read, "*Why Don't More Women Attain Enlightenment?*" The advertising said that he would talk about power, energy, clothes, make-up, money, and relationships. We women students were thrilled that Rama was going speak publicly about the Enlightenment of women. We knew that he is totally dedicated to empowering women and to spend just one evening with him and meditate with him could change a person forever. We invited everyone we knew and the ads drew hundreds of women from all over Southern and Northern California.

The night for the Southern California meeting finally arrived. It was indescribable to go to the Beverly Theater, where I had sat so many times and find it filled to capacity with only women. There were women of every educational and economic background. There were women in business suits, women in Birkenstocks, women in tie-dye. There were feminists, lesbians, radicals, mainstream, older, younger, married, single, simply hundreds of women, as diverse as women are. It was a dream come true: Rama empowering any and all women who came to hear him speak. He walked out on stage and sat down on a white couch.

Rama began to talk about women and power. He explained that women are naturally more powerful than men because of a fundamental difference in the structure of a woman's subtle body that allows women to conduct kundalini faster and more easily than men's. He explained further that the imbalance of the sexes in the world today is actually an inversion. Essentially, women are the source of power.

Rama said that for women to realize their true nature, they would have to tap into their raw power. This would require nothing less than a total revolution in how women think about men and about themselves. It was most certainly not going to happen if things are left in the hands of men since women have been culturally, economically, religiously, politically, and educationally repressed since the dawn of recorded history. "They have suffered to have their identities destroyed, their sisterhood splintered, their spirituality denied, and then been placed into an endless slavery to the men of this world."

My heart soared! Although I had spent a solid decade reading everything I could by, for, and about women, never had I heard the truth articulated with such clarity and conviction. Regardless of the seeming paradox of hearing the truth from a male, I loved the words, the veracity, the depth of understanding. Rama had done what I had postulated in graduate school, that a true Liberator would abandon every shred of any self-perpetuating agenda and join forces with the oppressed.

Any conflict I had about having a male teacher was so heavily compensated for, the notion held nothing for me anymore. If there is a chain or sequence in place which hands over information, generation to generation, era to era, Enlightenment to Enlightenment, and this male was not merely willing, but insistent on handing information to women, I was most certainly going to listen. It was the only sensible thing to do. In the end, I am far more practical than devotional. Besides, this particular Messenger had moved far beyond the petty and puny gender definitions of planet earth. There may have been a male body sitting on the couch, but the truth and power that was being made available to us that night was far above such contemptible human classifications.

Rama explained that the way a woman dresses has a power which can dictate how people treat her. A woman could use clothes as a type of shield, a protection from harmful vibrations. While women may be innocently walking down the street or past the Xerox machine, men throw sexual energy at them that is filled with hate, anger, and contempt. This energy has a certain consistency to it that actually erodes a woman's subtle body and eventually breaks down its ability to conduct kundalini. It eats away at a woman's life force, eventually bringing disease and speeding up the aging process. An escalation in the occurrence of breast and cervical cancer is no coincidence. If a woman is well dressed, impeccably dressed, men are less likely to notice her or feel so free to express such contemptuous feelings.

Although there may be an accompanying whistle or a suggestive smile, and some women may erroneously believe they enjoy the attention, the reality is that women are oppressed by the thoughts of men. These thoughts of domination and superiority make it clear to a woman that her primary purpose in life is to produce sexual pleasure for someone else. Rama said, "Sexual slavery is the ability to push the right buttons to receive the desired response when the individual who is being manipulated is either unaware that they are being manipulated or that they are unable to defend themselves. Men manage to perpetuate sexual slavery by making it seem that there is no other alternative, and by using social pressure, guilt, rejection, and other controlling mechanisms when a woman tries to buck the system."

Rama even mentioned that very high heels are actually power objects. There was a rumbling in the audience (the Birkenstock group). He jokingly remarked how it was an act of power to be able to walk in "those things." Men are intimidated by women walking well in high heels, not to mention that heels make significant weapons. A woman can use make-up, hair styles, all of these things to construct her appearance as an act of power and to help protect her from men's thoughts that she is an object put on earth for their observation, their perusal, their exploitation.

There was a strong sense that some of the women in the Beverly were getting very uptight. After all I had had an entire year to understand the things Rama was telling them in just one evening. I wanted them to listen with their minds and hearts wide open. I wanted them to understand that Rama believed in their power and their liberation. I wanted them to know that this was the one being on earth that could actually do something about our oppression that had gone on for thousands of years. But many of them had been so conditioned and damaged by society that they could only react. They couldn't imagine that they could take the very objects of their oppression and make them into objects of power.

Many women, while seeking liberation and power, only see the option of throwing away everything that had been foisted upon their lives. Though the intention is to reject male definitions and create their own, they are merely discarding external things. Not only does this not achieve the end they are seeking, but in some cases, it brings about the exact opposite. Those women who have discarded traditional female clothes, jewelry, make-up and hair styles often attract an even greater onslaught of negative attention.

I was not without compassion for the women who were finding some of the information difficult to accept. My before and after picture logging the last year were very different. I had not totally embraced the pantyhose regime and waxing, but I was trying to break free of automatically rejecting things. What I did have throughout this last year was daily meditation. Clearly, I was not very good at it or an expert on its benefits, but I knew that in just one year I was able to be more intelligent about my choices, more circumspect about my conclusions, and less susceptible to my conditioning. I had begun an internal revolution a year ago. These women were hearing about it for the first time that night.

After presenting a short lesson on meditation and meditating with us, Rama offered to answer questions. Dozens of hands went up. Rama called on a woman and she stood up. I recognized her from the clinic where I worked. She was a marriage and family therapist who was accruing volunteer hours at the clinic that were required by the state for her license. "Doesn't a successful career give a woman power?" Rama explained to her that the successes women are able to achieve are controlled by men. These accomplishments are seriously regulated. Although it may appear that a woman's "opinion is valued and her integrity admired, she is still viewed as a commodity." Rama went on to caution her that an education, a successful career and a "new white Mazda," did not really begin to equal a woman's true potential for power. I immediately remembered that just that morning, she had driven to the clinic and shown everyone her brand new WHITE MAZDA! I quietly giggled at how deeply that must have affected her.

Many times over the last year I had heard Rama iterate precisely what was on the mind of the questioner. I was anything but glib about it, and yet, I knew that this woman must have been overwhelmed by his remark. The wonder when it first happens is unparalleled. What a sweet secret. All of the other women in the audience had no idea about the level of intimacy that had just taken place. Rama looked deeply into the soul of this inquisitor and blessed her with a little miracle of knowing. He could have looked and chosen to not expose the extent of his understanding. Instead, Rama wanted this woman to know that he could see what was in her heart.

Suddenly a woman in the third row stood up and began to shout, "How dare you talk about the oppression of women! You are a man and you know nothing about being a woman. You have never been raped. You don't know what it is like to be a woman!" She was shaking and very upset. It was evident that she was not just having a difficult time with all of the information or that she was hearing it from a man, but she was expressing a lifetime of anger.

Rama stood up from the couch, walked to the edge of the stage, and knelt down. He sat back on his heels and looked tenderly at this woman. He listened at length to all of her pain and anger. He agreed with her every word and confirmed the profoundness of her grief. But the words are not what I remember the most.

As the two of them continued to talk, I began to notice great swirls of energy moving throughout the room. Currents of energy were swelling and shifting, running in a circular motion from the left to the right. They were filled with pain, grief, loneliness, and frustration. As I sat in my chair in the Beverly Theater, I saw something I will never forget. Rama began to pull all of this energy into himself. He sat on the edge of the stage, in quiet conversation with a woman in pain, while transmuting the energy of each and every woman in the theater. From the left, he took all of our emotions, our karmas, our sadness into his aura, and to the right, he sent out beautiful, clear, radiant, crystal light. Probably most of the women did not see this miracle of compassion and transformation, at least not with their eyes. But, I am certain that it changed their lives. It changed mine forever.

Chapter 17

Siddhartha or Simone de Beauvoir may not agree, but after fifteen years of aggressively searching, it seems obvious to me that Buddhism is ultimately and fundamentally feminist. No one could be more surprised to hear such a sentence from me than I. But since the search for truth requires fearless questions, abhors convenient answers, and once found, demands recognition, I simply have no choice.

The essence of feminism is that every woman must create her own experience. She must do this in the midst of a hostile world, regardless of disapproval; both external and internal. She must battle against history, embracing only her own definitions. Chances are high that she will have to take a stand against family, government, medicine, religion - any and all institutions that constitute the world she lives in. Moreover, because there is very little exterior support for this position, her strength, her courage, her fortitude must have a firm footing in her mind.

A feminist has to take responsibility for her own life philosophy. This is not just writing one's illusions to fit life's circumstances. Rather, it means engaging in the iterative process of writing and rewriting the thoughts and constructs of one's mind. This courageous task presents several gigantic challenges. First, she must be willing to coldly scrutinize the origin of her illusions. Second, she must be prepared to reject those ideas whose origins are rooted in misogyny, despite their familiarity or comfort. Third, she must be able to survive with the gaping holes that such discards create. Lastly, she has to sustain an indefatigable courage in her mind that cannot be bought, swayed or robbed.

And in the final analysis, there is yet one very large looming question: what is the mind? What, if anything, will be left after all of the opposing forces are demolished? What is a woman? After all of the conditioning, male definitions, biased history, and artificial trappings are stripped away, who will be left? Everyone has heard that "biology is not destiny" but what if the equation went beyond the physical? *"Thoughts are not destiny."* Can a woman live in such a way that she can discover the essence of being female? Remove all external influence, eradicate all internal prevarications, and, (if one considers reincarnation) mitigate karma; what is left? This process of diligently working to create one's own experience, is the essence of Buddhism.

I would feel greatly misunderstood if the reader thought that this conclusion was drawn lightly. At twenty, while working on a degree in Roman Catholic Theology, I hoped that the Church was ready for reform and I would be part of the new vanguard. With John XXIII at the helm, how could we lose? His death, and the death of his vision, catapulted me to study every religion on the earth, culminating in an M. A. in religion. This was not a cursory or academic investigation. I was driven. I had to know. That's why Patty nicknamed me, "Zoe No-half-measures Nicholson." Covering years, crystallizing in a moment, I systematically investigated how people on the earth address God.

There seems to be one determining factor, one thing that clearly demarcates all observable religions. Without exception they present an ontology that states that within humanity lies a condition that can only be obviated by something outside. To attain this spotless state, one must act a certain way, adhere to a series of rules, and embrace a set of beliefs. To question the code is to lack faith. To accept the most farfetched tenet is to display faith. Finally, faithlessness is to be repented. Simply put, God is an external answer to an internal question. Long for it. Score points for its approval. Search for it. Wait for it. The premise in this entire system, no matter the country, the century, or the culture, is that we are in a state of unworthiness perpetually waiting to be saved by something or someone outside ourselves.

Judaism, Hinduism, Christianity, Islam and all of their derivatives tacitly disallow the creation of one's own experience of God. Joan heard voices, Moses climbed the mountain, Muslims travel to Mecca, Hindus hope for a higher birth and all are awaiting the re-creation of another's publicized success. Certainly the most elementary study of these religions unveils unparalleled sexism, but more insidious and more inescapable is the fact that they have inherent in their systems, a built in fail-safe against ever reaching beyond the prescribed victorious experience. The method is simple. Great pedestals are built, paintings are hung, and candles are lit that create an uncrossable chasm between humanity and myth.

A journey through the "feminist" theologians only reveals a further adherence to the system. Women ministers and rabbis offer liberation by trying to retrofit one experience for another. Rosemary Radford Ruether or Elizabeth Gould Davis submit God in a dress. The closest to a true revolutionary is Mary Daly, who suggested that God is a verb not a noun. This removes the need to assign gender. Dr. Daly's later works reject her premise, but leave us with a battlefield for a mind, filled with trying to rewrite language and history to remove sexism from our words and thoughts. Ultimately, they all fall on the long side of the list, referencing experience with some external litmus test. None of them get to the root of things that is far deeper than scriptures, than gender, than exposing the lost civilizations of Matriarchy.

Much to my surprise, I was invited to participate in a "Feminist Think Tank." Feeling very complimented, I couldn't resist telling Rama that I was considering attending. He listened carefully and said, "Just remember, this time you don't have to stay." With that he walked away, leaving me with no idea what he meant. A few nights later I went to this meeting of the minds, eager to participate and meet the other attendees. After the introductions, the leader of the symposium turned to me and said, "We understand you have a male teacher now. How could you accept a male teacher?" With total enthusiasm, I replied, "His teachings go beyond gender." "BG! BG! Where would we be if everyone went BG!" she shouted. Twelve women waited for the answer. I quietly collected my coat and said, "I think you would all be more comfortable if I left." I went out the door and walked for several hours that night trying to sort it all out.

In the past, I would have felt compelled to stay and engage in high "politically correct" banter, if only because I was honored to have been invited. But, that night I saw that each woman was deeply involved in her own quest and her own language. My excitement to try to journey Beyond Gender was not part of their world. They were fueled with their anger, defined by their anatomy and protected by their thinking. To move beyond thought, to uproot the architecture of oppression was not an appropriate suggestion in that forum. What had happened to me? These were my sisters and it was not so long ago that I would have stayed for hours to demonstrate my understanding, my academic excellence, my superior political position. After walking for an hour or so, I smiled as I remembered Rama saying, "This time you don't have to stay."

The adventure to identify and annihilate the oppressor, to find radical liberation is a private one. It has to be invited, beckoned, maybe stumbled upon; but no matter the introductions, it evolves and blossoms. It was this realization that gave me the first clue that there is no internal problem seeking an external answer. The answer, the possibility of perfection, lies inside and the "problem" is outside. A baby girl and baby boy are not born with some sort of premonition of the master - slave relationship. It is an onslaught of countless forces pushing in from the outside. Religion was clearly not the answer. At best, it is part of the problem.

Buddhism is not a religion. Buddhism is a way of living one's life. It is a series of etiquettes that awards honor and respect to both the giver and receiver. Buddhism does not teach that there is a savior holding redemption stamps. There is no sin, no guilt, no delayed reward. There is evolution. There is perfection and clarity within: beyond gender, beyond description, beyond thoughts, beyond words. Biblical theologians knew that man took dominion over the animals by *naming* them. Feminist theologians declared that women are in a diminished position because the right to *name* had been taken from them. Even St. John said, "In the beginning was the word, and the word was with God." It seems as though everyone already knew that the essence of things, the pure expression of things, is buried in words. They just didn't consider what would be left after the words are stripped away. Maybe they thought that without words there will be nothing left.

Either way, there seems to be a great fight over who may name, who may assign words, who may use words. Buddhists have a great secret: on the other side of words lies Enlightenment.

The Passionate Heart

Existence is beyond the power of words
To define:
Terms may be used
But none of them absolute.
In the beginning of heaven and earth there were no words,
Words came out of the womb of matter;
And whether a man dispassionately
Sees to the core of life
Or passionately
Sees the surface,
The core and the surface
Are essentially the same,
Words making them seem different
Only to express appearance.
If name be needed, wonder names them both:
From wonder into wonder
Existence opens.
                    The Tao Te Ching

In Buddhism, not only is it possible to create one's own experience, it is pure practice. For a woman, for a man, Buddhism offers a way out of words, out of the lies that words carry, out of the oppression that words impose, out of the bondage of gender roles, out of the pain and suffering every earthling accepts as inescapable.

Chapter 18

Rama walked on stage in a three piece suit. He looked at ease, comfortable, natural, as if he wore a suit every day. He was handsome. He was classy. He was polished and debonair. It was unprecedented. It was foreign. It was shocking. We had grown accustomed to seeing our Teacher wearing trousers and an embroidered silk shirt. His beautiful shirts were handmade by one of the students, collarless and oriental in style. To see a spiritual leader in a suit was odd. To Americans, particularly Americans who preferred the Sixties, suits suggested conformity, corporate business, and classism. This was not an outfit for meditation, for truly spiritual people, or for supporting the stereotype of a Teacher that we all nurtured.

Rama modeled his outfit. "Do you like it?" If I am any representation of the rest of the students, I was very put off. This was not fitting into my definitions at all. It might have been easier to accept if Rama hadn't looked so at home in it. Naturally, it was tailored perfectly. That was no surprise. But he looked like a business man, a successful business man who wore a suit at least five days a week. I wanted him to look like a *spiritual* teacher, not a corporate officer. I needed him to look as I had known him to look, and this was shattering my little world.

After removing his laced shoes and sitting half lotus on the couch, Rama began to explain. The principle reason he was wearing a suit was to show us that he could, not just wear a suit, but become someone who looks as if wearing a suit is totally natural. Along the path of Self-Discovery, a seeker must learn to let go of self-definitions. They have to be, as in life, in a constant state of change. If a person feels that their hair, their dress, their demeanor are actually part of who they are, it sustains a stagnant sense of self. "I would never shave my beard." "My long hair is part of who I am." "I would never wear pantyhose." All of these ideas hold a person in a certain mind state. Buddhism teaches that there are ten thousand states of mind. At one time or another, a student on the path must experience every single one to eventually move beyond them all.

The Passionate Heart

Rama told us that it is important to break out of our self images. These images are really a composite of personal taste, reaction against what we find distasteful, expectations of others, and Madison Avenue or even Haight Ashbury. Regardless of their origin, self images are solid, confining, defining, and ultimately, just another illusion. Without casting any vote, we come to believe that what we look like is part of who we are. The axiom, "clothes make the man," was not only true, but something holding a man (woman) captive.

Self images, believing that we are a certain person, dress in a certain way, refuse to dress in another, hold us in a distinct segment of the world. A Buddhist, a person who practices yoga, strives to move through the world unnoticed. Unlike those who want to convert all they meet, or who prefer to do business with people of the same religion as themselves, Buddhists do not seek attention or practice such discrimination. Rama explained that in order to journey without notice, one should try to "blend." Impeccability is always key, but also, one should dress without calling attention to one's self. It is unproductive to create artificial barriers by insisting on one certain image. A closet should not be a fortress protecting a singular notion. It should contain costumes that give a person what they need to interact in the world without arbitrarily excluding themselves or unintentionally alienating others.

Rama said that to have one solid, reliable, predictable image perpetuates the illusion that a person is someone in particular. A woman or man begins to think that they are the person who acts a certain way, appears a certain way, thinks a certain way. For a Buddhist seeking liberation, freedom, and perfect meditation, it is an obstacle to maintain one image, one way of seeing themselves, or to hold on to one singular mind state. The goal in Self-Discovery is to become selfless, and in doing so, become "no one in particular." It is not the same idea as being charitable, like the Christians who treat their neighbors as they would like to be treated. It is giving and living without thought of a return on the investment. Changing clothes, changing homes, changing images releases a person to become as the world needs them to be. Like water seeking its own level, the practitioner of Self-Discovery seeks to be of service, pass unnoticed, and be no one in particular.

The Passionate Heart

That night, Rama, our spiritual Teacher, looked like a business man. He sat on the familiar blue flowered couch and spoke the truth, as he did for us each week. Replace the couch with a podium and he looked as if he was addressing the Rotary club. He could have been addressing successful middle and upper class business women and men. They would be able to listen. They would be able to hear him. They might have found the usual silk embroidered shirt and flowered couch too much of a barrier to even consider what he was saying. Dressed in a suit, Rama could have walked into any corporate meeting, dined in the best restaurant, stayed in the finest hotel, and passed without offending or drawing attention. Rama believed that he was no one in particular. Neither the silk nor starched white shirt defined him, dictated his travels, or denied him admittance.

Rama suggested that we begin to experiment with our own lives. Certainly many, if not most of us could not afford to go out the next day and buy a tailored suit. He told us that the price was not important. We should buy just one thing; one thing that is unlike anything we would normally buy for ourselves. It should be something that is professional, tasteful, classic, and impeccable. The task was to choose the perfect object. It could be a pair of socks, dazzling underwear, a different hair cut, an object like a briefcase or wallet, dress shoes, or an entire outfit. We were told to shop, walk through the stores, and take our time. Rama also recommended that if we could not step outside the self-imposed boundaries of our self image and we found ourselves gravitating to the same things as always, we should take a friend to assist in the selection.

I went home and opened my closet. There was Zoe. Every article on every hanger was most definitely Zoe. It was obvious that I had shopped for years with only one thing in mind, to find items that were, "me." I imagined holding up each hanger and asking close friends if they thought I would like the article and there was no doubt, they would say yes. There were things I had hung on to for years because they were so much a part of my life. Picturing them piled into a trash bag felt as if I would be throwing part of me away. I guess that was the point, wasn't it? To throw part of me away. But that wasn't the entire recommendation. What about selecting, buying, and wearing things that were not predictably characteristic? How would that change my life?

On Saturday, I took a hundred dollars out of the bank and headed for the mall. This was not an ordinary mall; it had hundreds of shops, thousands of people. If it wasn't in this mall, it didn't exist. As I walked from window to window, display to display, I realized that all I was doing was searching for items that felt comfortable, familiar, and non-threatening. From earrings to shoes, all I was doing was looking for things that easily fit into my established narrow world. With unnoticeable ease, I was instantly disregarding anything that was not in harmony with the stuff in my closet at home. Then I began to hear what my mind was saying during this see-saw of like / dislike, want / not want, it's me / it's not me.

It all circled around how I wanted people to view me. Before that moment, I would have insisted that I had no "image" that I wanted to portray, no statement that I was making. I certainly was not trying to gain or lose admittance to the world, nor was I trying to tell others how I felt about them and their particular image. But the conversation in my head was proving me dead wrong. That dress was too classy. That sweater was too sloppy. Those shoes were too dressy. That's too old. That's too young. Fat people can't wear that! Only pretty women can carry that off. That's too masculine. That's too feminine. It was non-stop and virtually without consideration. It was a total and unqualified litany of reactions to absolutely everything. I was accepting decisions and selections based on conclusions I must have made decades ago. I began to seriously wonder if I had made one *new* decision in the last fifteen years. Where did all of these judgments come from, and most importantly, did I even believe in them?

As with all tasks that a Buddhist Master gives their students, the task itself is hardly the lesson. To every customer in the mall, I might have looked like any other Saturday shopper, but in fact, I was deeply immersed in a multi-life and complex exercise in Self-Discovery. The more I questioned my thoughts and slowed down my unexamined judgments, the more I wondered who I am. Who is it that stands under these clothes, within these opinions, buried in thoughtless resolutions? It might sound poetic, but it was neither romantic nor nostalgic. It was desperate and immediate. I wanted to know who I am.

Now, walking through the stores, I was set on fire. My attention was brilliant and sharp. Every item, in every display, was refined and crisp. It was as if I had never been in a store before. Every floor and department was offering me a new identity, a different personality, a ticket to another culture, a path to find out how far I could expand the idea of preference, taste, and image. My five Twenties, folded in my pocket, were a passport and I had control of the destination.

First of all, one hundred dollars would not buy a suit or dress, at least not the type that Rama had in mind. Second, I wanted to really shatter my puny world and so it would have to be something that, for one hundred dollars, was very expensive. Third, I wanted it to be an item that I would feel compelled to use immediately, not put on a shelf and merely admire. Earrings were a reasonably good choice; I would never spend that much on a pair of earrings.

I cruised the jewelry counters. I decided that the most professional pierced earrings were small studs; gold or pearl. I already owned them both, though certainly not from that price bracket. Finally, I had to give up on the earring idea because even if I bought an expensive pair, wearing them would definitely not make me feel any different. Glancing to the left, I saw handbags. I love purses. I owned gobs of purses. But, one hundred dollars on a purse was unthinkable. It was not that I didn't like the more expensive bags, I just couldn't imagine paying so much for one and then actually carrying it around. I had always appreciated beautiful expensive leather handbags hanging on wealthy women's shoulders, but I was amazed that they wore them to the market, the ballpark, or to work everyday. Now this had potential.

There were racks and racks of purses: shoulder straps, zippers, pockets, snaps, Velcro, even magnetic closures. Every designer had a line of purses. It was a veritable ocean of purses. How could I ever decide? Then it dawned on me. I only had to ask one simple question, "Would Rama like it?" As fast as I could ask the question, the answer surfaced, like the floating response you get when you turn over a crazy eight ball from Toys-R-Us. I wasn't asking if Rama would like the handbag, per se. I was actually asking if the bag fulfilled the task. I was holding each bag against a precise unit of measure; "was it impeccable?" It was simply amazing. Rama had given me an exquisite gift on my shopping excursion. Now I wasn't looking for a purse or anything of any particular value. I was looking for impeccability.

I gave up on the racks. The best purses were in the glass cases requiring sales assistance. The price tags were hidden and the leather longed to be touched. Clearly the bag had to be black. It had to look expensive and tasteful, but not trendy. Then I saw it. I paused and pretended that Rama was shopping with me. "Do you like it?" I whispered inwardly. A sales woman offered to show me some bags. I pointed to the object of my attention. She ceremoniously handed it to me. Total perfection. It was beautiful, leather, black, big with shoulder straps and small pockets on the outside. If I saw a woman carrying this bag, I would think it was very classy. It was most certainly not something I would ever consider for myself. I dug the price tag out of the inside zipper compartment: $95.00. The deed was done. The bag was mine.

Walking down the aisle in the Beverly the next week was unlike any other. Familiar music was playing. The check-in tables were the same. As always, women and men were sitting, reading books or quietly talking, while waiting for the arrival of their Teacher. But things were palpably different. Each student had a secret, a special something that created an opening to another possible future. One week ago, their self-images had gone unnoticed, unchallenged. Their definitions had been just a little more solid than they were on this particular Tuesday. Seven days, one shopping trip, and these Buddhist students were just a little bit closer to becoming "no one in particular."

Chapter 19

The only piece of mail that is worse than a ninety day old bill is a rejection notice. I got fourteen. I had sent *The Hungry Heart* both "over the transom" and to specific editors whose work I respected. My notices did not address the quality of writing or the overall style of the book. I could have accepted either of those criticisms. Rather, each and every letter began with a paragraph expressing sincere admiration of my efforts on behalf of the Equal Rights Amendment and all fourteen ended with an apology that no one would be interested. To publishers, it was a marketing issue and they felt that the readership would not be interested in either the American Feminist Movement or the ERA. The men and women who read my poorly written manuscript explained that the topic would not sell books. The topic did not matter to anyone. It certainly mattered to me.

This was not the first time, or the last, that I have found myself in a curious minority. And even though it seemed to be a matter of course in my life, I have never expected it or met it with anything less than genuine surprise. It is not a galactic egotism that assumes that everyone will agree with ME, but rather an innocent assumption that eventually everyone will stumble onto the same discoveries I had. I figured that it was simply a matter of time, not wisdom. On many occasions, I found myself deeply embarrassed by this unassuming expectation.

Case in point. At the clinic where I was working, it was customary to provide an evening orientation for the new Marriage and Family Therapists. Although not one of my preferred duties, I participated in this tradition as a welcoming gesture to get acquainted with the counselors. The program consisted of a few consciousness raising sessions, which I equate to psycho drama games. This particular month, the CR session involved writing a list of six people whom each of us admire, telling everyone what the six people have in common and then reading the list aloud.

I breezed through the assignment: Gandhi, Mary Magdalene, Leonardo DaVinci, Cleopatra, Emily Dickinson, and Joan of

The Passionate Heart

Arc. (I intentionally omitted Rama, feeling that my apprenticeship was not something I needed to reveal to all of these shrinks.) My turn was first. I surveyed the list. The common denominator was obvious; they were all dead. Without hesitation, I proclaimed, "They are all dead." Without missing a beat, I listed their names. Nine psych majors stared at me. Apparently, I had revealed something quite disturbing to these women and men. I had no inkling of my faux pas until the others read their lists and proudly proclaimed what their selections had in common. Each of the nine had listed parents, spouses, children, best friends, school teachers and other living people. Their common identifier was mutual love and support.

Maybe they felt sorry for me. Maybe they felt that my life had not been as rich as theirs. Maybe they felt that I had somehow been cheated out of an array of healthy relationships. On the other hand, I felt utterly amazed that they could even compare MOM to Joan of Arc. How could their spouse hold a candle to DaVinci? What could their third grade teacher possibly have said that could measure up with Dickinson? In reality, I felt sorry for them. Their minds had tacitly dismissed everyone who was dead.

With the exception of Rama, almost everyone I loved, admired, and wondered with/about, was alive to me only through books. I adore history and authors. One summer I read all of Hesse's work in the order in which he had written them. After such a romantic summer together, how could I resist him? I felt more intimate with Lillian Hellman than any of my short term lovers. Virginia Woolf let everyone into her most secret heart. Emily Dickinson's poems and her remarkable letters gave her readers a level of personal revelation that is almost embarrassing. These people may be dead, but to me, they certainly offered love and support.

What had Martin Luther unleashed when he insisted that girls be taught to read? His intention was to eliminate the faithful's reliance on priests' biased interpretations by teaching people to read scriptures and make their own moral determinations. One of the many results of his reading crusade was that, for the first time, girls were taught to read. While it did not elevate girls' education to the position granted to boys, in time it opened up a world too large to ever nail shut again. Women began to read and thus eventually to write, write for themselves and for one another. Charlotte Perkins Gilman's *Yellow Wallpaper* would change the future for countless women imprisoned in their minds. Her little notebook and pencil, hidden in the pockets of her corseted dress, liberated thousands of women. Although her husband forbade her to write, as it would "excite" her, she managed to speak far beyond the grave through her tiny novel.

From grade school to graduate school, no teacher could coax me out of the library without a struggle. Admittedly, I was seldom reading books that had a relationship to any classes. When I was a sophomore in high school, my mother was beckoned to the Head Mistress's office because they found *The Many Loves of Dobie Gillis* and *Spencer's Mountain* in my desk. The Madams of the Sacred Heart were shocked (about the covers, they would never read them) and I was dumbfounded by their ignorance.

Was it that books were my teachers or that my teachers were in books? Regardless of the answer, until I met Rama, no living person challenged my mind, stirred my heart or spoke to my soul. Week after week, month after month, Rama astounded me with his eclectic knowledge, deep insights, revolutionary thinking and courageous conclusions. Nothing was sacred and everything was holy. No topic was trivial and no subject was beyond scrutiny. His mind bubbled over with endless understandings on an ocean of information. With Rama, no moment was boring, no discourse frivolous, no evening forgettable. I remember Rama telling us that his father simply could not figure out how his son knew so much about so many things. It was simply inexplicable.

Even if there had been no stirring in my soul that this man was genuinely spiritual, my intellect could not get enough. I wanted to hear every talk, listen to every word, follow every discourse. They were always intricate, provocative, literate, utterly new, and filled with humor. His sense of humor was beyond the normal human realm as it was never at another's expense. And no matter how closely I listened, never have I heard a sexist, biased, prejudiced, or flippant remark. His mind seemed to contain expertise on any subject, from every vantage point, surveying centuries of information.   It was wonderful.

Rama often recommended certain books. We would read something as a group and Rama would discuss it the following week.   It was nothing like the dry, academic, cursory discussions I had sat through so many times in classrooms. It was as if he actually knew the authors, the characters, the time periods.   From *Ulysses* to *The Lord of the Rings,* Stephen King to Dorothy Bryant, when Rama talked about them, he transported us across time and space and opened up worlds that heretofore rested on the printed page. Like his father, I too was unable to comprehend how anyone could know so much, in such detail and with such explicit understanding as my Teacher.

The diversity of titles was vast, as was the subject matter. Rama found inspiration anywhere and everywhere.   The authors and their domains cut across centuries, disciplines, and cultures.   Fortunately for my overwhelming desire for synthesis, Rama gave us a list of twelve recommended books. As with all things related to Rama's teaching, his criteria were above reproach. He explained that if one had only these twelve books, they would have access to the secrets of the ages, the essence of truth, and enough comprehensive information to safely navigate one's life.

1. *The Way of Life* according to Lao Tzu, translated by Witter Brynner
This is my favorite book in the entire world. When I was in my twenties, I copied it long-hand several times, wishing to memorize it.   These eighty-one short verses are brilliant, poetic, and infinitely inspiring. It was written in the Sixth Century B.C. China and is the basis for Taoism.

2. *The Bhagavad Gita,* translated by Swami Prabhavananda and Christopher Isherwood
The title means "The Song Celestial." It is a chapter from the Hindu Epic, *The Mahabharata,* in which Lord Krishna is instructing his student Arjuna.   It is the central teaching in Hinduism and Gandhi's favorite book.

3. *How to Know God; The Yoga Sutras of Patanjali*, translated by Swami Prabhavananda and Christopher Isherwood
Patanjali is an Indian sage who dates from 1500 years ago. Sutras are short teachings that were easily memorized, as there were no books at the time. His teachings are the essence of yoga and ancient methods of meditation.

4. *Shankara's Crest Jewel of Discrimination*, translated by Swami Prabhavananda and Christopher Isherwood
Dating from the Seventh Century, Shankara was a scholar and a teacher who founded many monasteries that are still present in India today. His writings are the classic Vedanta text.

5. *The I Ching*, Wilhelm Baynes Edition
The I Ching, or the Book of Changes, is a compilation by several authors, traversing several centuries. It is composed of sixty-four hexagrams that can be used as an oracle, by throwing coins or yarrow sticks. But regardless if the reader uses the *I Ching* to reveal the truth or predict the future, the verses weave in and out of time, telling the creation story of the universe and each individual moment.

6. *The Gospel of Sri Ramakrishna*, by "M"
Ramakrishna is thought to be fully Enlightened and the first one to be actually photographed, as he lived in the late 19th century. Although his "gospel" is greatly reflective of his time and culture, there is an essence of truth and wonder about his teachings. I am grateful to have been introduced to him, in that it led me to discover his holy and dear wife, Sarada Devi.

7. *Journey of Ixtlan*, by Carlos Castaneda
8. *Tales of Power*, by Carlos Castaneda
Both of these books are chronicles about Castaneda's apprenticeship to a Yaqui Indian teacher, don Juan Matus. Although Carlos' original intent was to write a thesis on the use of psychotropic plants in Mexico by the Yaqui Indians, he shortly found himself in a world of magic and truth. Embedded in Carlos' fascinating struggle to understand is the unparalleled wisdom and humor of don Juan, a Western sage.

9. *The Supreme Yoga*, a translation of the *Yoga Vasistha*, by Swami Venkatesananda
The Supreme Yoga is referred to as scripture. It is a whirlwind of stories in which the Holy Dharma is woven and rewoven on

a thousand different levels. As it says in the forward, it is best to read one page a day. I found it bright and happy, confusing and mystical, challenging and inspiring. It is a book that is better read by the heart than the mind.

10. *The Upanishads* translated by Swami Prabhavananda and Frederick Manchester
The Upanishads are the final verses of the Vedas, the oldest scripture in India and the original text for orthodox Hinduism. Differing from the Christian scriptures in that it does not serve as a history of a god once born and now gone, it encourages the direct experience of the infinite.

11. *The Tibetan Book of the Dead,* the Evans-Wentz edition
This may be the most esoteric book in the world; certainly it is subject to the most interpretations. Even the translator, Dr. Evans-Wenz relays that many of the teachings can only be passed from Teacher to student through direct transmission. Nonetheless, it is a guide for living as a Tibetan Buddhist: dying a little each day to desire and aversion to be reborn alive to light.

12. *Walden,* by Henry David Thoreau
These are short essays about Thoreau's two years and two months living in a tiny house on Walden Pond in Concord, Massachusetts. Nature is his god and their relationship is deep, intimate, and thoughtful. Clearly Thoreau's experience is genuine and poetic because of the purity of his intent. He is extreme, radical and quietly revolutionary.

Yes, it is true. There are no books by women. To which I answer, "No, not yet." I could spend time being angry about such realities. But, in the course of my studies with Rama, it was becoming apparent that to tarry in the worlds of anger and frustration about the inequality of the sexes served only as an interruption to getting on with living. It seems as though my idealism has flipped from the past to the future. The past demands realism - objective and inquisitive. The present requires silence and immersion. The future asks for faith and hope.

Chapter 20

I don't think anyone in the world loves words more than Rama. I don't mean words that lie, words that hurt, words that imprison. I mean words that create a new meaning, words that bring joy to the heart, words that open worlds, words that tell what has not been told before. Rama holds a Ph.D. in English Literature from the State University of New York, Stony Brook. He told us that since this was his first incarnation in the West, he wanted to learn the language. When Rama says he wants to learn something, this is no cursory understanding. Not only does he have a photographic memory, but a curiosity that knows no rival. Over the years, I have heard Rama recite from memory: Shakespeare, Poe, Kabir, Blake, Dickinson, Roethke, entire verses of the *Vedas, Bhagavad Gita, Upanishads, I-Ching, Tao Te Ching*, etc. Rama loves to learn as much as he loves to teach. Many times he has said that one should always be a student.

Rama invited us to see *The Merry Wives of Windsor* at the Old Globe Theater in San Diego. I have seen many plays by Shakespeare. I always enjoy them. Since I was 34 when I met Rama, I had already done many things, seen many places, read hundreds of books. That was not the case with many, if not most, of Rama's students. A large number of them met Rama when they were very young, under twenty-two. It was an interesting group of people whose primary focus was creating and maintaining a spiritual life. Although most had attended college, few were dedicated to building professional business careers.

Some students worked in the arts: music, dance, and acting. I knew several who were in the medical professions, particularly nursing. There was also a group of students in low-end professions, such as food services, temp workers, sales clerks, or whatever they could do to get by. To me, it was understandable. Spiritual seekers' desires run a different vein than average business oriented people. They want joy, fun, free time, fewer hassles, sunsets, and fulfilling relationships. It boiled down to what was central in one's life. For most Americans, it was family and security. For these students, it appeared to be inner peace and spiritual evolution. To Rama, these things were not mutually exclusive. Of course, he wanted all of us to have a spiritual life, but also to be educated, well read, and in professionally successful careers that offered financial advancement. The body, mind, and spirit were to be developed equally. Rama wanted his students to be successful in everything they did.

There was no ashram here, with the women confined to the kitchen. In fact, when Rama invited students to his house, *he* always did the cooking. This was not a community in which the students were asked to donate their savings and then spend their lives tending orchards and gardens. Ours was an ashram without walls. We lived and worked in the world. We were encouraged to have experiences, to make a good living, and enjoy our lives. Rama even told us to go and hear other teachers. He wanted our education to be as eclectic, progressive, comprehensive, and cultured as his own.

Over the last year, some students had taken Rama's career suggestions to heart and begun computer school. People were attending small professional schools, local community classes, and university courses. They were starting careers in programming and systems analysis. Each week, Rama would ask who got new jobs. A few people would stand and tell us about their new positions. The women were advancing just as fast as the men. Our shopping task had grown into an ongoing improvement program. We began to cycle through our wardrobes by throwing out something old and replacing it with something new and more professional. Slowly, but surely, we were becoming better dressed, better educated, and gainfully employed.

It was a curious thing. I had been going to meetings for almost two years and yet there was no sense that anyone was losing their individuality. It was a very diverse collection of women and men. Sometimes I wondered if we had anything in common at all. This was not a community in which people started walking and talking alike. I was never a joiner for the very reason that I couldn't understand why an entire association of people would want to have some group identity. But, this was different. These women and men were deeply independent and individualistic. One time Rama told us that the only thing that we had in common was that we believed in "the possibility of him."

That winter, I had occasion to visit my closest childhood friend. We had gone to both grade school and high school together. She was married with several children. I waited for all of the kids to get bedded down, her husband to excuse himself, and tell her of my discovery. "I have found him," I told her. "The one who can change everything is here, now." "He is fully Enlightened and I have seen him perform miracles." I thought that she of all people would believe me. She listened. She nodded at all of the appropriate moments. She smiled. Then she told me that such a thing was simply "impossible." I realized that she just didn't have room in her mind for such a thing to be possible. Her world didn't allow for it. I was starting to understand what Rama meant by saying, we believed in "the possibility of him."

If a student doesn't trust a teacher, there can be no true exchange. In the case of a spiritual Teacher and an aspiring student, it could never last. Too many times a Teacher makes suggestions or corrections that, without trust, a student could never accept, never consider, never be able to understand. Often, a student has to simply put the desire to understand aside and follow a suggestion blindly because the actual lesson can only be comprehended in retrospect after contemplation. It is through the growth that takes place by fulfilling the task that the student gains the ability to understand. The desire to know in advance doesn't work in this relationship.

Much to my surprise, Rama announced that we were all going to Maui. To me, it sounded like a pipe dream. I certainly didn't have the money to go on such an extravagant trip. Not only was it half way across the Pacific, but the hotel he booked was very expensive. The entire four day vacation was going to cost about $3,000. That was more than I made in a month at the clinic. Strangely enough, almost everyone was signing up for the trip. How could they possibly afford such a thing? I wanted to go. I had never been to Hawaii. But, I certainly did not have that kind of money. It seemed odd to me. Why not go some place that wasn't so expensive? Why not stay at the cheapest hotel?

The Passionate Heart

John, a student I had recently met, drove with me to San Diego for the Shakespeare play. I told him that I was very confused about the trip to Hawaii. Most of the students didn't have that kind of money. Why and how were they planning on going? John told me that I was the crazy one. He said that first I should sign up and then the money would surface. I replied that not only does money not just pop out of the pavement, but also how could I, in good conscience, go on such an extravagant trip? What did this have to do with spirituality? He laughed and said that I would never know if I didn't take the chance. More importantly, the money would never appear if I didn't at least have the faith to put my name on the list.

I sat through the play half-heartedly. It was not my favorite Shakespeare, although the Globe theater was exceptional. Even if it had been my favorite, *Merchant of Venice*, I would not have been able to concentrate. Hawaii, $3,000, this was a lot more than a hundred dollar purse which, by the way, was under my seat. I babbled all the way home about my conundrum. John marveled at my inability to picture myself in Hawaii. He felt no conflict. He did not have the money. He signed up.

The next Tuesday night arrived and, although conflicted, I registered for the trip. It was not necessarily an act of faith or even hope. The fact was that it was the deadline for signing up and if a UFO appeared with $3,000, I was going to be ready. The weeks rolled by, the money was not growing on the trees in my front yard, a deposit was due shortly, and my desire to go on the trip was becoming a major obsession. I did the only thing I could think of. I called Mom. Mom had money, that was not an issue. But, money for Hawaii was not an easy request. At the worst, I figured that it was the $3,000 phone call. Regardless of how painful it might be, it would be over faster than a root canal. I called, I begged, Mom finally said okay. Somehow I don't think this was the miracle John predicted, but I was going to Hawaii.

Patty and I drove to LAX and boarded the 727 headed for Maui. There were lots of other students on the plane. You could tell by the headphones on their ears, the shades on their eyes, and the smiles a yard wide. I had no idea what to expect once we got there, but two miles west of LA, I was instantly happy. Although it was a long plane ride, before we knew what was happening, we had leis around our necks and were on a bus headed for the Hyatt.

Looking out the bus window, I was completely overwhelmed. It is impossible to describe the beauty of the island. All I can really say is that I remember crying at the first ballet I ever saw. I was twenty-two. I sobbed all through *Les Sylphides* because I was ashamed that something so beautiful existed on earth and I had never seen it before. Maui was more beautiful than the ballet, more beautiful that my imagination had ever made room for, more beautiful than I thought God had granted the earth. Just to be alive, surrounded by the colors, the sky, the nature and the water, made my heart almost burst.

From there, it only got better. The Hyatt Hotel in Maui is humanity's glimpse of the Western Paradise. Oh, it was very big and very lovely, of course. But, everywhere you looked was either a Buddha or a glorious exotic bird. Hundreds of statues were displayed throughout the entire hotel and garden. Dozens of fabulous rainbow-colored parrots, macaws, and cockatoos sat on great hoops suspended from the ceiling. The pool swept under a waterfall and spilled indoors. There was an open air restaurant with little birds, like wrens, hippity-hopping from table to table, chirping only good news.

Opening the door to my suite, I found my roommate sitting on the lanai with two Pina Coladas, awaiting my arrival. I immediately swapped my city clothes for my shorts, sat on a lounge chair, and put my feet up on the railing. In full view, the Pacific was incredible, rivaled only by the blue sky that met her on the horizon. With a tiny purple orchid in my drink, what else could one possibly do, but toast Rama?

The itinerary was simple. There were meetings on each of the three nights, a day trip to Haleakala National Park, and the rest of time was totally free. I didn't care if I ever moved from the lanai, but I had rented a convertible and made some plans with Patty. Fortunately, nothing was on the agenda for the rest of the afternoon. I sat. I gazed at the ocean. Mostly, I smiled.

The Passionate Heart

Something was very different. Something felt very different. I felt very different. It took several hours to realize that I was not thinking. The torrent of thoughts that usually poured through my mind was gone. It wasn't that I had stopped my thoughts. This was totally effortless. I was completely functional; in fact, my senses were crackling. I could find thoughts when I needed them, such as "How about another (virgin) Pina Colada?" But the thoughts that habitually led me around, dragged me around, suffocated me, were nowhere to be found. My mother, my teachers, my boss, my past; the perpetual blah, blah, blah was silent.

We met with Rama at 8 P.M. He was the ultimate host. He was funnier than ever. He told us that we should have a wonderful vacation and thoroughly enjoy ourselves. It was time to forget all about the mainland and have a talk with a fish. He recommended para-sailing, snorkeling, scuba diving, hiking, swimming, or just sitting on the beach. The only directive was to have fun. Everyone was cordial and happy. I had never known this group to be so light-hearted. People who had never said a word to me were gracious and affable.

Rama ended the meeting early, suggesting that we stroll through the gardens and along the shore before going to bed. In the courtyard, I discovered magical statues of Buddha hidden among flowering trees and winding paths. There were statues of fierce growling dogs that were originally made to guard Buddhist temples from evil spirits. The architect who built the Maui Hyatt had traveled throughout Asia and brought back several million dollars worth of Buddhist artifacts for this phenomenal paradise. I was appreciating every single one. I wasn't Zoe the next-door neighbor, the clinic assistant director, the angry feminist, the bibliophile. I was just a perceiver, a perceiver of intense beauty and wonder.

The next day, Patty and I drove the fabled Hana Highway. The tour book said that it had over six hundred twists and turns. It must have been a gross under-estimation. Curving and swerving in our yellow Mustang, it became hilarious. There were sugar cane fields, banana tree groves, gorges, valleys, waterfalls, hillsides, and breath-taking ocean panoramas. As the car snaked forty-five to ninety degrees, this way and that, we gasped, pointed, shrieked and roared over the incomparable splendor. Then we began to notice these state signs along the road that read: "Scenic Area Ahead - 1 Mile." Who could have possibly placed the signs? Who could have made such a determination? How could one mile be any more, or less, beautiful than any other on this fabulous road? At first Patty and I believed these misguided signs and looked for that special "Scenic Area." Then it became silly. We grew hysterical with laughter over these incredible perjurious signs. Eventually, the lush scenery was almost too much, like eating too many pink roses on a birthday cake.

On the morning of the second day, Rama met all of us at Haleakala National Park. The forty-mile drive to the park ascends from sea level to over 10,000 feet. People go early in the day in hopes of finding the view free of clouds. The Haleakala crater is twenty-one miles in circumference, seven miles long, and over two miles wide. It appears to be a wasteland filled with cinder, lava flows and mini-craters. Rama warned us the night before to be very sure that we would be able to make the hike in and out again. The air is very thin and the walk steep. He advised us that there was no shame in not making the hike. It was better to wait at the top than to inconvenience everyone by not being able to easily walk down and back up the path unassisted. That's all I needed to hear to decide to stay atop and be content with watching.

Embarrassed by my inability to hike with everyone, I found a secluded spot. With a full view of the path down the barren crater, I sat on green grass concealed by tropical bushes. Rama led the group. They walked in for at least a half hour and stood still for an hour more. Many times Rama lifted his arms to the sky. I could only imagine what was being said. As the time passed, I began to regret my decision. Moreover, I regretted that I didn't even attempt the walk. Eventually, I felt like a slob who was obviously missing out on something marvelous.

Rama led the walk back to the top. Nervously, I busied myself with my camera. Out of nowhere, I heard, "Hi." I turned and looked. It was Rama. He was standing only five feet away. "Hi," I sheepishly replied, embarrassed to have my laziness exposed. He smiled affectionately and slowly walked away.

The Passionate Heart

Maybe I could have hiked down with the group that day. I might have even survived the trek. But, that special moment with my Teacher was bigger to me than any crater.

The Passionate Heart

Chapter 21

The third and final night in Hawaii arrived. Rama spoke. He asked us to take a moment and notice how comfortable we were. Even though the hotel was very expensive, we were at ease. We may have been vacationing in one of the wealthiest spots in the world, but we did not feel awkward or out of place. Regardless of our financial circumstances on the mainland, this magnificent setting felt natural. The hotel and the land had a level of refinement that was appropriate for us. It was not just a lovely place to visit; it was actually suitable for our evolution. We were seekers of light.

In the East, it is understood that people who are seeking light and perfect meditation need to live in refined and secluded environments. In Tibet or Japan, the finest buildings, placed in the most beautiful areas, are the temples. Monasteries are intentionally built on premium locations with the best views. It is not a matter of preference or social reward. It is physics. It is mathematics. Meditators find it easier to access higher regions of the mind and stop thought for longer periods of time in certain places as opposed to others.

Rama called them "power spots." What distinguishes one spot from another is the amount of power it has. Haleakala is a power spot. The Anza Borrego desert is a power spot. The Hyatt in Maui is a power spot. Each one is very different and each one has a different type of power. In the case of the hotel, it is the land that drew the architect. It is the land that attracted such beauty. The land had actually enhanced our meditation. The beauty, the serenity, the seclusion, the ocean elevated our ability to meditate.

I would never have believed it unless I had experienced it. Upon reflection, it was true. Since the moment I had unwound from the city and the plane ride, my thoughts had noticeably and significantly slowed down. On the island, meditation was effortless and I was consistently happy. It wasn't the surface and volatile happiness I knew back in California. It was a deep contented happiness. I had not really considered why. I would not have attributed it to the land or the ocean. I certainly would not have guessed it to be the artistic and luxurious surroundings of a resort hotel.

To me, being spiritual meant placing a ceiling on acquiring material things and shunning extravagance. Somewhere I had picked up and nurtured the notion that, if it was genuinely spiritual, it could not be associated with money. Maybe it was my disgust with the Vatican and how the church regards (disregards) the poor. Most of the saints and spiritual people I admired were poor. I thought that meditation, stopping thought, and selfless giving were more in harmony with the image of a begging bowl and wandering barefoot through a forest. But now my experience was contradicting all of these ideas.

Buddhism is taught through the simple and pure method of experience. A Buddhist is a scientist of life. They break the boundaries of precedence, experiment with their lives, and draw their own conclusions. Regardless of what the stories of holy women or men and the scriptures relay, a Buddhist tries things first hand. Even if the conclusions are contrary to what others have found, they still trust their own results. A Buddhist Teacher creates the conditions for an experiment and the student has their own experience.

My Hawaiian laboratory was presenting me with a unique and unfamiliar body of evidence. My expectation had been a fun four-day vacation, but I thought it would only be a momentary flicker of indulgence. I figured it would be a series of photos to take home and then I would merely resume my practical life. The unexpected fact was that I was feeling more at home in Hawaii than in my home. I was feeling more myself in this foreign environment. In a world I had only dreamt about just four days ago, my mind seemed to be more my own. What had my Teacher revealed to me and moreover, what would I possibly do with this lesson? I listened to him as never before.

Rama told us that there were lines of power running throughout the earth. Power is neither good nor bad. It is simply power. If we understand this, we can use power to change our lives, shift our states of mind and possibly aid us in stopping thought. Tibet was the sublime example. It is the purest power spot on the planet. The energy and power lines of the Himalayas are the best on earth for meditation and spiritual advancement. Had the Communist Chinese not seized Tibet, Rama would be living there.

Rama always wanted to give us practical information that we could directly use in our lives. He explained that there are actual components one can use to survey the power of a certain place. Often, it is remote, with a minimum of human vibrations. This could be because of elevation, being surrounded by water, dangerous terrain, unfriendly climate, or just too difficult to reach. The monasteries in the snowy Himalayas appear to be hanging off the edges of a cliff. This was not done to keep the monks in, but to keep the other people out and keep the energy as pure as possible. Haleakala crater, the Grand Canyon, the desert, remote islands are naturally insulated from the pollution of human vibrations.

Another type of power spot attracts people. You can tell there is power in the land because the people prosper who live and work there. Greenwich, Connecticut has a certain power. While just a mile away, Port Chester, New York has quite another. One might presume that the wealthy people bring the power to Greenwich, but the truth is just the opposite. People prosper because they live on powerful land. They actually draw the lines of energy through themselves and their lives reflect the quality of the energy.

Rama cautioned us that, as with all natural resources, the power can be used up. For example, Beverly Hills used to be rich with pure power, but it has been spoiled by the greed and intent of the people living there. Los Angeles, once the capital of the American Dream, is running on fumes now. Unemployment is up, business is down, the power has run out.

Another way to assess the land's power is by observing the types of buildings and businesses that are there. From churches, graveyards, golf courses, libraries, factories, corporate parks to the city dump; each manifests precise and reliable indications of the power in the land. These are actual physical expressions of the land's energy. For example, the lines of power are clear and exact in Manhattan, New York. From Central Park to Wall Street, the United Nations to Harlem, the Upper East Side to Soho, it is a kaleidoscope of energy. Every Manhattan native can say exactly where a dancer would live, a student, a financier, a homeless person, an entrepreneur, a superstar or a welfare mother. It is not the people arbitrarily building tribes. It is defined by the land.

In addition to accessing power in the land, a person can collect and store power. The best way to collect power is through meditation. By sitting and stopping thought, the practitioner creates an opening for power to come into the world. If a person sits in the same place in their home when they meditate, they can actually create a "power spot." The area actually collects energy. One would take particular care of the area and place special objects there. With the example of the hotel, the power in the land was further increased because of all the beautiful gardens and sacred objects. The more care given, the more power is collected and stored.

Finally, Rama asked us to consider that to achieve perfect meditation, full liberation, and the merge with light, it would require us to significantly upgrade our lives. There was no need to feel hindered or imprisoned by our current financial circumstances, but if we genuinely wanted to progress, we would have to live in better neighborhoods and lead more refined lives. It is not a matter of preference or social reward. It is physics. It is mathematics. Now, through our own experimentation, we had proof that meditators find it easier to access higher regions of the mind and stop thought for longer periods of time in places that had power.

For us, the hardest part of this lesson was that we would have to eliminate our Western ideas that money is evil and career advancement is contrary to spiritual growth. Rama explained that money is inherently neither good nor evil. It is money. It is paper. It is a representation of energy. He said that it would take just as much effort to make a little money as a lot. Forty hours a week is forty hours a week regardless of the pay. In fact, higher paying jobs tend to wear a person down less than the lower paying ones. The important thing is what you do with the money. Money can actually aid in Self-Discovery if it is used to create a life of liberation and power.

Rama advised us to take all of this information home. He told us to remember the refinement, the energy, and the feeling of our vacation in Maui. We should recollect the beauty of the island, the vastness of the ocean, and the silence of Haleakala. Our apartments should be just as lovely. Our plants should be just as well tended. Our meditations should be just as elevated. The aesthetic of our lives needs to be just as refined because we are seekers of light. Finally, Rama said that everything we had experienced on our trip was ours to keep, to take wherever we go, for all eternity.

The next morning, it was time to go. I felt melancholy and nostalgic. I had left Costa Mesa in innocence, like a tourist with extra rolls of film. I was returning with more to consider, to change and to grapple with than ever before. I felt an apprehension that I may be a tourist in Costa Mesa now, with my home in some silent remote spot that I would never see again. There was entirely too much to think about.

Patty and I went up the steps of the DC10 and walked down the aisle of the first class seats. I heard a friendly voice call out, "It looks like you two had a good time!" I turned around and saw Rama smiling at both of us. "Yes," I answered, "the time of my life."

The five hours back to the mainland was infinitely longer than the trip going to Hawaii. My mind was sifting and sorting through everything Rama had said the night before. As usual, it was not so much evaluating what he said, but rather it was realizing the enormity of the consequences of what he said. If liberation and power did have a relationship with land and money, what would women do? What could women do?

Politically, things were not improving. Equal numbers of women and men were graduating from college, but the glass ceiling was stopping women from reaching top management positions. Women still represent only 40% of the work force in the Fortune 500 companies. Sexual harassment is widespread and is being used as a tool to keep women from advancing. There are more women doctors and attorneys than ever, but the women are being locked out of the tenured positions. If we rely on the court system to enforce equality, with the average litigation time being eight years, it will take four hundred and seventy years for women to achieve equality in the workplace.

The Passionate Heart

Flying east over the Pacific, I began to see that glass ceilings, sexual harassment, gender bigotry, and male legislators were merely symptoms, not causes. Women did not have the power, the raw power they needed to move forward. For the most part, the energy lines of the earth were governed by men. Men owned the best properties. Men decided who would travel where. Men controlled women's access to the power lines of the earth. Men were not just regulating women's career and financial advancement, they were stopping women's ability to progress spiritually as well.

For women to achieve lasting liberation, they will have to discover their own power lines. Women will have to invent their own ways to collect and store power. Women have to get the information, experiment with their lives, and have their own experiences.

I knew Rama was telling the truth. He was giving away the very secrets that had kept men in power for centuries. He was breaking the chain of silence. He was offering women a way to access power. He was creating an opening between the worlds. Rama was the real "power spot."

Chapter 22

In a meeting in early March 1985, Rama distributed blank 3 x 5 cards. He said that these little cards would change our lives forever. After teasing us for a while, Rama told us to draw two small squares along the left border. "Next to the top box, write LA. and by the bottom one, write Boston," said Rama. Then he told us to put the cards away and out of our minds, not unlike telling someone "Do not open the drawer with the elephant in it."

For over eight years, Rama had been privately teaching only on the West coast, with centers in LA, San Diego, and San Francisco. He felt that the moment had arrived to open a meditation center in the East. Rama saw that he would be teaching some of his students in Boston. It was the Dharma. He explained that many of us would join with him to start this new Boston center. He already knew the precise number and this evening was going to be an exercise in our ability to "see" the right thing to do.

Although it happened rarely, there were special occasions when Rama suggested that decisions should be seen, as opposed to made. It is because there is one truthful decision waiting to be uncovered. At these unique times, Rama would direct us to close our eyes, meditate deeply, and then simply watch what happens. Our higher selves would know what to do. The principle at work here is that the truth exists beyond attraction and repulsion. If we could eliminate desire, we would always be able to see what was the Dharma. As the first line in the ancient Chinese Zen poem, *The Hsin Hsin Ming* says, "The Great Way is easy for those who have no preference."

After a long explanation of Rama's newest dream, newest scheme, he told us to close our eyes, meditate for a few minutes, and check off the box that would design our fate. I did not need a few minutes. There was no way I was moving to Boston. Sixteen years ago, I ran for my life to the Pacific Ocean and away from the Midwest. Upon graduating from college, my husband and I drove straight for the shore, turned the car east, and rented the first apartment we found. It was eight doors from the sand in Hermosa Beach. Anything east of the Harbor Freeway, let alone the Rockies, was out of the question.

The beach meant youth, freedom, sunshine, surfboards, and leisure. The rest of the country meant family, children, neckties, and pensioned work. I arrived at the beach looking for a world that did not endorse the draft, did not reject non-traditional roles, and promoted questioning authority. I sometimes mused that since the most revolutionary people moved to the shore lines; the citizens of the sea must do the same. Are the free thinking fish, whales, and dolphins setting up households near the land? Bored with the status quo, is each of us looking out at an inhabitable world contemplating the unknowable possibilities? Regardless of the chimerical nature of my wonderment, the Pacific had been a dream come true for me, and Boston, or any city over three miles east, was not a possibility.

I opened my eyes, marked LA, and we took a break. Patty checked Boston! I couldn't believe my ears. She had just graduated from Chiropractic school and had begun developing her practice. I asked why she had checked Boston and she assured me that she was just as surprised as I. She had not made the decision; the decision had made her. And so my best friend was leaving LA. Patty was the epitome of Southern California to me. She loved the ocean, the sand, the West. How could she make such a dramatic change?

I returned to my seat for the rest of the meeting with my head whirling. A count had been taken and almost half of my community was moving to Boston. I was deeply shocked. Rama talked about Transcendentalism, Walden Pond, Harvard, MIT, the Charles River and the excitement of shuffling one's life around. I felt personally untouched. I was going to stay in the West. I had a job, a house and a life in California. I hated snow, tire chains and rotating wardrobes. I had made my (counter) cultural migration years ago.

As the week rolled by, Patty and I spoke several times. She was enthusiastic and apprehensive. She had no idea what it would mean to her career. At the least, it would require getting a license to practice in Massachusetts. She simply found herself checking the box next to Boston and the repercussions were not under consideration. This seemed to be the case for many of the students who volunteered to make the move. They had meditated for a minute or two, and watched their pen do the checking. It was the Dharma.

The following meeting was on March 17, St. Patrick's Day. Rama told us a hilarious story that no matter where he is on St. Paddy's day, his father finds him and insists on singing a *fine Irish tune.* He said that his father knows that it drives him crazy and is motivated all the more. This year, Rama thought that he had gotten the best of the situation by not being home to answer the phone. Upon his arrival at the house, he listened to his answering machine. And there it was: Dad singing chorus and verse of "My Wild Irish Rose." And then, filling the room with absolute rhapsody, Rama sang a beautiful Irish lullaby to us.

Rama proceeded to say that some students had not seen correctly the week before and because it was St. Patrick's Day, they would have another chance to determine their fate. Blank white cards were passed out again. He said that a few had chosen Boston who should have checked LA and vice versa. This time, the clearing meditation was longer. Rama advised us to make a genuine effort to put aside personal preference and listen to the Dharma.

I drew two boxes. I wrote LA and Boston. I closed my eyes and searched for an affirmation of my previous decision. I opened my eyes, checked LA, left my seat for the break, and turned in my card. Wandering the theater lobby, I asked several people if they had changed their original choice. A couple of them had switched to Boston.

Leaning against the vacant concession bar, I watched Rama walking through the crowd. He was making his way over towards me. I grew increasingly restless as he drew nearer and nearer. Finally, he reached the bar, stopped, and looked at me. "Checked Boston, huh?" he inquired. The veritable shred of etiquette I knew forced me to say, "Yes." Rama smiled and said, "Good, you will be much happier there. You have no idea how much better you will feel in Boston." He walked away.

The Passionate Heart

I waited for a moment, rushed to the administration table, and asked for my card back. I tore it in two and put it in my pocket. Without considering any of the consequences, I filled out a new card and placed a very anemic check mark next to Boston. Not unlike my impetuous agreement to fast for the ERA, I found myself lurching into an unknown future. The second half of the meeting was a blur. I vaguely remember Rama asking for people to guess the final number of Boston-bound students. A man hit the number exactly -- 184.

The week was an avalanche of realizations: my job, my lease, my pets, my friends, my beloved sunsets vs. blizzards, boots, mittens and the unfamiliar Atlantic. I stood in the center of my living room at least a dozen times, surveyed the situation, and simply gasped. How would I handle moving? What would I do with the hundreds of books? How could I drive my car and a rental truck? Where would I land? What would I do when I got there? Seven pairs of sandals, beach chairs, sun visors, and my Weber grill looked stupid and wonderful all at the same time. I didn't own a *winter* coat or a turtleneck sweater.

As the days peeled by, things slowly began taking shape. One by one the puzzles were being solved. Patty was going to rent a truck with a friend and I could stow my things with them. I had a huge garage sale and dumped the bike, the grill and the beach chairs. Every time a friend left the house, they carried out one of my beautiful plants. I gave notice at the clinic and started interviewing replacements. I was letting go of countless things that people had given to me over the last sixteen years. The memories were fading and their grasp was weakening. With each item being sold, given away, or thrown out, I was uprooting and reordering my inner life.

When my last week in California arrived, I fell even more madly in love with the land, the foliage, the stucco, the freeways, the ocean, and the sunset. The feelings I had for the people in my life swelled until I thought my heart was going to burst. I knew hundreds of women. I had built my own network of women. I had a woman doctor, a woman vet, and a woman therapist. I knew the woman who led any and every type of community activity: electoral politics, the battered shelter, AA, Al Anon, the Freedom of Choice movement, the abortion clinic, lesbian rights, gay rights, music, poetry, astrology. And my special friends, how would I live without them? What had I done?

With every box packed, every tear shed, and every friend kissed, I got in my VW bus and drove due east. I was knee deep in maps, cassette tapes, bubble gum and emotions as I headed for the Nevada border. After I smoothed out some of the fear, I found myself talking to Rama. It wasn't out loud. It wasn't even with words. It was more a sense of the closeness of my relationship with him. It felt as if he was in the car with me and we were driving across America together. I recognized him because the feeling was similar to the quiet, the calm and the depth I had only known while in his presence. My senses were alert and my mind was sharp in watchfulness. The road was even, the clouds defined, the sky friendly, and the adventure welcoming. My past was miles behind, the future was completely unknown, and the present was in constant motion.

I had read many stories about students going on a journey on behalf of their Teacher. They always explained that while the student is in transit, their Teacher is with them. While Yogananda traveled all over the world at the request of his Teacher, Yukteswar, he knew that his Teacher was actually traveling with him. This is not metaphorical. This is not desire or wishful thinking. This is a genuine merging of energy because of the mutual intent. When a Teacher gives a student a task, it is understood that while performing the task, the Teacher is present. It is part of the contract. It is the very nature of the relationship.

As my bus motored east, I started getting clearer and clearer. I started getting happier and happier. I started getting lighter and lighter. Memories, miseries, attachments began peeling off me. Hour after hour, I was actually discarding the weight of the world as I had known it. My mind was sifting through all of the things that had happened to me in California over the years. I was married, divorced, taught school, owned a bookstore, worn a hundred hats, danced a thousand dances, and dreamt a million dreams. Like snapshots in a photo album, they had all found a place and become embedded in my mind. Somewhere while traversing Texas, Illinois, Ohio and Pennsylvania, the pictures were fading. My whole being was opening up to the road, the sky and the horizons of change. Rama's pure kundalini was sweeping my mind and washing me clean. It was filtering the energy in my subtle body, like a dialysis machine diffusing impurities.

3,200 miles, four motels, six bags of Doritos, one speeding ticket and Boston was in view. Maneuvering through insane one-way streets, I eventually found Cambridge. The tiniest line on the map was Gray street, the home of my dear friend, David. Somewhere between deciphering that men are the enemy and all women are sisters, life demanded that I examine this fool proof algorithm more deeply by catapulting just enough kind and loving men into my life to make it smack of an unacceptable simplicity. David was one such man.

I met David in 1972. There was something significantly different about David. He was not afraid of feeling. Although his feelings were often melancholy, David lived life through his heart. He tenderly loved the ballet, fine music, poetry, and the human condition. Upon completing a tour of duty in the army stationed in Germany, David worked on his Ph.D. in psychology at Harvard. He invited me to land at his apartment while I figured out what I was going to do.

One of my favorite things about David was his love of Jessie Taft. As I never stopped pestering David about therapy and how it worked, he let me read his favorite book on the subject. In it, Jessie Taft writes that there is some type of "magic" that occurs between a therapist and a client during an open and trusting hour together. She doesn't explain it away with a lot of quantifiable data. She acknowledges that the healing process happens in a place that is outside of clinical analyses and theoretical protocols. She, like the fox from *The Little Prince*, knows that "It is only with the heart that one can see rightly; what is essential is invisible to the eye." David lived by that advice.

David's apartment was part of Cambridge's rent control program. It was a one bedroom, third floor apartment for $313 a month. The shocking price and expansive front windows made up for the noisy radiators, two long flights of stairs, and wildly leaky plumbing. I arrived late in the day and we carried a minimum of things upstairs for the night.

Naturally, the primary objects in his apartment were books. They were everywhere, on tilting shelves and piled high on the floor.

The next morning David had to run off to class. Before his departure, he gave me directions to the University, which was just ten blocks away. As if Harvard wasn't enough, Radcliff was even closer, which I knew was the home of Emily Dickinson's handwritten manuscripts. After a very anxious meditation, I dressed and headed down the stairs. The sidewalks were cobblestone and streets narrow. It had been eighteen years since I had lived among rows of trees. They were Oak, Elm, Maple, and filled with birds. They were tall and green and sculpted the paths. California had made me forget how wonderful trees are.

After two blocks, I was on Massachusetts Avenue with the University in full view. I began to pass by students, professors, shopkeepers: the citizens of Cambridge. There were men pushing baby carriages and women carrying briefcases. As I walked past each person, I noticed something remarkably different. They weren't staring at me. They weren't looking at me. They weren't checking me out. They were minding their own business, going to their own destination. They were in transit.

In being confronted with this blinding reference point, I began to realize that in Southern California, every passerby had taken a long judgmental eyeful. They didn't just bother to look, they formed an opinion, made a survey, cast a vote. Like Olympic judges, they gave people a rating as to their acceptability as inhabitants of planet earth. "What a dog!" "You're fat." "You're ugly." Not only did they formulate a thought, but also the thought took form and was deeply felt. It was actually painful. One time while eating an ice cream cone as I crossed Pacific Coast Highway in Laguna Beach, a couple of girls in a convertible yelled out, "You shouldn't be eating ice cream, you fat pig." It wasn't just my pride that was hurt, the thought actually carried a feeling with it and from that moment on, I carried the pain with me everywhere. My subtle body had been so constantly pelted with negative thoughts that I made my own insults and I believed them.

The Passionate Heart

But, here walking around Harvard, around Cambridge, I wasn't feeling any such thing. The women and men were all different sizes, wore glasses, carried books, and didn't assume the right to form and foist a verdict at one another. My step became lighter. My shoulders became squarer. My eyes rose off the ground. My chin lifted off my chest. I was passing by unnoticed, unjudged, or better yet, freely.

All my life I had been told that I was too smart. One night at the dinner table, my future father-in-law told his son that he shouldn't marry me because I was entirely too smart. I guess they felt that women should be stupid, maybe they would be easier to control that way. A couple of years later, while sitting on my favorite beach chair reading a book, with a pencil behind my ear, my husband paraded up and down in front of me exclaiming that I was the only person on the beach with classical music on the radio, reading a philosophy book. Not long after that, he told me to "Stop buying books!" But, between Radcliff and Harvard, all of the women looked smart. It was not a detriment.

In the first few weeks, wandering the neighborhood and through a score of bookstores, I began hating myself less. I began thinking that it was okay to be big and look intellectual. It wasn't that I had essentially changed. It was because I wasn't living in an ocean of disapproval. I wasn't being bombarded with thoughts that women should be blond, in a bikini, and look as if they ate two lettuce leaves yesterday. I wasn't being used as a dartboard sustaining painful and damaging thoughts about what a woman should or should not be. Best of all, my cache of painful thoughts began melting away, leaving my mind. My self-image was radically changing.

Recalling Rama's sentence, "You have no idea how much better you will feel in Boston," made me think about the little check mark on my (third) 3 x 5 card. No matter how deeply I had loved the land and sea of Southern California, Rama knew that I would be happier, more comfortable, and freer to be me in Boston. I had no way of knowing until I experienced it for myself. My love of books, my preference for classical music, my literary way of viewing life were not eyesores in Boston. I was not an eyesore in Boston. My subtle body did not have to survive the negativity that I had become so accustomed to while living at the beach. My mind was becoming more my own. I was proud to be a tall, smart woman walking down the street, carrying books.

Chapter 23

The move to Boston was the biggest thing I had ever done by myself. In the past I always had a partner, a group, some friends, or even family to shore up doubts, confirm the wisdom of the plan, share in the workload, and join in the outcome. Certainly I never thought that I could do something so extreme, so irreversible, and so very unpredictable by myself. Although Lakshmi was a community of several hundred women and men, we did not necessarily share a mutually defined dream. We did not have one another's phone numbers. We had not made any type of commitment to each other.

This was a journey between one student and one Teacher. This was a relationship that did not reference any greeting card occasions, school traditions, or family ties. Even more mysterious was that the longer I stayed and the more I got to know the others, the more it became apparent that each student had a solitary relationship with Rama. Each of us saw and heard our own individual Teacher. He was someone wholly distinct to every one of us. Although we sat in the same hall, listened to the same words and meditated together, each of us was having a unique experience.

For many nights I asked myself why had I moved? Why had I quit my job? Why did I leave a life that I had spent almost two decades building? It was not because Patty moved; we had gone in different directions before. It was not because I understood Asian etiquette, certainly not well enough to warrant such a change. There was only one answer large enough, strong enough, deep enough; I loved Rama. I loved everything about him: his mind, his heart, his passion for life, his vision. I loved how he made me feel. He challenged me. He talked to me as if I could be even more than I had dreamt possible.

Rama seldom talked about love. He said that it was something you shouldn't diminish by talking about it. But now and then, Rama would pause and say, "Why else would I do any of this, but out of love?" I was just starting to comprehend the size of this love, the inexplicable depth of this love. It was not the utilitarian bargain that most people label love. It was not the magnetic attraction that couples *temporarily* call love. It was not the familial obligation that people express on holidays. It was unearthly, unprecedented, uncontainable, irresistible. It existed outside of desire and aversion. It was the Dharma.

David made arrangements with the Cambridge rent control board to turn his apartment over to me upon his departure. It was a great deal, not just because the rent was cheap, but the location was terrific. It was near the subway, the universities, and best of all, in the heart of a community that valued education. The power lines in Cambridge are some of the best in the world for people who want to learn, read, study, and grow. Sexism and racism were certainly at a minimum. It was not unusual to see a man wearing a snuggly or a same-sex couple. From my point of view, it was the most civilized place I had ever lived.

Naturally, I immediately wanted to visit Walden Pond and Ralph Waldo Emerson's house in Concord. The pond was surprisingly small. It was early summer and very beautiful. People were hiking around the water and picnicking in secluded spots. Thoreau's famous house of twenty-six months was not there any more, but the foundation had been memorialized with an exact layout of the floor, placed precisely where the house had once stood. The minuscule size was a shock. How did he ever fit three chairs in there?

After the pond, I took the tour through the Emerson house. Books were everywhere. There were free standing shelves in every room as well as built-in shelves all along the staircase. As the group was being ushered in and out of the tiny rooms, and escorted to the second floor, I lingered behind. I couldn't resist stopping and reading every title on the shelves that belonged to the man who wrote *Self-Reliance* and *The Over-Soul*. There were all of my favorite and familiar books from the East: *The Upanishads, The Bhagavad Gita, The Tao Te Ching,* etc. And, there were all of the European mystical authors; Besant, Blavatsky, Leadbeder. They looked like my shelves at home, except I had books by Emerson's protégés.

Finally the night arrived to see Rama. Lakshmi was officially opening in Boston. I didn't know how the others felt, but I was elated. A totally new Zoe was walking through the

The Passionate Heart

door. I was presenting my Teacher with a whole new person, the product of his instruction. I was proud of all of the changes I had embraced and endured. I felt clean and shiny entering the hall. This was the first time I felt as though I had actually done something to deserve seeing my Teacher.

Rama walked on stage, knelt down near the edge, and sat back on his heels. "I have something important to tell you. I have decided to leave spiritual teaching," he said. If I live to be a thousand, I will never forget his exact words or my exact feelings. I was devastated. The chasm between my expectation and the reality engulfing me was immeasurable. 3,200 miles seemed like nothing in comparison. Five minutes before, I felt as if I had gone to the Himalayas, and back again, to get a cup of snow for my Teacher. Now I felt as if going to the moon would be insufficient.

That night I wanted to be a student more than any other moment in my life. For the first time I had felt a sense of worthiness, like a kid who actually practiced the scales all week. What could Rama possibly mean? Why would he ever do such a thing? He was heavy. He was ponderous. He was most serious. This was no list on a yellow pad or some teaching device. It didn't matter if Rama had just changed his mind, his mind had changed him, or it was simply the Dharma. The reason was not going to alter the outcome. Lakshmi was going to close at the end of the summer.

Rama explained that he needed to build something completely different. In previous incarnations, in other cultures, other countries, Rama had been working with people who naturally had a deep sense of tradition and etiquette. Eastern families and society understood and respected communities seeking Enlightenment. Here, in the United States, people simply did not understand. This was his first incarnation in the West and he said that he had not been accustomed to teaching Westerners. The type of teaching that he had been doing was not working. We were not advancing.

A community dedicated to meditation and Enlightenment needed to be insulated from the violence and anger of the U.S. Had we been in India or Tibet, we would have been carrying forward centuries of tradition and been born to families who not only knew but accepted that we were different. The advancement of women was particularly difficult because both East and West, women are being held back. Women did not have a chance anywhere on the earth to fully realize their potential.

Rama explained that it had taken him some time in his own cycle to fully understand what was happening. Methods that would have been appropriate and far more successful in the East were not working here. Rama was seeing that here in the U.S., men and women seeking light have to take responsibility for their own lives, their own well being, their own livelihood. Career and meditation have to be perfectly melded. For Americans, the study of Self-Discovery would have to include economic advancement.

To move to higher states of attention and to meditate perfectly, we would have to have fully integrated lives. To go beyond the states we were currently traversing, we would need to collect and store more personal power than our present lives could ever create. And so, at the end of August, Rama was closing Lakshmi. He would be spending the entire summer recapitulating everything he had ever taught us and defining what was ahead.

Rama explained that in several months, he would be starting a new program - Vishnu Systems. This was not going to be a center devoted exclusively to the study of meditation. Vishnu Systems would be a complete program for American women and men who were seeking Enlightenment. It would include economic advancement, martial arts, career seminars, and, of course, meditation. There would be an application process and absolutely no one would be exempt.

To qualify as a member of Vishnu Systems, a student would have to choose one of four professions. They were the performing arts, medicine, law and computer science. Rama described it in great detail. "To reach higher states of attention, the mind had to be strong and tight." These four careers demanded a certain discipline, a type of mind that could hold a lot of information in place. In addition, they would afford us the economic mobility we needed to live as we should and allow us to travel as well.

The Passionate Heart

For women, it would mean that we could be independent and attain positions of respect and power. Women in particular need to have lives that develop and sustain self-esteem. Service positions could not create the autonomy, confidence, and self-reliance women needed to progress on the path. The situation for women was especially sensitive because women not only have to combat the conditioning of their present lives, but also confront centuries of tradition that hold them in bondage.

Rama said that we could take the whole summer to decide if this was what we truly wanted. If it was not for us, there was no shame, no sense of failure; we had simply gone as far on the path as we could. He assured us that if it was what we wanted, it was most certainly do-able. "Everyone in the room has what it takes to do this," he said.

Who was this Teacher? Was I his student? How was I going to deal with this new twist of fate? This was not my sweet Teacher sitting on a couch pointing to his heart chakra. I wanted him back. I just wanted to meditate and receive Darshan. I was deeply disappointed. After all I had just moved across the country. The least he could do was give me a week of bhakti bliss. It sounded as if I would actually have to DO something. I didn't want to go to computer school. I could never be a programmer.

I don't think I was alone in my feelings. Other students were riveted to their seats as well. The rubber had hit the road. The writing was on the wall. The dealer was calling in the cards and I was not sure I wanted to play this new hand. The break was not the usual milling around in idle chatter. It was more like surveying the wreckage. It was obvious that Rama was serious and if we wanted to continue sitting in the Clear Light with him, we would have to get serious too.

I got myself home to my/David's apartment. I was living in a totally different world now. If I didn't want to apply to the new program, what would I do in this strange and foreign city? And, even if I wanted to continue, there was never a guarantee of being accepted in the application process. What did Rama really have on his mind? I knew I really needed to examine that. At the very least, I owed him that much, he deserved that much.

There is a certain sentence Chuck told me years ago that haunts me at least once a day. "Everything you've got, for everything you want; everything you want, for everything you've got." No matter how I have tried to shake off the resonance of this expression, it sticks to my soul like a wad of pink bubble gum on running shoes. Being the practical Virgo, the pragmatic accountant of life, I can never turn away from a deal that offers what I want, what I need. First, he has what I want. Second, what else would I do? Third, everything he said about women is absolutely true. Fourth, how hard could it be? Finally, I came for the Blueprints; I can't leave without them.

Later in the week I met with a few of the women from my community. They had already begun making phone calls. There were several technical schools in the area that offered certificates in computer programming. They required an entrance exam and in five to eight months, one would be qualified as a junior level programmer in COBOL or Assembler. It all sounded reasonable.

Then Patty arrived, she had already visited a technical school, passed the entrance exam, applied for financial aid, and enrolled in their program. Patty had just finished Chiropractic school, gotten her license and didn't look back. If she could do this, then what was my excuse? I didn't have a career. My degrees were not making me any money. One by one, women were applying and being accepted in computer science programs. Waitresses, typists, nurses, therapists, saleswomen, and secretaries were all saying, "Yes." They believed. What was my excuse?

As horrible as my family karma has been, there was one notable plus. My father's trust provided me with unlimited funds for the sole purpose of education. Although dependent on my mother's approval, if I could convince her, I would have the money to go to computer school. Besides, compared to graduate school, it was not very expensive. I called Mom and we talked about it.

The Passionate Heart

I think that somewhere inside this woman, who never worked outside the home, she understood that I was facing a different kind of life than her own. I was thirty-five, divorced, and never placed any value on "hooking" a husband to pay the bills. I was never going to have a traditional family, no matter how much she wanted one for me. In spite of the fact that she had never touched a computer, she knew that they were most definitely the wave of the future. Pushing aside any hesitation she had about my life taking yet another tack, she agreed.

I spent a few days taking practice entrance exams. Math was never my favorite subject. I had done well in geometry, but algebra and calculus were (murder) mysteries to me. Besides, I hadn't taken a class, or a test for that matter, for over ten years. The only math I knew was from calculating astrology charts, not simple, but hardly advantageous. I took the twenty-five minute exam, passed, and signed up to begin the following week.

Why is it that the things that seem the most scary, the most demanding, the most incomprehensible, take just a few moments to be realized? There must be something in the step, in the motion, that appears to be so very foreign that you can't even fathom doing it. Could it just be the word, *never*? I could *never* get on a roller coaster. I could *never* move to Boston. I could *never* go to computer school. Maybe all I have to do is get rid of the word - *never*.

On July 22, 1985, I began computer school. There was a Lakshmi meeting that night. I walked in as I had so many times before, not knowing what was going to happen, going to happen to me, going to happen to all of us. As I stepped just inside the entrance, I looked to my right and there was Rama, sitting in a chair. I smiled and said hello. He looked at me and said, "Wow, you look like you've been to beauty school." I grinned like a five year old and innocently replied, "No, today I started computer school."

Chapter 24

Computer classes began at 7:30 AM. While this might sound reasonable to most people, it was nothing short of catastrophic to me. Lutherans, Jews, even agnostics, can hit the alarm clock, jump out of bed, shower, dress, commute, and viola -- the day begins. Lakshmi students sit in meditation for an hour each morning. My day began with: hit the alarm clock, jump out of bed, make coffee, shower, drink coffee, sit down, drink coffee, continue sitting, get more coffee, finish sitting, coffee... To be at class by 7:30 AM meant getting up at 5:30 AM.

There were twenty-five people in my class. Although we kept it to ourselves, twenty-one were also members of Lakshmi, nineteen of whom were women. It was very inspiring to see these Buddhist students taking on the discipline of COBOL. I knew that most of them were holding down one and, in some cases, two jobs to pay their way through technical school. I knew they were working well past midnight and still getting up at 5:30 AM.

The temptation is to skip meditation and I am sure all of us have tried it once or twice. But, it doesn't take long to figure out that it is a very bad idea.

In the beginning of building a meditative practice, it can seem as if nothing is happening, particularly while sitting. For me, it was a gradual process, like focusing a microscope or turning a kaleidoscope. My life and mind slowly started coming into view. At first, the mind is uncharted, the waters rocky, and the weather unpredictable. Thoughts have been pouring through unchecked, never being held accountable for their origin, their intent or their outcome.

People often remark that when they start meditating, they are overwhelmed by what they find going on in their minds. They may even assume that meditation is responsible for kicking up the storm, but their minds were always in a tidal wave. They just hadn't looked before. After a while, with perseverance, the sea calms down and one can take command of the ship and navigate safely.

But almost immediately, meditation begins affecting the rest of the day. Life becomes more manageable. Circumstances that previously would have confounded or stopped someone in their tracks, are understood and overcome. Complex problems lose their grip and solutions surface. Accidents are circumvented. Meditation affects everything from coping with traffic to time management. And so, like body builders who know they can never stop working out and runners who can't stand to miss a day, an experienced meditator does not want to face a day without putting in their time. As Rama has said, "Meditation, don't leave home without it."

As the weeks went by and writing computer programs got more complex, Rama's plan became clearer. To develop efficient code, a programmer has to hold the entire program in their mind and follow the logic throughout, from beginning to end. It requires a certain discipline, a focus, a strength. It was a natural for meditators. The two activities, meditation and programming, have a direct and powerful relationship. Programming was like lifting weights that develop muscles in the mind. One can then apply this mental strength to control and, eventually, stop thought. The better the programmer, the better the meditator, and vice versa.

The women and men in class who meditated were finding that programming was not nearly as hard as they had presumed. It was fun, like solving puzzles. The real obstacle was changing one's self-image that they could not *be* a programmer. Each of us held in our minds a certain image of a) what a programmer was and b) what a spiritual seeker was. The two concepts seemed to be mutually exclusive. The judgment was that computers were cold and stilted. We did not want to be either.

Wrestling with whatever was happening in computer school, was nothing compared to dealing with the inevitable closing of Lakshmi. All summer long, we met with Rama while he recapitulated the essential lessons of the last several years: purity, humility, selfless giving, psychic self-defense, personal power, and most of all, meditation.

Beneath the surface of this in-depth review, Rama was telling us something very specific. Seeking liberation, seeking light, was not a spectator sport. It was not something a person could do by sitting an hour each day and attending a weekly meeting. To be successful, it must permeate one's entire life. Every moment of the day, every thought, every interaction either added to or subtracted from, one's state of attention. Up to that point, we had been showing up and expecting it to be done for us. I remembered Rama telling me in the desert that I was behaving as if this was a movie and I was not really participating in the process at all. Now the time had arrived to really commit.

The old program was about meditation and, by this time, we had all of the information on the subject we needed. The new program would be about increasing personal power and thus reaching higher states of attention. Rama compared our minds to a high-rise building. He said that although we had a hundred floors, we were only accessing the first ten or so. To get to the higher floors, we would have to create lives in which our practice encompassed everything we did. Programming was not just about computers, increasing our incomes, and building solid dependable careers. It was about intent.

There was a poignancy all summer. It was sobering and deeply wise. One of the most magical things about my association with Rama was that no matter how much I didn't want to hear what he had to say, or follow through on a suggestion, the resonance of truth was always irresistible. I was free to disagree and often did, but my soul knew better. Rama had begun talking about computers over two years ago and I had dismissed it as out of my realm. I was too old for such a change. My nature was too philosophical to embrace computers. I pictured myself as aesthetic and programming as insensitive. Now, I was living in Boston, excelling in COBOL, making new friends in the group, and deeply examining the level of my intent. Why was it that genuine appreciation and visceral understanding only seem to occur when facing loss?

Adding to this sense of loss was that half the community was on the other coast. It wasn't that I knew and would miss them individually, but rather that all of us would never be in the same room again. It was a dissection, a disintegration of something that had been very beautiful. I would never sit with these people again. I would never know this certain camaraderie again. We had a culture, a language, a humor about us. I would never see Rama sitting on the couch again.

On August 31, 1985, my Teacher, this magical being who moved stars and made me laugh a thousand times, sat on a carousel in Disneyland and closed Lakshmi. We were on our own. I was on my own. I was alone.

Life went on. David accepted a job in the West and returned to his homeland, California. I was living by myself. Certainly, I was more fortunate than many of the others in that I was attending computer school and saw people I knew everyday. Much to my surprise, I got a 98 in COBOL. I actually liked the language. It was logical, rational, dependable and well within my reach. Assembler was cryptic and more difficult, but nothing like I had expected. Going into the final exam, I had a 94.

Every morning I meditated. I sat and gazed at my yantra or a flower. School was over at 2:00 P.M. and I went to movies in the afternoon. In the evenings I studied, although not much. Life went on, but it was most certainly different. There were no weekly meetings. There was no interesting and challenging discourse to ponder each week. I had no Teacher. I was back to my life of books.

One day in late November a letter arrived. It was from Rama. It was an invitation to attend a meeting in LA. Rama would be explaining a new program in detail. Anyone interested in studying with Rama in the future would have to attend.

School that day was like no other. The excitement in the halls was palpable. Most of us had no idea how we would afford a trip to LA, but that was not going to get in the way. The meeting was the day before our final, but that was not going to get in the way. It would mean that twenty-one of twenty-five students would not be in class that day, but that was not going to get in the way. Nothing was going to get in the way. Money was pooled, homework was shared, hotels and flights were booked. We were going to see our Teacher.

Four hundred women and men gathered in LA to see Rama. We met at the Wilshire Ebell Theater where I had seen my first ballet. Looking around the room, I could hardly believe my eyes. This was no collection of itinerant new-agers, no hodgepodge of social cast-offs, no crowd of counter-culture revolutionaries. This was a gathering of impeccable women and men. This was a hall filled with Buddhists who were seeking liberation. There was a fresh and visible respect, not just for the program, not just for their remarkable Teacher, but for themselves.

When I stopped looking outward, I felt it too. In these few months, I had uncovered a whole new range of self-esteem. I had moved across the country. I had confronted life by myself. I had learned to program. I had actually *done* something. I realized that my meditation and my respect for my Teacher had transformed my life. I was a woman with intent, living and working in the world.

The Passionate Heart

Chapter 25

When I was ten, I wanted to be a Daughter of Charity of St. Vincent De Paul. This was not just a flimsy wish that occasionally floated through my mind. I had dolls in full habit, read scads of books about nuns, wrote to the Mistress of novices, and constantly pretended I was in the convent already. Age twenty, I was a Catholic wife. I taught marriage classes in a Catholic high school. I had a degree in Roman Catholic theology and often knew more doctrine than the nun and priests I taught with. At thirty, I was deeply immersed in the Woman's Movement. I expressed it politically, socially, spiritually, romantically, and professionally. My life has always been integrated and filled to the brim. I never understood people who lived as if life was a checker board, with each interest in a separate unrelated compartment.

When I arrived at the hall and met Rama, my understanding was that this was my *spiritual* Teacher. I thought that he would teach me to meditate, challenge my point of view, expand my vision, and enhance my life. I imagined that this association would color my life, add shading and depth, and push me to live more fully than I would attempt on my own. I never considered that being a student, a Buddhist, a meditator would become the center of my life. Of course, I knew it would affect everything in my life, but I did not intend to make it my entire life. I had a life -- one with purpose, direction and commitment. I didn't build a box around my spirituality, like weekly church goers, but I thought of it as an adjective as opposed to a noun. Although naive, it was true.

Just as I had not lived an ambivalent life, I had not found a perfunctory Teacher. Rama told us that students actually attract a particular Teacher and by examining that, we could learn some things about ourselves. Rama was dedicated, definite, positive, and always did everything whole-heartedly. He took his teaching very seriously. Everything had to be done perfectly, impeccably, and fully. If a student wanted to learn, Rama wanted to teach them. This was the bargain struck between Teacher and student. This was his total commitment. This was his life.

I arrived one day asking for the Blueprints. I wanted to learn to meditate. I wanted more out of life than I was able to create on my own. I wanted to become more than my limited imagination conjured up. Rama said yes. I might have assumed that this was going to be an adjective in my life, but my Teacher knew better. I said I wanted liberation. He agreed to teach me. He knew my life was going to have to change dramatically.

Having been a teacher myself, I have always been awestruck by Rama's teaching methods. Week after week, month after month, Rama patiently unfolded lessons, tasks, truth. He would offer suggestions and recommend small adjustments, changes that when totaled up equaled an intense shift of awareness. His belief in me was so much greater than my belief in myself, I would find I had accomplished a task before I even had a chance to undermine it. When I taught high school and had a goal in mind, I would enthusiastically tell the students all about it. If they thought it was out of their reach, they would derail themselves before they even got started. Looking back, I can see that I should have asked only as much as they thought they could do or would try to do. Ultimately, if one of them failed, it had been my impatience that created the opening for failure.

Three years and two months had passed since I first walked into a meditation seminar. I had been an angry woman who owned a failing bookstore. I was lost in the world of books, searching for meaning. I wanted liberation for all American women and had come face to face with the male combine. In retrospect, I can see that these women and men were not so very different from myself. We were seeking more than life on earth had to offer. Neither sex, drugs, rock-n-roll, nor the American dream were enough. We wanted answers. We wanted light. We wanted liberation.

Now I looked around the room and saw the same faces, but that was as far as the reference could be made. These women and men were dedicated, definite, positive, and living life whole-heartedly. We were as comfortable in our professional clothes as we had seen our Teacher demonstrate for us just a year ago. Each of us was now firmly planted on a productive and lucrative career path. Our minds had embraced a discipline. Our lives had direction. We were a reflection of Rama's work. We were his students. He was our Teacher.

The one thing we all had in common, Rama and students alike, was that we had a distinct purpose that permeated every aspect of our lives. We did not sustain a distasteful job to support the rest of our lives. We did not wait for the weekend to do what we really wanted. We did not save up for a two-week vacation that was supposed to make the rest of the year tolerable. We did not relegate our spiritual quest to one hour on Sunday or even one night a week. Our journey, our interests, our careers, our entire lives were expressions of being Buddhists.

Finally and most importantly were the women. These women were not in a subordinate position. These women were not merely equal. These women were members in a community where the advancement of women was the priority. We did not wait for the men to lead the way on any ground. We did not sit in the back of the hall nor feign self-esteem by serving refreshments. Our Teacher had made it very clear that the primary focus of his current incarnation was the Enlightenment of women. That told me a lot about Rama and it told me a lot about these women.

The dreams of these women were larger than pro-choice legislation or constitutional rights. The hopes of these women were bigger than establishing a female ministry in Christian churches or female rabbis rewriting the Talmud. These women believed that a woman could be enlightened and they were risking their entire lives on their belief. Their souls drew a Teacher who wanted to change the entire world, regardless of the magnitude of the dream, the difficulty of the task, or the unknowable result.

After months of being on our own, we had come to LA to hear what Rama had to say. For me, this time alone had deepened my commitment, ignited my dedication, and strengthened my resolve. This reunion confirmed my estimation of the talent of this Teacher and demonstrated the promise of these students. Although I have never been absolutely sure where we may be going, it is obvious where we had been and the distance we had traveled.

Rama Seminars would begin in January. They would be held in LA. It did not matter where we lived. Attendance was not required. Seminars would be open to the public. There would be no private meetings or accepted group. Rama would teach anyone who came to hear him. By now we had been taught enough to maintain the level of our commitment. Naturally, Rama would be teaching Kundalini yoga and all that it entailed. He assured us that these meetings would not be watered down or a step backwards.

At this point in my apprenticeship, I knew and had experienced enough to understand that what a Teacher is doing or saying is not the principle component of the teaching process. The most important thing that occurs is the transference of energy, ki, kundalini. Several times when we had gone to movies with Rama, although he never said a word or even so much as gave me a glance, my state of mind had been significantly shifted. As soon as he arrived, the movie theater would pulse with energy and fill up with clear iridescent light. No matter if it was animated mice or Harrison Ford on the screen, it was as deeply meditative as any seminar I had ever attended. LA, Boston, Timbuktu, if I was invited and I could sit in his presence, I would be there.

The flight back to Boston was packed with students anxiously studying Assembler books. The final exam was early the next morning. I did a decent job with my test and on November 27 graduated with honors: COBOL -- 98 and Assembler -- 96. When school ended so did the money from my father's trust and I had to find a job. Patty got one right away as a systems programmer in the I.T. department at MIT.

In mid-December I got a call from my brother. His company was looking for a computer professional to evaluate a system they were considering to purchase for their product catalog. He offered me the job. It was too much to believe: $24,000 a year, unlimited travel, open expense account, a company car, and *required monthly trips to LA*. The plus side of this was very heavily weighted. But, because of karma or maybe God's intergalactic sense of humor, there was significant ballast on the minus side. The job was in the automotive repair industry and primarily located in Milwaukee, home of my mother. This

157

was my Hobson's and Sophie's choice combined. I *had* to choose the side that guaranteed monthly trips to LA and yet sacrifice my beloved distance from my mother.

Christmas was packing boxes instead of wrapping them. On December 26, movers carted my stuff to Wisconsin. I sold my VW van. Alice and I flew off to America's Dairyland. My brother picked us up and let us stay at his house while I looked for a place of my own. It would be several days before the computer system would arrive, before my car would be delivered, and my things would arrive from Boston. I surveyed the suburbs and immediately knew where I wanted to live. The east side of town was out of the question, as that was where I had survived my first seventeen years. I chose a village on the west side. Both my brother and sister-in-law assured me that there were no rentals in that part of town. Although the newspaper confirmed their prophecy, I was not convinced. There was power in the land there and nothing else would do. I drove the perimeter for two solid days refusing to give up on my quest. Finally and suddenly, a FOR RENT sign went up on a window and by 5:00 PM that day I was a lease holder.

After the movers left, Alice and I arranged our stuff. That day the UPS truck pulled up and delivered sixteen large boxes. I had absolutely no idea what was in them. All I knew was that my brother's company manufactured top-of-the-line equipment for auto-body shops and they were deliberating about acquiring this particular computer system as one of their product offerings. My instructions were to do everything possible to investigate the wisdom of this proposal and report back in six months. If they did buy the distribution rights, I would be the obvious choice to head up the effort.

Since it would mean a very substantial purchase to the software developers, I was given *carte blanche* to travel to their installation sites, assist in their trade shows, learn the program, test the software, and spend time at their corporate headquarters in LA. With both reluctance and excitement, I plunged into the sixteen boxes that had taken over my living room. Ten terminals, two enormous industrial printers, one dot matrix printer, two mini computers, one modem, three printer stands, and thirty miles of unidentified cabling emerged. No matter how hard I looked, how hard I wished, how hard I cursed, there were no manuals to be found.

I phoned the home office. They assured me that no manuals had been packed. There were no manuals. Clearly these were not Apples, not PCs, not Macintoshes. These cable connectors must have been stolen from the Kennedy Space Center. The printers could have handled the US Mint. I was knee deep in the unknown. They asked if I had a soldering iron and an ohm meter, *Oh sure!* Adding to my diminishing self-confidence, the program had been done in BASIC. I didn't know any BASIC. As if it would be terribly consoling, they told me that they were dedicated to the success of this project and would spend as much time on the phone as I needed to get on-line.

I took off for the ACE Hardware store. I got a Weller soldering iron, an Ohm meter, and a speaker phone. At first, I was irritated with the entire fiasco because I knew that a guy would have viewed this as one big adventure. Why did guys instinctively know how to wire lamps and repair frayed extension cords? Where did they learn that stuff and why were girls uninitiated in these electronic mysteries? While I was with the girls in Home Ec perfecting shepherd's pie, the boys were learning things that would actually come in handy. Besides the obvious discrimination of arbitrarily segregating classes by gender, it carried the explicit message that each house needed to have one guy and one girl to cover all of the household situations life would present. It was 1986 and this was not proving to be a reliable theory.

To my amazement, I was up and rolling in two weeks. All ten monitors were cabled in a daisy-chain. Both computers had been opened and their pins moved appropriately, the printers were churning, and I was learning the inner workings of auto-body repair. It was an entirely new culture: repair, replace, paint booths, unibody, estimating, etc. I went to a national trade show in Chicago to hang around the booth. I noticed hundreds of men crowded around a demonstration in the next aisle. Curious to see just what could possibly be so interesting at an auto show, I parted the ocean of men to reveal four women in short shorts repeatedly attaching and removing radial tires with electric devices that screwed and unscrewed the lugs. I was most definitely in the enemy camp.

The Passionate Heart

Over the next few months I helped with several on-site installations. I came to find out that this was a very unpopular position. I was one of the representatives of the company who made the machine that would be tracking the paint man's time spent on the red Chevy. Now he would have to clock out for coffee and clock in from coffee. This miracle machine would instantly flag the boss when the paint man had moved the red Chevy outside of profitability. While spending time in body shops, I learned that men hate intruders and, in almost every case, it was a woman who actually ran the business.

Eventually, I broke down and told mother that I was living fifteen miles away. She came over that day and in less than twenty minutes she rearranged my silverware drawer, refused to drink out of the glasses I had, and told me that she was ashamed of how I looked. Of course, she was utterly dumbfounded as to why I didn't want her to know where I lived. What is it that happens in the birth process that pits two females against each other? I certainly wanted liberation for *all* women and this did not exclude my mother. But I knew that, even if it were handed to her on a golden tray, she would only accept it if a man had approved the offer.

Chapter 26

The commute to the meetings in LA was heavenly. I booked any flight I wanted, stayed at the hotel of my choice, and dined at the best restaurants while charging it all on an American Express card that wasn't even mine. I spent the days with the software company and evenings with my Teacher. Though my salary was not very much, the perks provided for me were more than my employer ever imagined. In reality, I was learning a lot about the automotive repair industry, mini-computers, and Corporate America. I wore a suit everyday and had an exquisite briefcase. I made a habit of going to restaurants the moment they opened for dinner and the service I got was always first rate.

People treated me with respect. They made the natural conclusion that I was a professional career woman. The obvious drive I had for perfection in everything I did they attributed to my character. They never would have guessed that the more I immersed myself in their world, the more I was able to leave it. No one suspected that I was a Buddhist simply using my life as my practice. It was miraculous.

In April, Rama made a "suggestion." After three years, I knew that a suggestion from Rama meant something very specific. If you ignored it, you would never know what was on the other side. If you procrastinated, you would diminish the power behind it. If you accepted it, you would find something magical. Adding even more weight to this equation, was that the more difficult the task, the greater the consequences. To the newcomer, it might appear that we were being asked to do something extraordinary. But to a true student we were simply receiving the requested instruction.

The way of a Buddhist is to live in the present. A Buddhist believes that there is only this moment and to believe otherwise is to live in illusion. The past is gone and the future is unknowable. The goal of this study is to break through illusions, determine the truth, and practice Self-Discovery. Many times, along the way, I have had to remind myself about all of this. This was one such time.

The Passionate Heart

Rama suggested that to plant ourselves firmly in the present, we should get rid of everything and anything from the past. He used his own tape series to illustrate the point. If we were listening to Rama's tapes from five years ago, we would be holding him in a certain place. Obviously he had changed many times since then and by holding on to the old tapes, we were blocking truly knowing whom he had become. The same was true for us. If we were holding on to old descriptions of ourselves, we were stopping our own progress.

I had no trouble finding examples to validate what he was saying. When my adorable Lickie died, I thought I would never get over it. It happened the night we saw *The Merry Wives of Windsor*. My adventurous poodle had wedged under the fence and taken off for whereabouts unknown. When I got home, she was nowhere to be found and I took off in my van to find her. I drove the streets for hours calling her name. I phoned the police. They finally admitted that she had been hit and was at an emergency clinic near the house. I banged on the door and with great effort and convinced the night tech to let me see her. I knelt next to the cage, opened the door, picked her up into my arms and said my grateful good-byes. She was the one who lay on my bed when I was sick. She was the one who always greeted me at the door. She was the constant, bright, and silly love of my life. Lickie died in my arms.

For weeks I thought I heard her in the night, felt her lightly jumping on the bed. I did not want to let her go. I held her in my mind and found only deep emptiness in continuing to do so. As I reconciled that she was gone, the hole diminished. Eventually, the pain of her death transmuted into a respect for her sweet spirit. Alice knew better. Alice was always in the present. There were many times we were so broke that I had no idea where the next dollar was coming from. I worried myself sick about it, but Alice only referenced the present. Her bowl was full: life must be fine.

Rama suggested burning or destroying all of our old tapes, posters, pictures, and journals. He was beckoning us into the present. I knew he was right. I also knew that what he was recommending was not extraordinary for spiritual seekers. Had I entered the convent, I would have left everything behind me and walked through that door fully expecting to have no past. Many convents and monasteries initiate the new members with at least a year of being completely cut off from the world: no newspaper, no radio, no TV, and no family contact. While we weren't practicing our spirituality by leaving the world in such a fashion, we were still aspiring to liberation. The past was one of many captors.

When I returned to Wisconsin, I got out all of my tapes, photos, and journals. I petted the tapes tenderly, as I loved the first series most dearly. One by one, I tore up the photos. No more little girl. No more unhappy high school student. No more married housewife. No more angry political prisoner. With each picture, I said farewell to a memory, a notion of who I was. The journals were not quite so easy. I had kept elaborate writings, poems, and drawings for over twenty years. I loved these beautiful diaries. They were just blank books when I bought them and today they were my story, my roots, my journey. Slowly I ripped apart the bindings and shredded the pages into pieces. With all of these things deposited in one green trash bag, I prayed that my faith in my Teacher would mitigate my grief. Only time would tell.

Being daringly honest is a sword I often wielded merely to dazzle the listener, but the event of being honest with my brother and his company was not such an occasion. I had done my job and done it well. I knew that purchasing the computer system would be a mistake and regardless of the personal ramifications, I had to tell them. The fundamental deciding factor was that auto-body repair is wholly dependent on the insurance industry. Insurance companies had been way ahead of them in developing computer systems. My report said that in just a few years auto-body shops would have to have software that could directly communicate with the insurance companies. The system I had been looking at would be obsolete.

Essentially, I fired myself. I gave back the American Express card, the computers, and the car. I was not the slightest bit disappointed to be leaving Wisconsin once again, as I had fifteen years before. I bought a used car, packed, put Alice in a pet crate, said good-bye and drove west. Four days later I was in Huntington Beach California, on the doorstep of my friend Adam. With his help, I found a beach apartment in less than a week.

I was home. The sand was a block away. The magnificent sun set everyday just for my amusement. I tried to never miss the show. But at night, something was terribly wrong. I could hear everything that was gong on in the apartment upstairs. A woman was crying. A man was shouting. And many times I would hear a crash, a thud, someone falling on the floor. She was begging him to stop and he was relentless. I couldn't stand it. I called Adam and asked if I could sleep on his living room floor. This went on for several weeks.

I wanted to help her. I wanted him to leave. I wanted her to throw him out. I called the landlord and the police came by. They said there was nothing I could do. One night it was particularly bad. Emotions were high, tempers were way out of control, and I heard a cat scream, hit the wall, and silence. That was it for me. One of us was moving. The cat did not agree to this drama. The cat did not ask to be a party to some ugly arrangement. There was no mutual consent here. The next morning, while the tenants were out, the landlord entered the apartment and found the cat, dead on the floor. He served an eviction notice that day.

Shortly thereafter, the apartment was rented to a young couple. It was their first serious relationship and their first home away from their parents. As I lay in my bed those first few nights and heard them making love, giggling, playing like children, I marveled at the diversity of the human condition, of the human experience. It was all incomprehensible. A man and a woman could hurt each other, but it was a cat that finally pushed the situation to its limits. I could not sleep under the noises of pain, anger, and injustice; but in just a few days of the shiny new couple's arrival, I acclimated and slept soundly, never awakened by their happy antics again.

In the course of my many nights sleeping on Adam's living room floor, I met his housemate, Craig. There was karma here. There was a relationship here that would prove to go far beyond anything I had ever expected to happen to me. Craig was a musician. He and his wife had a band that performed in

Las Vegas, Reno, and Tahoe. There was something special about to unfold and neither of us knew what it would be.

Shortly after my arrival in California, I got a job as a technical recruiter. I had actually sent my resume to this firm looking for a job in computer science, but they called and said that they were interested in interviewing me for a different type of opportunity. Eight hours a day, I called computer professionals and asked them if they were available for work. If I found a match for a project requirement and they took the position, I was paid $385. I liked the job and was doing fairly well with it.

That summer, Rama changed his entire program. He was now going to be teaching Zen. The focus of this new series of seminars would be Tantric Zen. These meetings were available to the public and anyone could attend. Adam and I went to the first of a four-night seminar in early September and had a wonderful time. This course of study was fun and entirely new. "This is the study of the Ten Thousand States of Mind," explained Zen Master Rama. "It is a practice in which you can learn to recognize and enter into happier and more expansive states of mind at will." Tantric Zen is based on the idea that nirvana is samsara and samsara is nirvana. Rama said that it means that the highest truths of Enlightenment are not separate from the moments and actions of our daily lives.

On the second night, I sat in the middle, on the left. Half way through the first segment, I got an uncontrollable urge to leave. It was something I had never experienced before. I could not sit still. I wanted to get up and walk out of the room. Nothing could be more rude than to leave while one's Teacher is talking. It would be a very serious breech of etiquette. Inside my mind, I was engaged in a full-blown argument with myself trying to find the will to simply stay in my seat. It was terrifying. It was violent. It was angry, and many times, I did not think that my *polite* side was going to win.

Finally, Rama announced the break. I don't remember hearing anything that had been said the entire night. All I could do was find Adam and tell him that I was leaving. I tore out of the building, got in my car, and took off. I drove west on the

The Passionate Heart

Santa Monica freeway towards home. My mind was spinning out of control. What was wrong with me? Why did I leave? The exit came up for the San Diego freeway and for some inexplicable reason I headed north instead of south. Home was an hour south. I knew nothing that was north.

Suddenly from out of nowhere I looked to the right, and there was Craig driving 55 miles a hour, going north on the San Diego freeway, and waving at me. He motioned for me to get off the freeway and talk to him. I managed to exit and stop the car. Passing me on Melrose Boulevard, he pointed for me to follow him. We ended up at a House of Pies restaurant. Where was he going when we met on the freeway? He was just out for a ride. Why was I going north? I had no idea. In the course of drinking coffee and eating pecan pie, I handed Craig my ticket for the remaining two nights.

That night, I sat on the shore for hours asking the Pacific why I had left. Craig went to see Rama both nights and had the time of his life. Apparently, as I was leaving, Craig was arriving.

Chapter 27

For two weeks, I could think of nothing else but why I had left the hall. At the time, it felt as if I was going to explode right on the spot. Running out of the room was a matter of survival. What bothered me most was that I hadn't thought about it in advance and I have never been a spontaneous person. I wrote a letter to Rama. The essence of it was that I felt I had only been taking advantage of him all of these years and I wanted to have something to give. I told him that I was teaching beginner's meditation classes and would be bringing people to see him whenever possible. I signed it, "I love you and am learning to love better each day." Since there was no formally accepted group at the time, I had not actually resigned from a community. It was that I needed some time out to appreciate what I had.

My friendships with Adam and Craig began to grow. I started aikido lessons with Adam's teacher. I was very clumsy and nervously laughed constantly. After my first class, the Sensei said, "One day you will catch on to this, and when you do, don't hurt my boys." I was astounded and later Adam told me the Sensei said it because he thought I had an exceptional amount of ki. Adam and I began teaching little meditation classes wherever we were welcome. My favorite place was an alcohol rehabilitation center.

Craig's band was performing in Las Vegas in early October. Adam and I drove out to catch the Friday night show. Saturday morning, we went hiking at Red Rock National Park. It was a beautiful day and the park is spectacular. The rock really is red and wedged against the blue sky; they created a majestic combination. When I got to the top of the cliff, I looked up and was deeply struck by how much the sun had contributed to my life. It kept me warm, tanned my skin, shimmered on the ocean, nourished my plants, cast beams through my apartment windows, and set ablaze millions of times with color. I wanted to give something back. I wondered if anyone thought about giving something back. And so, I stood on the edge of the mountain and meditated on the sun from noon until 1 PM, asking what could I give in return.

The Passionate Heart

That night we went to the Pointer Sisters show at Caesar's Palace. I couldn't see them very well. I kept asking my friends what the sisters were wearing and what they were doing. Monday morning, I went to work and got out the list of phone numbers to begin making my usual calls. Slowly, I began to realize that I couldn't bring the numbers into focus. I couldn't read the dial on my phone. No matter where I looked, the center of things disappeared in a blur.

I called Adam, asked him to pick me up, and take me to an eye doctor. When the ophthalmologist examined my eyes, he became quite alarmed. He left the room and returned in five minutes with an address. "I called ahead, he is expecting you," he said. Within an hour, I was sitting in an examining room with my eye lids wired open and dye coursing through my veins. The doctor took Polaroid pictures of my retinas, flashing one every 4 seconds, for a full minute on each eye.

The next morning, I sat in the eye surgeon's plush office as he cautiously explained that I had burned severe holes in both my right and left retinas. He was obviously very disturbed. It must have been difficult to tell a 37 year old computer professional, avid reader, obsessive seamstress, that she would never read again, never thread a needle again, never sit in front of a monitor again. He said that retinas are as thin and delicate as wet tissue paper, the burns are permanent, and the holes will never close. "There is no pigment in the tissue around the edges of the burns, so there is no possibility of new tissue growing," he reluctantly explained. He apologized and said there was nothing he or anyone could ever do about it.

Instantly my life changed in ways I could never have imagined. My bookshelves were one big blurry fog. My astrology charts were indecipherable circular patterns. My sewing machine was only a reminder of what I would never be able to do again. My PC was now a symbol of the life I could have had, but would never know where it might have led. I could not drive and had to be taken to the grocery store. I would stand in front of the dairy section and ask, "Is this yogurt or sour cream?" I could not see if a traffic light was green or red and had to ask strangers on the corner to help me cross the street.   Everything was just barely out of reach, just far enough away to break any relationship.

I was swamped with conflicting feelings.   I was not blind.   I could see shapes and colors.   My peripheral vision was intact. But, as soon as I looked at something, it disappeared.   It was like watching a movie on a screen with a giant hole in the middle.   I could catch the moon out of the corner of my eye, but as soon as I tried to bring it to the center, it was gone. Since there was no external indication that I had even the slightest disability, people didn't know how to react when I asked them to read a label or tell me what the crosswalk signal was.   They would glare at me as if I was lazy or stupid.   Later on I discovered that strangers were only willing to help if I enabled them first by explaining that I could not see.

It was odd to watch the people in my life go through their own reactions and see who was going to have to comfort whom.   My mother wanted to come to California and "take care of me."   I was very direct and told her that was impossible.   My brother flew in to encourage me to enroll in the Braille Institute.   I would do no such thing.   I heard that Patty took it very hard and spent a day circling Walden Pond trying to reconcile it. My friends, Maria and Laura, invited me to their home in Amherst.   I accepted the offer.   The highlight of the trip was touring Emily Dickinson's house.

The most interesting thing was that people seemed to have a limit or expiration date on their concern.   At first, they treated me like a poster child, doting on my every whim, bearing gifts, searching for something they could do to create compensation. This melted into an awareness: never asking me to look up movie times or offering to shop with me.   Then I had to ask for help, a ride, or a phone number.   I found this phase was very difficult.   I grew resentful due to their complacency as I was in the constant state of humbling myself.   Finally, the entire structure broke down, as if they felt it had lived its due course, like the flu or a broken ankle.   I was supposed to be normal by now and my inability to read a street sign or road map was voluntary and rude.   One girl charged across a crowded room and said, "You are such a snob.   Why won't you wave back?" She never gave me a chance to explain that at thirty feet, faces and waving hands ran together as if in Monet's Giverny.

The Passionate Heart

Internally, I oscillated among a whole pallet of feelings. I felt sorry for myself and hated anyone who would not join me at that level. I despised myself for having created this viscous, self-imposed cloudiness. It seemed so unnecessary, inescapable, and impossible to understand. Ultimately, I was angry every time something reminded me of what I had done. I might have just been asking what the soup label said, but inside I was furious. Many times I ended up alienating the very people who were trying to accommodate me because I didn't want to be accommodated. I wanted to read the label myself.

Meditation became a point of desperation. I felt an urgency to expand my interior vision. I got inspired to write a small book on meditation and a friend bought a huge white board for me that covered an entire wall. It wasn't long before I lost interest. I wanted to see Rama again but could not bring myself to do it. It seemed insincere to show up now. I said I left because I had been on the take and I was not going to reappear now that I was needy. I thought I should work this out by myself. I would go back when I had something to give. While Craig and Adam went to the monthly Zen seminars, I stayed home and wandered through my life.

In December, I got a call from my brother, Fred. Mother had been in a serious auto accident. She was not expected to live. I asked if I should fly there immediately and he said no. Fred wanted me to wait and come when her condition was clearer. The very next morning, he phoned again and said the doctors felt she would not last more than two days. I should come right away. It was the longest plane ride of my life. I prayed the entire time that Mom would be gone before I arrived. I did not want to see her dying.

I hated her and I loved her more than any woman on earth. I could not forgive her for drinking all of those years and I wanted to make them all go away. I wanted her to love me and it was way too late. We were from different worlds and we never bridged the distance. What made it worse was her insistence that we were so alike. Every time she said it, I felt invisible, unknown, unknowable. And yet, I knew there was an educated, powerful woman buried deep inside her pain. She had been widowed at forty-five and, in her blind

Catholicism, she never saw herself as anything but a married lady. It was as if she had committed suttee and for her remaining thirty-one years and she was only waiting to join her husband in heaven, in "the great golf course in the sky."

Fred and his family found me walking the airport corridor and sadly relayed that mother had died while I was in the air. It was a moment they have never understood. I was visibly relieved. My prayers had been answered. To them, I appeared cold and heartless. To me, it was that I didn't have to witness Mom's pain for one more second. I stumbled my way through the next few days: selecting a casket, ordering flowers, sleeping alone in my mother's unfamiliar house. I felt like an outsider, an alien. My family was comfortable in their routinized Christian procedures and I knew I had said my good-byes thirty-one years ago when mother decided to stop living.

Returning to California, I missed her. But then, I missed her since I was eight years old. It was just more final now. It was hopeless now. My grief was that I had always held out a wish that mother would wake up one day happy to be alive and that was impossible now. In time, I would have to let all of my anger go, like burning photographs.

I had heard that Rama was going to have a meeting on December 31. If I went, this would be my fourth year in a row. It was the best place to spend New Year's Eve. Everywhere else on the earth would be filled with intoxicated people making hollow promises and pretending to be celebrating life. I simply could not resist the opportunity to bring in 1987 with Rama. Besides, I had to find out if I felt any different sitting in his presence than I did in September.

I wanted to sit in the front row so Adam and I got there very early and stood in line. The theater was small and intimate, not like the sprawling Beverly. I got a front row seat on the far right, directly in front of the stairs that led to the stage. It was glorious. It was wonderful. I felt at home. I loved Rama and realized just how much I missed seeing him. He was funny, warm, and magical. So much had happened to me in those three months, it felt as if it had been years.

The Passionate Heart

We took a break and I stayed close to Adam. I was afraid that people would see me across the room, expect me to see them and give them a friendly special smile. But of course I could not recognize them any more. To avoid the possibility, I returned to my seat as soon as the doors reopened. Finally, Rama came walking down the aisle. He started up the stairs. With one foot on the first step, he turned to me and said, "Time to come back, don't you think?" I smiled, nodded timidly, and looked away in a whirlwind of shame and ecstasy.

Two weeks later, Rama held a meeting for the women and men who at one time had been students. There was going to be an application process and a private community again; Vishnu Systems was going to begin. All of us were welcome to apply.

Rama asked if there were any questions. I raised my hand. Then, one of the most radiant moments of my life occurred. Rama looked at me and said, "Zoe?" He called my name. It is a singular and inexplicable joy that happens when a student first hears their Teacher say their name. Who really knows why it happens or when it happens. In my heart, I imagined that Rama knew I would not be able to see him look my way and nod as he had called on me in the past. It was his impeccable etiquette that prevented me from losing face by not being able to see and respond. Ultimately, it didn't matter why. My moment had arrived. I heard Rama say my name.

"I was cruising for power in a place where I did not belong," I heard myself say.
"Yes, I know," he replied.
"They told me I would never be able to read again," I told him.
"We'll just see about that," he said.

Over the next few weeks, strange things started to happen. At first, I noticed that I could see a red traffic light. I was astonished. Then one day, I saw Alice's whiskers and the expression on her face. Very slowly, but just as surely, things started coming into focus. My hideous scrawling was getting smaller and smaller. The vanilla yogurt was not looking anything like the cottage cheese.

I went to the ophthalmologist for my monthly appointment. He peered into each of my eyes with his fancy electronic device. He was visibly upset. "The holes seem to have gotten smaller. That's impossible." he said. I hardly knew what to say. "Yes, I've been reading with the help of a magnifying glass," I told him. "This has never happened before. I never thought they would heal in any way," he assured me. "I understand." I *reassured* him.

Each day, for the next six months, the holes in my retinas closed just a little bit more. Each day, I could see just a little bit more. With bifocals, I began reading most text. Sitting close to my monitor, I could make out characters. My astrology charts started coming into focus. I began driving again. Although the moon would still slip in and out of view, if I were fast, I could catch a flicker of a glimpse.

When I was a little girl I especially loved stories about miracles. I read all about Bernadette and the children of Guadalupe. I was fascinated with the roses that rained on St. Theresa's bed. I had hoped that when I became a nun, I could have the name Sister Raphael. St. Raphael was an archangel and patron saint for the sick and dying because he cured Tobias' blindness. I wondered what it was like for Mary and Martha to see Jesus cry and bring their brother, Lazarus, back to life. I knew, even at the age of five, that miracles were very special things, things God gave freely, for nothing on earth could provoke such an action. And I was right.

The Passionate Heart

Chapter 28

According to Zen Buddhist cosmology there are ten thousand states of mind. Each of them presents a different view of essence and experience. Most people access only a few of them during their lifetime. The purpose of practicing Zen is to gain entry into any and, ultimately all, of the ten thousand states of mind.

Zen Master Rama was an entirely different Teacher than any I had seen or read before. He presented Self-Discovery with absolute continuity. In the four years I had been a student, spiritual references included: Hindu, Buddhist, Taoist, Native American traditions and Tantra. Actually, anything that was instructive and inspiring was included; poetry, music, literature, historical figures, and of course, computer science. Rama was able to gracefully wear a three-piece suit or tuxedo, discuss Mozart or Tangerine Dream, lecture on *The Hobbit* or Vedanta. He could do all these things because he freely traversed any and all of the ten thousand states of mind.

For me, the evidence of Rama's ability to travel from one mind state to another was indisputable. I had sat with him in halls, theaters, Hawaii, the desert; over four hundred times. Not only was each and every event completely different, but even in the course of one meeting or gathering I had seen Rama transform dozens of times. From my limited understanding of his fluidity, he became whatever the circumstances required. Whatever a student needed to hear, whatever feeling best expressed the message, whatever addressed the situation honestly, Rama was able to do what was needed wholly and unconditionally. It was as if Rama estimated the possibility for liberation and simply fulfilled it.

In traditional Zen terms, Rama is Enlightened. He has experienced all ten thousand states of mind and has gone beyond them to the "state-less state." He had gone beyond desire, aversion, and beyond thought. In Buddhist terms, it means that Rama can act only in harmony with the Dharma. Since there is no singular mind that is being held as a prisoner of attraction and repulsion, he cannot act any other way. To put it simply, Rama is the Dharma. He is the truth itself, in all of its fluid facets and fluent expressions.

I may sound as if I know what I am talking about, but the reality is that I understand the principles of Buddhism academically. It is my experience, in all of its skepticism, in all of its demands for proof, in all of its suspicion, insists that Rama is fully Enlightened. As I hold on tightly to my academic theories, my educated ideas, my accomplished cynicism against my experience, I still have no alternate explanation.

I can't even speculate on the fantastic benefits to being Enlightened, but I do know some specific advantages to being a direct student of an Enlightened Teacher. My will, heart, and mind are stronger, larger, and clearer than I ever would have accomplished on my own. My life experience is now conversant with the waking, dreaming, and meditative states. The world I see when my eyes are closed is larger and more complex than when my eyes are open. I am living a life I never would have thought possible, as is true for every student whom I know personally. Not only have I witnessed hundreds of miracles, I have been the beneficiary of a documented major miracle.

Rama's mind is so strong and disciplined that he can hold a thought or an image and everyone in the hall can feel it too. He is able to actually loan his state of mind to someone -- to an entire room of people. That is why it is so much easier to learn to meditate sitting with Rama. Instead of wallowing in a room filled with human thoughts and images, a student who is sitting with Rama is automatically engulfed in a pure meditative state. The ability to perceive it, to feel an image, to stop thought depends on the student's effort in their own private practice.

On very special occasions, Rama would take us on extraordinary journeys through his mind. One night Rama told us about a particular incarnation he had in ancient Egypt. He was the High Priest in the temple and we were actually his students at that time. He told us that, during the meditation, he would show us what we looked like and the place where we studied with him. The only instruction he gave us was to focus on the sixth chakra, the third eye.

Up until then, when Rama made such an offer, I would listen and follow the directions, but never really saw the world he was opening up. That night I sat in my straight back chair, closed my eyes, listened to the electronic music, and concentrated on my third eye. Within just a few seconds, I realized that all of us were sitting on backless, stationary seats on top of a flat pyramid. It was nighttime and the sky was filled with stars and a three-quarter moon. There was a warm breeze that I distinctly felt blowing on my face.

Rama was standing in front of us talking. His hair was long and dark brown. He was wearing a floor-length white robe. It was collarless with cuffed long sleeves. As if there were no difference in the lessons being presented in either world, Rama was instructing us to meditate. "Close your eyes and focus." My hands were resting on my knees, my back was straight, and I closed my eyes.

After a moment, I heard Rama say, "Come, dance with me." I opened my eyes and he was standing on top of the pyramid, directly in front of me. I stood up, lifted my arms and, as if to begin a formal waltz, placed one hand on his shoulder and rested the other in his open hand. As I raised my right foot and brought it back down, it did not touch the ground. With each step, we slowly rose higher and higher into the night sky, turning ever so slightly.

When the music stopped, I gradually opened my eyes to find myself sitting in Los Angeles. As certain as any seminar had ever been - was my knowledge of the meditation class in Egypt. My recollection of it was as vivid, crystal clear and physical as my memory of where I had been that afternoon. There was no sense of having been in a dream. There was no feeling of just waking up. I had simply been to another place, as surely as I was now in a LA Convention Center conference room.

Rama asked us to tell him what we saw. Many students raised their hands and shared their experience. They had seen the flat top pyramid. It was night and the stars were spectacular. We were all sitting on square blocks. Rama was wearing white. I did not raise my hand. I did not want to say out loud what had happened to me. It was too personal, too magical, too precious to be talked about.

The Passionate Heart

In ancient Egypt and Atlantis, women were not oppressed. I would not say that women and men were equal. That is a shallow statement that implies that identical opportunities afford both genders the possibility of fulfilling their potential. It is as ignorant as saying that birds and fish are equal or fire and wind are equal. What could such a statement possibly mean? How would it apply?

Although I do not have a distinct memory of life in those distant times, I do have an internal awareness that women were completely different from anything one could reference today. It was not a world in which men and women had equal opportunities to compete in business or that parenting was shared. It was not that women and men could freely select from a list of open possibilities. The implication of such a provincial concept is that somehow there were no genders, as if they blended into one another or equality translated into the genders being indecipherable. Clearly, that was not the case.

In ancient worlds, in previous yugas, women and men were very different. The distinction in their occult structure was obvious and their lives reflected an understanding of this essential difference. Each gender had their own particular power. Each gender had a special individual energy. The worlds in which they lived were evolved and wise enough to create cultures in which everyone was prosperous. They knew that as one person advanced, they all advanced.

Today, we are lulled into complacency upon hearing that it is illegal to discriminate against women. In the Sixties, we felt victorious when the classified ads stopped segregating jobs as Male or Female. In the Seventies, we felt hopeful because the Supreme Court declared that a woman's body is her own property. In the Eighties, we are expected to feel enfranchised because a woman was appointed Supreme Court Justice. We are supposed to feel that things are improving because a liberal man will admit, when asked publicly, that he would consider voting for a woman to be President *if she was qualified.*

The cry goes out that things are better, better than ever. A woman may enter the profession of her choice. Shelters and clinics receive government funding. Girls and boys are attending cooking classes. Females in the military are being recognized as soldiers and veterans. Insurance companies are being investigated for discrimination. There are even women's sections in bookstores. What more could you ask?

Feminists respond that professional latitude does not deflate the Old Boys Club. Federal funding for abortions is being cut back. Co-gender classes are not really displacing inequality in the school system. Women have always been full participants in the business of war. Investigations of insurance fraud are not unseating the unbridled power the industry had in blocking the Equal Rights Amendment. What are the books in the women's section? Reports on hormone replacement therapy perpetrated by the pharmaceutical industry? How to satisfy your man? How to compete in a man's world? How to catch a man? How to compete and not alienate men? etc.

Then the strife breaks out among the women. Those in the center want the women on the left to lower their voices for fear of losing the few strides that have been made. The women on the right argue that they don't want equality and women should be back in the home, in the kitchen with the children.

All the while, the men continue building a culture, a world that doesn't even allow for the ultimate questions, the radical questions, the *only* question: What is the true potential of woman? What is the natural power of woman? What is woman?

My remembrance of another time, another world, in which women were accessing their intrinsic power, catapults me to a grief much deeper than the one caused by job discrimination, the ineffectual legal system, or the arbitrary limitations of pink blankets shackled on innocent female babies. It demands that I ask questions much larger, much more painful. What will it take for women to really access their power? Is this even possible in the current civilization? Can we, as women, survive the pain of knowing the truth?

Much to my personal dismay, I seem to be incapable of being satisfied with less. Why me? Why should I care? Why can't I live and let live or be satisfied with the celebrations of women winning the Nobel Prize, a seat in Congress or even a term in the White House? I have no idea. It was one of the dozens of questions I wanted to ask Rama.

Rama had been invited to appear on the Larry King show. Over the last fifteen years he had written several books and been a guest on both radio and TV. I wanted to call in my question for many reasons. I wanted every woman in the United States to know that he believed in them. I wanted women to know that he was working for the Enlightenment of women. I wanted women to know why more women don't attain Enlightenment. I wanted to know.

Assuming that getting on the air might be difficult, I called the Larry King phone line two hours before the live show was being aired. The operator took my name and my question. She told me that my call was in the queue; I could hold on and my question would be considered, but it was not guaranteed. She added that I should mute the TV to avoid play-back. I sat on my floor, my phone in hand, and waited.

Finally, I heard, "Huntington Beach, you're on the air." "I would like to know why there aren't more women in the position of teaching, Enlightened women?" I asked.

"History speaks for itself. Hopefully, you will be one of the women who changes that. A lot of women have not been given access to Self-Discovery and the advanced teachings. In the seminars that I do there is no discrimination whatsoever. It is just very unfortunate. It is just the history of the world."

The Passionate Heart

Chapter 29

In the Spring of 1987, Rama held an unusual meeting. The sole topic for the evening was, "Sex, Drugs, and Rock-n-Roll." Rama said that he would talk at length about each subject and answer questions. It was going to be a night of absolute, unabridged truth, and although we may not want to accept it, we were going to hear it.

Certainly sex was the most complex and difficult of the three. Rama had never prescribed celibacy for his students or claimed to be celibate himself. His recommendation was that for a Buddhist seeking liberation, the real issue is detachment and that did not necessarily translate into refraining from sex. As Rama explained, "If you find yourself having sex with someone, engage fully, but otherwise sex should not be on your mind." As with every moment in life, the idea is to be entirely mindful in the present.

For men, the point was having a controlled and disciplined mind. Men lose power by thinking about sex or focusing on the person they currently desire. The mind should not be wandering aimlessly through the past, wasting the present, or wishfully constructing the future. Bob should be fully present while having sex with Sally, but when he is not with her, he should not be thinking about her. It could be argued that Sally is pushing her way into Bob's mind, but regardless of the source, Bob needs to be in charge of his own mind. The mind, body, and spirit should be integrated - that means all three, at the same place, at the same time.

For women, the same principles of mindfulness apply, but the issue itself is far more complicated and the results much more significant. While a man can easily engage and disengage in sex, the consequences for a woman, particularly a woman seeking liberation, are serious and often deleterious. A man can go to bed with a woman and leave with his energy intact. In fact, he can, and ordinarily does, leave with more energy. This is not the case for women. Rama explained that when a man has sex, he doesn't have to open himself or his energy field. But a woman naturally opens herself, and therefore her energy is totally available. She usually leaves the experience with less energy, less power.

"The primary place where women lose energy is sex," Rama continued. A woman who is dedicated to raising a family has agreed to use her energy this way. It is the Dharma for her, her karma. Sex is a critical issue for a woman who is dedicated to elevating her attention, meditation, and stopping thought. She needs this energy, or Kundalini, to sustain health, advance economically, establish self-reliance, and attain higher states of mind.

There were several women in the community who had children. Being a mother did not necessarily disqualify a woman from spiritual advancement, but it certainly made it more difficult. From the moment of birth there is an energy line from mother to child. Mothers had this additional responsibility. If a woman was considering pregnancy, Rama always cautioned her to be strategic. A child is dependent on a mother's energy for a long time.

Someone asked Rama about abortion. He explained that an embryo did not have a soul. It was not a person. To remove an embryo was no different from removing any other organ. It does have a severe effect on the woman's subtle body and the procedure may cause physical trauma, but it was not killing anyone or anything.

I was glad to hear Rama address abortion so frankly and clearly. I have always felt it was each woman's individual choice. I had publicly lectured on it and urged people to understand that the decision of when life begins was private and not the domain of government. I appreciated that Rama was not glib about it either. He acknowledged that it can be difficult and painful.

Over the course of my life, I have had two abortions. They were both difficult and painful. In my heart, I believe that life begins with breath, with birth. I never thought that abortion was wrong. But I discovered that no matter how resolved I was ethically and spiritually, the procedure was deeply emotional. Maybe it is just part of the universal consciousness of women. Maybe it is just a female body mourning over the interruption of its natural biological process. No matter what it is, I resent that the anti-abortion people think that the pro-choice people feel nothing about life. From my point of view, they are dead wrong.

Rama had told us a hundred times, in a hundred ways, that a Buddhist must examine their life by asking, "Is this adding or subtracting power?" No matter how much we didn't want to hear it, no matter how much we wanted it to be otherwise, the reality is that women lose energy in sex. Certainly a woman may survey the situation and figure that something in the relationship compensates for the loss. But ultimately, women who are practicing Self-Discovery must understand and accept that sex with men diminishes their power supply. It isn't personal. It isn't negotiable. It is structural.

Some of the women in the community had already dealt with this and made the decision that, at least for now, they would avoid having sex. My guess is that just as many women made the decision to not decide. They preferred to disregard the theory and hold the notion that, if they refused to believe it, they could deflate its truth. Although not the wisest of choices, it is certainly a widely accepted method of denial.

Rama was compassionate, but he just could not, would not, lie to us or abate the impact merely to gain our approval or reduce the distress. Over the last four years Rama seldom pushed the issue. But on this night, he wanted to uncover the truth; moreover, he wanted us to hear the truth. This night, we had to invoke the detached side of Buddhism, the side that was a strategist of life.

Rama asked a man to tell the women what men really think of a woman after they have had sex with her. Although this student might have felt trepidation, or have been accused of disloyalty by his comrades, he knew, (as we all did) that when Rama asked a question, lying or even glossing over the truth was a waste of time. "Once a man has sex with a woman, he never respects her again." Rama confirmed his answer and added that it was universal and unequivocal.

My feelings on the subject were deeply mixed. While my experiences with men validated what he was saying, I did not want it to be true. I wanted to access, maintain, and exchange power when and where I deemed appropriate. This sweeping proclamation was much too binding and too general to easily accept, especially for the rest of my life. I wanted to believe there was some exception out there, not just for myself, but for every woman who was in a relationship with a man. If it was the absolute, unswerving truth, women were in greater danger than even *I* had considered. I was not weak-hearted about confronting the terms and conditions of liberation, but this was untenable.

Rama continued, "Sexual desire is simply in DNA. The species wants to propagate itself." Most of what we feel as attraction is largely biological. Over the centuries, women have had to use sexuality to ensure their social position. If "wrapping" men were not a required survival method, there would be a lot less sex going on. While men use sex to gain power, women have been forced to use sex to guarantee civil and social rights.

I could not argue with it. Many times, I had read similar ideas in radical feminist literature, but I also had tempered it by attaching the mental footnote that it was mostly written by lesbians. Their reasoning seemed obvious, entirely appropriate, and positively understandable. Now the difference was that I was hearing it from my spiritual Teacher. It was not a theory presented by a cultural subset of the world, affirming their position, but rather a statement made by someone who had no ulterior motive. If anything he was once again exposing the secrets of the opposing (oppressing) camp.

The abject inequality of this dynamic was far more disturbing than the imbalance of power in Washington DC. I could only speculate about the age of this oppression, the size of this oppression, the depth of this oppression. But what of the remedy? How could this ever be changed, corrected, reversed? We have trouble reaching out to battered women who are held hostage in their fear. We haven't even ensured every woman's right to birth control and abortion in the U.S.. And what of women around the world?

Switching to the subject of drugs was a relief. My assessment of this group was that almost everyone had some type of experience with drugs. This was familiar territory. In the Sixties, usually the first place a person looked for liberation was drugs. It was a way out of pain. It was a way out of monotony. It was an effortless rebellion. In the days of *Leave it Beaver* and *Gidget*, there weren't a lot of alternatives.

Rama said that this subject was very simple. Drugs were completely unacceptable, under any conditions, at any time. He began by explaining that the mind is made up of bands of attention. These bands have a certain elasticity with a natural limitation that regulates both expansion and contraction. The practice of meditation strengthens and tightens these bands. Drugs artificially loosen these bands and stretch them beyond their normal healthy ranges. Drugs can destroy the mind, making meditation and mindfulness impossible. Rama also made it clear that he had worked very hard assisting us in tightening our bands of attention. To take drugs, thus creating an irreparable elasticity, was ultimately disrespectful.

I am sure that many people would have preferred to have heard something else. There were lots of sentimental notions about Carlos Castaneda and his Teacher's use of psychotropic plants. But Rama was not allowing any leeway on the subject. He told us that the states of attention we achieved through meditation would be ours forever. They were appropriate levels, revealed in perfect measure. Whatever doorways were opened through the use of acid were dangerous and unreliable.

A woman raised her hand and asked about a particular street drug called *ecstasy*. In the Sixties, it was called godspeed. She said it was reputed that *ecstasy* opened the heart center. Rama laughed and joked, "If that were true, I would dispense it myself. Nothing opens the Heart chakra but meditation and the rise of Kundalini." *Ecstasy* was a form of speed (amphetamine) that had no genuine spiritual benefit at all.

Rama shared with us that the higher regions of meditation were much more interesting than anything drugs had to offer. The worlds that are waiting on the other side of thought are real and, once discovered, are available anytime inside the mind of the perceiver. Finally, Rama said he knew that many of us had taken drugs when we were kids and he had spent a lot of energy repairing the damage. If we were so stupid as to take drugs now, he was not going to heal the damage again.

The Passionate Heart

Many times I think Rama would have preferred to be a rock musician. Although musically eclectic in both exposure and taste Rama loves rock-n-roll. One particularly fun night, Rama told us that a sure-fire way to record our passage into old age was our reaction to popular music. "If you find yourself saying the same things your parents did about popular music when you were a teenager, you know you have gotten old." If we thought the current music made no sense, the lyrics were ridiculous, or the songs had no melody, we had graduated to that special place reserved for *adults*. The singular thing we could do to guarantee staying young was to keep up with the changes in popular music.

In 1984, Rama started his own band - Zazen. Three of his students were the performers and Rama produced the music. At first, the men in the band assumed that Rama didn't know much about orchestration and composition. At one meeting, Rama asked a band member to tell us what had happened. He stood and shared with us that the three musicians figured that Rama would give them directions about the feelings and shadings of the music. They expected Rama to direct the music through meditation.

It didn't take long for them to find out that they had no idea who they were dealing with. Rama's understanding and direction were precise, exquisite, and astute. They would tape a section. By playing it only once, Rama knew every note, every intonation, every nuance. Rama listened and set the number of tracts, changed the timing, tapped out the percussion, selected sounds, designed albums, created album covers, named songs, etc. Rama's suggestions were always perfect and he accepted nothing from the band but absolute perfection. They would mix and remix until it met Rama's unparalleled standards.

May 10, 1987, Zazen made a live recording of *Occult Dancer*. Side one was named *Day* and side two *Night*. It represented a single twenty-four hour period in the occult dance of life, or the dance of an Occultist: Rama. That night, while the band (surrounded by tons of electronic equipment) played the music, Rama danced for us. He had told us about it in advance but I had no idea what to expect. I did not know if Rama had formally studied ballet, jazz, modern, or any type of dance. I did know to expect the unexpected.

The lights went down. The band began to play. Center stage, Rama began to dance. Although impossible to describe, the best I can say is that Rama combined Tai-Chi, ballet, jazz, and magic.

It was as if everything Rama had ever taught us about meditation, shifting states of attention, power places, and bridging the worlds came together. Years ago, I had seen Rama shift the energy lines in a room by simply moving his hands, moving a finger. I had seen light pouring out of Rama changing colors every ten seconds. I had seen the stage disappear and the theater collapse, revealing the night sky. Now they were all happening at once.

Rama and the music were one and the same. Rama's entire body was performing mudras. With each step, a new world opened. With each spin, the energy lines shifted. With each rhythm change, the vibration of the light wavered. There was no stage. There was no theater. There was only the music and the dance. The Dancer was power itself, revealing Day and Night in the worlds of the occult.

Chapter 30

As my sight was continuing to sharpen, I was able to look for work again. My resume was rather unusual since the first job I had after graduating from a technical school was "Director of Computer Research." Nepotism had worked out well for me, but the title was difficult to explain. After a few interviews, I decided that the truth made the most sense. I simply looked at the interviewer and said my brother hired me. I had been wrong in thinking I should hide it. People were congratulatory, if not jealous.

In addition, I told them that my vision was somewhat impaired. Although I may be sitting extremely close to my monitor and occasionally use a magnifying glass, I could do my work. Surprisingly, it was not an issue. Any apprehension I had about it was unfounded. Close work was not a problem, but I couldn't compensate for things far away. If a person tried to get my attention by giving a "high sign," I couldn't tell. The worst was if a person was meeting me in a public place. I would tell them that *they* would have to look for *me*, but it still made me very nervous. The happiest place was the front row in a movie theater. There I could see everything.

My third interview was with a hospital systems company owned by an order of Catholic sisters. They were converting all of their small independent computers to one large integrated system. I was hired as a systems analyst for $36,000. I worked with two women on the radiology component. I had my own cube, my own password, my own responsibilities.

My immediate supervisor was Michelle, who had quite a reputation. She was said to be tough, demanding, and unpredictably impatient. I knew I would like her and I did. I probably learned more from her about corporate computing than anyone else. Michelle's attitude had no room for mistakes, procrastination, or sexism. She had a tremendous amount of responsibility and responded to it by organizing her files, tasks, and life to exactitude.

The Passionate Heart

I felt as if had made the quantum leap of my life by going to computer school and getting a systems analyst job. My mind has always loved complex and diverse things. Now I had the joy of combining mental development, earning a living, and spiritual practice. To my dismay, Rama continued to insist that physical development was just as important. I hated the entire idea. I learned at a very early age to use my mind to deflect attention away from my body.

Like it or not, Rama talked more and more about martial arts. He wanted every student to study karate or judo because these forms had sparring and competitions for belt ranking. His intent was not just self-defense, but to confront and overcome fear. Rama said that we needed to get serious about this if we were genuinely interested in meditation because the higher regions of meditation require both courage and physical stamina. My puny compromise on the issue was taking tai-chi.

My aversion to martial arts was about using my body. I was too ashamed, too uncomfortable to put on a gui, exercise with a class, and call attention to my clumsiness. I knew it was self-importance, but it made no difference. Feeling guilty, I was compelled to find something radical to shift my opinions and sensibilities about violence and self-defense. I got a crazy notion that I might be able to loosen things up a bit by learning to handle a pistol. I hated guns. I hated movies with guns. I hated everything about guns. It might be a good place to start.

I called an indoor range and signed up for a class specifically aimed(?) at women. I arrived at 10 AM for a lecture and two hours on the range. Except for me, every woman was dropped off by her husband, who left her with a kiss and the household gun. It was clear that *he* had decided that the woman of the house should know how to use the revolver too. The instructor showed us how to load, unload, fire, and clean revolvers and semi-automatics. Then it was time to use the range.

I was handed a nine millimeter semi-automatic, a hundred rounds of ammunition, earphones, and five paper targets with drawings of men. I hung a target on the line and hit the electric button to send it out a hundred feet. With my earphones in place, I loaded the clip and waited for the instructor to watch my first round of fire. He came over, showed me how to brace my hands, and where to point the barrel. He had no idea that I could not see the site on the gun or the picture on the target. He had no idea that I hated guns all my life and had never heard one fire before. He had no idea that I was a silly Buddhist trying to overcome an aversion. I placed my feet shoulder length apart, pointed my gun, and squeezed the trigger. Once, twice, ten times. "Wow," said the instructor as he reeled in my target. "You should keep this, you just qualified as a security guard!"

I loved it. I guess that's all one needs to overcome anything -- success. I bought a membership at the range. I rented a gun and shot on Wednesdays, *Ladies* 1/2 price day. I don't know how or why it came so easily to me. I dabbed a little White-Out on the sight and could see the gun, but the target was pretty blurry. I stood squarely, concentrated on my navel center and seldom missed. A couple of years later, at a range in Connecticut, a woman interrupted me while practicing. She introduced herself and explained that she was interested in helping women learn self-defense. She asked me how big my bedroom was. I said twenty by fifteen feet. She reeled the target in to twenty feet and said, "Then that's all you need." I never missed again.

It seemed that if I gave anything half a chance, someone would show up to encourage me. More than anyone else in my day-to-day life, Craig had been there for me. He had driven me anywhere, everywhere. He patiently read to me. He played music for me. He never let me feel alone in my out-of-focus times. His birthday was coming up and I wanted to give him something that matched my appreciation. His favorite artist was Paul Reps, who wrote *Zen Flesh, Zen Bones*. Craig made the most ridiculous, simple and pure calligraphies; just like Paul Reps. I wrote to Reps's publisher to see if I could reach him and buy an original calligraphy for Craig.

I wasn't sure how old Reps was, but I did know that he had been friends with Christopher Isherwood; had actually met Ramana Maharshi, an Enlightened Hindu Teacher; and had known many direct disciples of Ramakrishna. Reps spent much of his life in India and the Orient studying Vedanta and Mysticism.

Six weeks went by and a plain postcard arrived. "I would be most grateful if you and your friend, Craig, would spend my ninety-second birthday with me. I will be wearing a straw hat and sitting under a tree, across the street from the post office. I will wait for you from 1 PM to 2 PM. Sincerely, Reps" The return address was Kamuela, Hawaii. I decided that instead of buying a Reps drawing; I would to take Craig to Reps for both their birthdays.

We flew to the Big Island, drove to the tree, and there was Reps. Watching these two men was amazing. There was instant recognition. They said little, as there was little to say. Reps invited us to his house, took out his ink, brushes, and paper. Craig and Reps spent the afternoon creating joy, chaos, and laughter. Years later, Rama told Craig that he had been a monk in Ramakrishna's ashram. Maybe Reps knew him then.

Impatiently I sat percolating my usual incessant questions. I wanted to know everything. I wanted to hear about India and the Holy men Reps had known. I wanted to know if Reps had been the real Larry Darrell in Somerset Maugham's *The Razor's Edge*. Finally, I blurted out all of them at once. This happy old man looked at me and said, "All lies, all lies." I was shocked. What did he mean? Hadn't he met all of these people? Hadn't he traveled throughout the East? Reps replied, "The past is all lies. There is only now. The rest is lies."

At this time my life was wonderful. I loved my job. I loved my apartment. I had good friends. And I had an Enlightened Teacher. Life was sweet. Monthly meetings were in Georgetown, Washington DC and at Wolftrap in Virginia. I flew into Dulles Airport and stayed in Fairfax, Va. It was fun to be back in the capital, where I had marched so many times for pro-choice and women's rights.

The May meetings were in Virginia. Rama discussed career development. Students stood to announce new jobs and salary increases. Everyone applauded in support. Women were making amazing leaps in their professional lives.

The Passionate Heart

Waitresses, saleswomen, and nurses were becoming systems analysts, programmers, and data architects. After just a few years in computer science, many of these women and men were making more money than their parents.

Rama said that the next step was obviously New York. "If you can make it there, you can make it anywhere." The New York market was excellent for the computer industry. There, we would learn professionalism, fascinating financial applications, and street savvy. Everyone was very excited about it. The cultural leap from LA to New York was gargantuan and this group loved an adventure.

Rama asked if anyone would prefer to not move at this time. A few hands went up, mine among them. He asked us to stand up. I gulped and slowly rose from my chair. One by one, we explained. "I just got my first real computer job with a cube and am learning a lot about systems analysis," I offered. "Fine," Rama responded. At the break, Rama asked to speak to the people who were living in Southern California. He told us that the energy was very tricky there and we should make an extra effort to get out into nature on a regular basis. He suggested the public gardens near Mt. Wilson.

Memorial Day was just perfect to visit the gardens. Craig and I took off early to meditate there. I had been thinking about a new puppy. Now that it was certain that I could commute from California to New York for meetings, I didn't have to wait anymore. It was time for poodle number four, so I brought an *LA Times* with me. After sitting in silence for an hour, I perused the pets section of the classifieds. I knew she was in there. I found an ad: Poodles, 6 wks, blk, F&M $150. Within two hours, the most perfect, little, black, adorable, poodle was sitting in my pocket. Mary was her name and Alice was not impressed.

Just booking a flight to JFK gave me the willies. I had never been to New York and it sounded terrifying. Another student who lived in LA was going to commute with me. Waiting in the boarding area, I couldn't find her. Once in flight, I still couldn't find her. Arriving at the biggest airport I had ever seen, she was nowhere to be found.

191

The Passionate Heart

I was galvanized with fear. I could not rent a car. I could not read a map. The best I could do was claim my suitcase and take the tram to the Hertz office. I called the hotel to see if she had left a message. No luck. I just folded on to my suitcase and disintegrated into a pool of tears. In less than a minute, three women were standing around me, asking how could they help. They were students from my community. They were staying near my hotel. They would drive me there. They were the most beautiful women I had ever seen.

When I got to the hotel there was a message from my lost friend. She missed the flight and would be a couple of hours late. I checked in and, as promised, she arrived shortly. We put on our business suits and took off for our first meeting in New York.

We met in a very beautiful hotel ballroom. Looking around, it could have been an IBM conference or a real estate seminar. Rama arrived, as always, dressed even more impeccably than the month before. He told us he loved New York. More precisely, he loved what he saw New York was doing for us. Many of the students had already found work on Wall Street, the World Financial Center, and the World Trade Center.

Rama raved about the trees, the cute houses, and the small towns surrounding the city. He said that city living was not a good idea; better to work in the city and live in the country. The train commute would be our time to read computer books and the Wall Street Journal. "Look around and notice the professionalism of the commuters because some of the most successful business women and men in the world take these trains. They are not afraid of success. They are educated and intelligent." Rama reminded us that we came here to learn independence, corporate business, cultural sophistication, and pride in our careers. In New York, we would practice Tantra.

Tantric Buddhism is the most esoteric branch in all the Buddhists traditions. It is the fastest, the most dangerous, and the most misunderstood. It is known as the "left-handed" path. While most forms of Buddhism offer hundreds of lifetimes to perfect meditation and mindfulness, it is said that

192

Tantric Buddhism can bring a person to Enlightenment in one lifetime.

As with all forms of Buddhism, the practice is meditation and the goal is Enlightenment. The aspirant strives to stop thought, dissolve the ego, and eliminate desire and aversion. But in Tantric Buddhism, one sees "Nirvana in Samsara and Samsara in Nirvana," explained Rama. Since Eternity and perfection are in all things, a student of Tantra goes into the center of life and interacts directly with the world. Thus, the challenge is much bigger, as is the possibility for mistakes. Rama said it is like driving a Porche around a hairpin curve. It is dangerous and requires extraordinary control, but you get there much faster.

The word Tantra means the joining together of opposites and the idea is that the opposite of everything is present in its polar expression. Purity is in the cosmopolitan city; solitude is in a crowd; detachment can be found in attraction. To practice Tantra, a Buddhist does not remove themselves from temptation, from desire, from passion, but goes into it and faces it head on. In Tantra, everything is an opportunity: sexuality, possessions, beauty, business, money, success, etc. The world is the ashram and Enlightenment is hiding everywhere.

By tradition and wisdom, Tantra is always directed by a Teacher. A student needs to be guided through the perilous turns. The Teacher can point and say, "That way is safer." As always, a student is free to experiment and make their own decisions. But in Tantra, it is particularly easy for a student to get lost in their own desires, careen out of control, and accrue some serious karma. Certainly New York was the perfect place to practice Tantra.

After the break, Rama asked to meet with the people who had not moved to New York. I met with the other errant students. I knew what was coming. I knew he was right before he even said a word. I not only understood the importance of what he had just told us, but I could see the difference in the students who had moved and those who had not. The New Yorkers looked polished, at ease, awake. We Californians looked trendy and laid back. This time, Rama did not have to ask. This time, it was not a matter of etiquette. This time, I wanted to make the move for myself.

Two weeks later, it was a done deal. I had said good-bye before. It was getting easier. Bye, blue Pacific. Bye, wonderful job. Bye, cute apartment. Bye, dear friends. Mary, Alice, and I got into my little Prelude and drove east.

Chapter 31

My two little furry friends and I drove for five days and wound up at a Ramada in Elmsford, New York. Fortunately, they accepted pets, so we could come and go as we pleased. It took much too long, but eventually we found a place to rent. It was a hand-hewn log cabin, surrounded by trees and only ten minutes from a train station. Mary and Alice loved it.

My first trip to the city was ultimately silly. I had only seen New York in the news, movies, and TV. I wanted to visit every scene in every place, I could recall. I started with *Alice In Wonderland* in Central Park from the opening of *Rhoda*. I went to the Dakotas, where John Lennon had been assassinated and home of *Rosemary's Baby*. Radio City Music Hall, where Michael and Kay read about the attempted murder of *The Godfather*. *Breakfast at Tiffany's*. Rockefeller Center. FAO Schwartz. The New York Public Library, scene of *Ghostbusters*. Beekman Place, home of *Auntie Mame*. On Christopher Street, I found a plaque commemorating the Stonewall Rebellion.

I rushed to the Plaza Hotel hoping to see Eloise's room. I waited in a short line to ask the concierge about their most famous resident. Behind me was a woman wearing a mink coat, guarding Louis Vitton luggage, who shook her head in disbelief as she overheard my inquiry. The concierge told me the room had been closed years ago, but there was a full-length painting in the lobby around the corner. As I stood admiring the portrait of Eloise and her turtle, Skipperdee, the mink laden woman joined me. "I love Eloise too, but I didn't have the nerve to ask," she tittered.

Standing on the corner of 5th Avenue and 50th Street while paging through my tourist book, I asked a business man if the building across the street was St. Patrick's Cathedral. He stared at me, rather bewildered and said, "Why yes, I walk past it everyday and never noticed. It *is* St. Patrick's Cathedral." Finally, saving my favorite for last, I sneaked into Macy's locker room where Kris Kringle put on his glorious red velvet suit in *Miracle on 34th Street*. From the Guggenheim to the Metropolitan Museum of Art, *Starry Night* to *Joan of Arc*, Broadway to Wall Street, New York was utterly fantastic.

The Passionate Heart

As the days went by, the thrill of my adventure began to fade. I simply wasn't prepared for the poverty. Nothing could have braced me for dealing with the homeless. Women in Blackgamma mink and Nikes stepped over beggars; confused women and men talked to the unseen. The distance, the indifference, the suspicion were all too much to reconcile in one heart. How could I possibly respond to ten or twenty people a day asking for money? I cared but had no way to express it. I wanted to help, but I was overwhelmed.

One day, while sitting in a taxi with a friend, I saw a man run down the street, stumble, and fall. Another man ran after him, drew something out of his jacket, and held it to his head. "What is it? Is it a gun? I can't see, what is it?" I shouted. I had to stop it. I didn't think or care to think. I had to stop it. Throwing my purse on the floor of the cab, I jumped out and ran into the nearest shop. "There is a man in trouble, call the police!" No one moved. No one looked. In total disbelief, I went back outside. Two uniformed officers came charging down the street. In just a few seconds, it became apparent that it had been a plain-clothes policeman apprehending a suspect. I slinked back into the cab, not knowing if I should laugh or cry. Laugh at myself, cry for the world. Cry over my stupidity, laugh at my innocence.

When I got to Grand Central, I really needed some chocolate chip cookies and a diet coke for the train ride home. A man began to follow and pester me for a hand-out. I kept telling him, "Not today." He stood next to me at the Fields counter and intercepted my change. I lost it and spouted, "Fuck off!" Instantly, I was deluged in shame. How could I have said that? How could I, who is going home to a poodle and a cat in a lovely wooded place, do such a thing? What happened to my compassion? I knew that being a bleeding heart in Manhattan was impossible, but how could I have strayed so far? What was happening to me?

At the very next meeting when Rama offered to answer questions, my hand shot up. "I am out of balance in regards to compassion, I know being a liberal is over, but I told a homeless person to fuck off." "That's okay," said Rama. "Is it?" I blurted out. "As long as it is not done with hate or anger. Trust your body. It is okay to say fuck off. Why spend all you have on this person? If it was the right thing to do, I would spend all day with them, but I am not supposed to be working with these people now. It is their karma. It would be wrong to pull them out of their cycle, to lift them out of the lives they have," explained Rama. I had struggled with this question before, as it says in St. Luke, "What then must we do?" I knew that Rama was saying the same thing Jesus had said about the poor two thousand years ago.

Rama paused. The entire room dissolved in an ocean of light. It felt as if he and I were talking alone. "Does that answer your question?" Although I felt unsettled, I followed the lines of etiquette and said, "Yes, thank you." He acknowledged my hesitation and continued. "You don't have to save the world, Zoe. It is enough to just walk past them, go to work, and light up the floor, light up the building." Rama spoke very slowly, very gingerly. "You have already given to the United Way. What you are doing is enough. You are helping by your contribution here." I could not actually see his face, but I could see his gestures. I could feel his kindness. "The word compassion is misleading. Each person is living the life they are meant to live. Some of the homeless chose their lives. They do not want things to change."

With that, Rama moved on to the next question. A man asked about anger. In the course of his response, Rama referred to me, "I did not answer Zoe's question solely with words. The words were the least significant thing that occurred." He said that when he answers a question, he transfers an entire block of information, an understanding, that creates a change in a student. "As I answered a question for Zoe about compassion, I shifted something in her structure so she will come to understand the true answer. She will see it unfold in the circumstances of her own life." What did he mean? What magic had he done to me? What would happen? Like watching New York movies, I could only wait and see.

At the end of the meeting, Rama announced that the next seminar would be very unique. It was going to be about being inaccessible in New York. We needed to learn how to blend with the local culture. As part of our practice and etiquette, we should be fluid and not draw attention to ourselves or make other people uncomfortable. It is a form of selflessness, of diminishing the ego. Though generally unspoken, part of being a Buddhist is passing unnoticed, leaving no trace.

Rama said that it would be a fashion show. He asked us to wear our very best professional outfit. We would walk across the stage, one by one, and he would critique our appearance. It would be a chance to have a private moment between Teacher and student, as well as hear his advice on our business attire.

Now, the act of choosing what to wear, hair style, jewelry, make-up, everything for this fashion show was a task. Some students were able to go shopping for new clothes. My finances dictated that I would have to find an ensemble in my closet. I spent the entire week rummaging through my meager selection. Which suit was an easy choice, I only had one that was acceptable. Shoes were always an embarrassment. I wear size 12, and the industry has delegated only the most utilitarian shoes for feet my size. Even after making every decision, from earrings to pantyhose, I prayed that I would be invisible.

Rama began the evening with an explanation. He said that since most of us were Californians, we were at ease talking to people on the street, striking up a conversation with people at the gas pump and shopkeepers. We got involved wherever we went. In LA, we walked down the street as if we had no place to go, enjoying the local scenery. Women casually hung their shoulder bags solely on their shoulders. We commuted in separate cars.

Now we were going to be New Yorkers. We had to learn the local customs about trains, subways, streets, bagels, and coffee *regula*. Rama asked one of his woman students who had lived in New York City to demonstrate how to walk down a street in Manhattan. She pulled the shoulder strap of her purse up and over her head, wearing the strap across her chest. She showed us how to hold the bag close to our body. "Always walk briskly, with total intention, as if you have a certain place to go and cannot be deterred," she said.

The workplace in New York was professional. Interviews were tighter. Leather briefcases, not canvas, were appropriate.

Resumes must be clean, clear, and precise. All references had to be in perfect order. The cozy California schmooze would only get us in trouble here. Sharpened skills, exacting programming, and computer expertise won work here, not clever conversation and winning smiles.

The dreaded moment arrived. The men went first, as the women sat and watched. I was a wreak. My hope that the line would pass quickly was soon dashed. Rama called each man forward, one at a time. He directed them to walk to center stage, make a full turn, pause, and slowly exit. A flood of emotions flashed through me. I can't do this. I am going to trip and fall. He is going to notice my enormous feet. He is going to say something about my weight, my posture, my height. He doesn't understand that because of size, I can't buy stylish clothes.

Rerouting my obsessive attention off myself and onto the stage, it became apparent that no such thing was happening. Rama was sitting in the front row. As each man quietly, slowly made his journey across the stage, his Teacher lovingly greeted him. "Hello." "Hi." "Good evening." A few were called by name. Everyone received an individual comment. Many were stopped and told something in particular about their suits, ties, haircuts, shoes, even socks.

Something most extraordinary was going on. This was no "fashion" show. This was a pageant of gestures between Teacher and student. Those who were shy and apprehensive were encouraged. Those who were afraid were reassured. Those who had performed the task well were honored. Watching more closely, I could see that there was a brilliant duet being played by each student and Rama. The student's energy was being reflected back at them through the attention of their Teacher. In the greeting, in the comments, in the intonation, Rama was telling each man something specific about the condition of the student's energy field.

As if that wasn't enough, as each student walked by, Rama shifted the structure of his subtle body. Rama occultly scanned the student, assessed precisely what was needed, and made the adjustment. While Bob was focusing his attention on getting across the stage, Rama was infusing Bob's aura with Kundalini. Listening carefully, I heard Rama make private remarks to a few men about their past lives. This was all a magical and intricate play of gestures, honor, and respect. Rama was telling each man exactly what they needed to make the next transit in their professional advancement. It wasn't about clothes or fashions, but about an entire being, walking across a stage and pausing in front of Eternity to receive a very personal and extraordinary boon.

The last man made his turn and took his seat. Rama called for the women to begin. We were not lining up by our names, so for once I wasn't last. I just wanted to get buried in the crowd. I ended up somewhere in the middle. It seemed to be going very slowly and I was inching forward. As the woman directly in front of me disappeared onto the stage, I thought I was going to faint.

It was my turn. I took a deep breath, bolted on to the stage, made a swift single turn, and charged off. Rama called my name, "Zoe." I gasped, crawled back, and stood center stage. I was wearing my navy wool Villager suit, a hound's tooth gold and white long sleeve blouse. I had on my pearls and two matching gold pins with diamonds and rubies (they were my Mom's). In my suit breast pocket, I had arranged an antique lace hankie. Rama asked everyone to stop and notice how I had arranged my accessories. "This looks like you have been in business for a long time," he said. I was nervous and thoughtlessly mouthed the words, "A very long time." Rama corrected me, "No, now what I am saying is you look like you have been in business a long time." I caught my breath, said thank you, and tiptoed off stage.

Taking my seat, a tidal wave of thoughts flooded through my mind. He had said so much to me in those few words. I didn't have to be ashamed. I didn't have to be embarrassed. He didn't make fun of my size, or my shoes, or anything. He gave me a special moment, an eternal moment. He made a comment that diffused my fears about being too old, too tall or too anything. Rama was telling me that I looked as if I had been in business a long time. I had been in business in past lives. And I have that power to draw on whenever I needed it.

To each woman and each man, Rama had said such things as, "nice suit," "great color," "now that's sharp," "good tailoring," "now look at the cut of this jacket across the back," "terrific shoes." And all the while, as students paraded past their Teacher, there were infinite exchanges occurring in countless worlds.

After the main event was over, Rama said he had a few suggestions that would help us do well in Manhattan. One, no more meditating on the train. It was not working. There were too many thoughts and too many dreams going on in those passenger cars. "Read the Wall Street Journal instead." Second, starting tomorrow morning, meditation would expand from one hour to ninety minutes. We had been practicing long enough now that ninety minutes was the appropriate amount of time. It had to be done in the morning before going to work. Third, physical development was not an option. Because the city was aggressive and violent, we needed it more than ever. We could choose between high-impact aerobics, karate, or judo. Seven classes a month was the minimum requirement. Finally, there would be monthly reports in calendar format. Each day, we would check off our meditation and mark the days we had gone to martial arts or aerobics class. At the end of the month, we would hand in our calendar to him.

Chapter 32

Much to my dismay, practicing Tibetan Buddhism in the West creates a lot of room for misunderstandings. On countless occasions, I have wanted to say to someone, "I am a Buddhist," foolishly thinking it would immediately establish a certain standard and credibility about my life. I've always wanted to tell a potential landlady/lord that I am a Buddhist, as if they should instantly accept that everything would be kept immaculately clean. Maybe if I wore ochre robes, people in the workplace wouldn't get so concerned about my "spinsterhood." But then reality sets in and I know it wouldn't help at all because people in the West have no idea what it means to be a Buddhist.

Tibetan Buddhism has a powerful and ancient tradition. People in the United States do not understand or respect what that means. We are the ones who unabashedly hold a bicentenary celebration. Searching my early childhood for some trace of tradition, all I could find was Santa Claus, the Easter Bunny, and the Good Tooth Fairy - all guardians of the Christian ethic, goodness and suffering bring rewards. I found Buffalo Bob, Mother Goose, and the Brothers Grimm. Primarily, I found Disney, who made sure we all got the message: the prince is on the way, blondes have more fun, single brunette women are evil, and mother love is blind. And not one of them can boast a tradition of over a thousand years.

For six centuries, young Buddhist monks have annoyed, treasured, mimicked, admired, frustrated, and deeply loved their Teachers. Teachers have tricked, protected, guided, confounded, encouraged, and deeply loved their students. No matter how ridiculous, how heroic, or how astounding the Teacher - student relationship is, it is a well-known tradition.

Teachers have handed the baton directly on to the next generation. There is a lineage, a precedence, and a cache of stories with names and places that validate and certify ancient, respected, and, sometimes, incongruous Buddhist principles. Easterners build temples revering them, establish customs based on them, and teach their children all about them. While Westerners often find these same principles repugnant, suspicious and, in extreme cases, criminal. If wisdom truly comes with age, the infant(ile) Westerners have a lot to learn.

Stories proliferate about aspiring monks waiting for months at the monastery gates to demonstrate their intent. Families are greatly honored when their young child is recognized as a Tulku, and gladly wave good-bye as their son or daughter is taken to the ashram for the rest of his/her life. Monks long for tasks of impossible proportion to affirm their dedication to the order and their Teacher. The more eccentric and foolish the Abbott appears, the more wisdom is ascribed. Generations memorialize these traditions through the arts. Children hear the stories again and again. All because they are handed down, Abbott to Abbott, Lama to Lama, Buddhist to Buddhist.

Intrinsic to this tradition is the tenet of ancestry. In Buddhism, it is believed that upon initiation to the order, one joins with all Buddhists, past, present, and future. It is one unified force bringing light and truth to the world. All of the Enlightened Ones support advancement of every Buddhist and every sentient being. Sometimes, Rama respectfully called this assembly of ancestors, "The Company." He warmly referred to them as his employers. The obvious implication being that Rama does not, cannot, act outside of the collective Dharma of Buddhism. Having reached Enlightenment, Rama and "The Company," are one.

Rama told us a story about a meeting of the Company. It seems they all congregate on occasion, from yuga to yuga, to swap outrageous stories about their adventures and their delight in prodding and taunting their students. As the single most important characteristic of a Buddhist is an unmitigated sense of humor, these meetings often dissolved into uproarious laughter. A great competition broke out among this conclave of Teachers as they offered accounts about the imaginative and ingenious tasks they had devised to assist in their students' progress.

The Tibetan Lama, Marpa, told his peers about one of his students, Milarepa. This tenacious student approached the Lama Marpa for instruction, as Milarepa heard that Marpa had learned the way to Liberation from his Enlightened Teacher, Naropa. Although Milarepa had a questionable past,

The Passionate Heart

Marpa knew there was hope. This inventive and dedicated Teacher told his undisciplined student to build a house out of stones and earth. Three times, Marpa stopped the process mid-way and told Milarepa to disassemble the house, return every stone to its original place, and begin again. Not until the house had been built from the foundation up, a *fifth* time, did Milarepa win the approval of his Teacher, Marpa. (Milarepa went on to become Marpa's best student and finally attain Enlightenment.)

Not to be outdone, Rama told his business partners that he had come up with a task that would win any challenge in any yuga. In addition to the magnitude and unlikelihood of the task, Rama had taken on not just one or two students (as was the norm) but hundreds. Rama explained that he had found a group of people who longed for Enlightenment but who knew nothing about patience and hard work. He set them on a long and arduous path to learn the art of computer science, acquire professional business skills, develop successful careers, and work in the Mecca of finance, New York City. Obviously, Rama easily won the competition for creating the most outrageous, intense, and effective scheme in all the universe to further his students' evolution.

Having heard Rama tell this amazing yarn, I realized not only did I have quite a task in front of me, but now it included Rama saving face with the Company. Of course, believing in ancient Buddhist traditions, it also meant I had the support of every Enlightened Teacher -- past, present, and future.

I had arrived in New York in early July. My resume, though eclectic, offered some highly valuable skills. I had been a teacher, business owner, director of computer research, technical recruiter, and systems analyst. I had a BA, an MA, and a computer technical school certificate. I had above average written and verbal communication skills. I had a navy suit and a leather briefcase. By October 1, I also had well over thirty unsuccessful interviews.

I was despondent. I had tried everything I could think of. I had prayed, meditated, and cleaned my closet a dozen times. I had run out of money long ago, and now even the train ride into the city for an interview was a major investment. Clearly I was doing something wrong.

Rama had given classes on how to write resumes and how to successfully interview. Most of the women and men had already found jobs in COBOL, DB2, C, systems analysis, data architecture, and various esoteric technologies. Several students had looked at my resume and said it was fine. A couple of times, Rama spoke specifically to those of us who were having problems finding work. He said that we needed to do a systems analysis on our lives. We were losing energy somewhere. "Make a list of what you are doing to collect personal power and a list of how you are losing power." I was sick of looking at my lists and trying to reconfigure my life.

One night, a man I hardly knew approached me at a meeting and asked if I would look at his resume. He was having a tough time finding work and he had a hunch I could help him. I warned him vehemently that I was having trouble myself. He insisted. He said that he didn't know what it was, but there was some specific reason he was asking *me*. Maybe we could help each other. Arrangements were made to meet the next evening at a Mexican restaurant.

We ordered margaritas and swapped resumes. Although we had seldom talked before, the conversation never waned. He had a Ph.D. from MIT, been very successful in research and was trying to make the switch to programming. We started going over what we had done with our lists. Since there was no investment, no front to uphold, no hidden agenda, it was rather like talking to someone on an airplane, someone whom you knew you would never see again. We had no time for shame and were highly motivated to get to the bottom of things.

In the course of the discussion, I mentioned that most of my "stuff" was in a friend's garage in California. He stopped, stared at me, and said, "Oh, safety measures." I said, "No. I have no safety measures." I twisted and turned, squirmed and stumbled, defended and insisted, "No. This is what I really want to do." He was not about to let it go. "None of this is going to work if you have left room for alternate options. Burn all your bridges and get rid of the safety measures."

The Passionate Heart

All the way home I was more than uncomfortable. My new friend had pointed to the core of my will. I was holding out. Somewhere deep inside my subconscious, I was making room for something else to happen. I was investing half-heartedly so that, just in case this didn't work out, I would have another option available. It was my energy leak. I had been collecting power and losing it by splitting my attention, splitting my intention.

I looked around the cabin and saw that although I had moved from California to New York, I had kept much of the California dream alive. I may have burned my past two years ago, but by now I had recreated an entirely new one. I had accumulated a whole new series of drawings, photos, cards, writings, letters, tapes, etc. Once again, everything had to go. I tore drawings off the walls, piled up the writings and photos, unraveled the tapes and threw them all into the fireplace. I called my friend Craig in California and asked him to send all my boxes that were in his garage to my New York address.

October 9, I got a call from an agency about an interview. It was with a bank on Wall Street. They needed an analyst and tester for their mortgage system. They had seen my resume and were interested. Although Monday, Columbus Day, was a civic holiday, the manager would be in and would like to interview me. I was definitely available.

I got up extra early and meditated for ninety minutes, no skimping. I wore the exact outfit I had worn at the "fashion" show, including the same lace hankie. Although the train was almost empty, Grand Central was as busy as ever. I took the #4 Express downtown and read my Wall Street Journal. Walking up the subway stairs to the corner of Broadway and Wall Street, I found the entire district deserted. The Exchange was closed. The banks were closed. The brokerage firms were closed. The sidewalks were open but empty.

At the top of Wall Street is Trinity Church, at the bottom is the East river. It felt as though it was mine alone that day. I was the only person walking down the sidewalk of the most powerful street in the world. Noting the numbers on these famous buildings, I paused one block from my destination. I stopped to catch my breath and remember what I was really doing. Gazing vaguely into the window on the corner of Water and Wall, I realized I was standing in front of a florist shop and in the middle of the display was a statue of Buddha. I bowed slightly and asked for his good wishes.

It was a short interview with a young man who had just been given a promotion. He was looking for someone to take over the position he had just left. He asked about writing specifications, panel design, and test scripts - everything that my militant manager Michelle had drummed into my head. We shook hands and I left. To celebrate Columbus Day, I walked over to the World Financial Center and took the tour on the top floor. When I got home, I wrote a short note to the man who interviewed me. "In 1492, Columbus sailed the Atlantic. 496 years later, I sailed down Wall Street. I hope my journey is as successful as his."

A week later I got a call. They offered me the job. By Halloween, I was the lead analyst for the mortgage systems for one of the largest banks in the world. Every morning I got up at 4 AM, sat for ninety minutes, marked my daily meditation calendar, and took the 6:40 to Grand Central. I was working on Wall Street. I had made the journey from LA to New York, from religion teacher to computer analyst, from the past to the present.

One day, several months later, the manager called me into his office. He invited me to sit down. He asked if I knew why he had hired me. I said I had no idea. He opened his drawer and held up the Columbus Day card I had sent him. He smiled and said, "I hired you because of this." I knew better. I knew I got the job because of the Buddha in the window, the Buddhas in my order, all the Buddhas who worked for "The Company."

Chapter 33

On the outside, we looked like computer professionals. On the inside, we had the hearts of aspiring monks. Both observations were true, but essentially we were human beings and human beings love attention. Every student longs for attention and a personal relationship with their Teacher. The human operating system is simple - one person figures out what the other wants, needs, or prefers. And then they become that. A classic example is a high school girl who develops an unprecedented interest in football at the exact time she meets the handsome quarterback. Another is a young man who takes to the dance floor as soon as he discovers that the woman he wants loves to dance. It is the natural play of attraction and aversion.

The etiquette in Buddhism dictates an entirely different dynamic. The more a student wants to be noticed or singled out, the more a Teacher ignores them. When a student develops a hint of humility, the Teacher may glance their way, smile, even say hello. This ancient and discreet process is used to validate a student's progression.

Frustrating as it might be, the principles of etiquette are never openly discussed. Everything is done through inference. A student just finds themselves in the same predicament, again and again. They are permitted to take as long (or as much embarrassment) as they need while the Teacher patiently waits. It might take a naive student months to realize that their proud gyrations are not creating the desired results and that the attention they want cannot be solicited. Eventually, they stumble on a flash of humility, receive an approving gesture, and witness the wonder and discipline of their Teacher's attention. At the time it is very easy to miss the delicate nuance of a Teacher's apparent indifference, but the fact is, a Teacher is never indifferent.

An Enlightened Teacher does not make these decisions, not in the conventional sense of observation and deduction. Once a Teacher has achieved Enlightenment, there are no more *personal* decisions. They are not people. They are a field of energy; the perfect pure energy of Enlightenment itself. This energy is naturally drawn towards the refinement of humility.

Because Enlightenment is completely selfless, it gravitates towards that which needs it. Many times I have watched Rama navigate through a sea of students. He wanders, pauses, has a brief conversation and moves on. Or he might ask a student to step aside for an in-depth conversation. Eternity decides. Rama's Enlightened mind communicates with the student who needs it most. It operates without manipulation, expectation, or desire.

In a traditional Buddhist monastery monks don't expect to see their Abbott. They know there are benefits simply from the Abbott living there, meditating there. If and when the proper moment arrives, the Abbott will spend time with a certain monk. It is because the monk reached a certain point where a direct relationship is called for. Maybe they need a special push to make the next jump in their spiritual evolution. The Abbott may spend a day, a week, a month with that particular monk. Once the work is finished, the Abbott may not talk with that monk again for several years. The decision is always based on energy. Enlightenment interacts whenever it is needed, wherever It can be of service. It cannot be bought, earned, or enticed. It is always a gift.

The exchange between Teacher and student may include words or tasks, but the most important interaction is taking place between energy fields, between occult bodies. The student's occult body has a specific structure, a certain vibration. In the course of a conversation or working on a task, the Teacher presents a student with the precise configuration of energy needed to create an opening for change for that exact time and situation.

If a Teacher approaches, the wisest thing a student can do is try to meditate, stop thought, or at least be silent. The reason is that if the student can turn off the internal chatter, they will find it easier to *feel* what the Teacher is saying. The principle works like a tuning fork. The student's energy field may be off key or vibrating at a frequency that is ready for the next step towards refinement. The Teacher presents the perfect pitch, the most exquisite chord that is just within the range of the student. It is an opportunity for the student to match the tone or refine the quality of the note.

The Passionate Heart

Rama's students did not live in a monastery. This was not a group of monks who left their previous lives and families behind, dedicated themselves to the order, and vowed to spend the rest of their lives in monastic life. This was not a group of students who worked in the garden and kitchen, prepared to wait years for a single moment of attention. We were Americans - impatient and filled with self-importance. Rama had several hundred students who lived and worked in the world. Nonetheless, the traditional Teacher - student dynamic was exactly the same. Rama used the modern world to teach the ancient principles of Buddhist etiquette.

In 1988, Rama devised a method for each student to have a personal, private, and powerful relationship with him. As with everything Rama does, it was resourceful, fun, ingenious, aesthetic, selfless, educational, effective, practical, and centered on the welfare of others. In other words, it was magic.

The plan was to develop graphical software. Each month, we would show Rama what we had done and Rama would critique the work. What sounded simple, which was its most beautiful asset, was infinitely complex. The software would be an exact reflection of our energy field. It would be a mirror of our state of attention. As the software was displayed on a screen, Rama would see exactly what each student had been doing all month and what they needed to progress. Something as simple and subtle as selecting a shade of blue would give Rama a forum to make suggestions, adjustments, and observations.

Rama never gave personal advice. If asked, Rama always said it was for the student to figure out. If someone asked about a relationship, Rama would say, "Oh, no, I'm not going to get involved and tell you what to do." But, by referencing our software, Rama could directly interact with each of us and avoid getting ensnared in our petty human dramas.

We formed teams of five or six people. We chose our own themes and Rama offered some suggestions of his own. All of them were either games or educational packages. They were to be fun and beautiful. Our first assignment was to design the opening sequence of screens to introduce the package.

The next month, Rama would look at them and make recommendations.

After the break, we sat with our newly formed groups and waited to tell Rama the topic we wanted. I joined a team of five women who wanted to create an astrology package. Rama walked throughout the theater, spending time with each group, refining the selections, expanding the ideas, encouraging the teams.

When Rama reached our row, we asked him about an astrology package. Rama said that astrology was very special to him because his mother was an astrologer. I had never heard him speak of her before, "She was very developed psychically and spiritually. She was interested in women's liberation before it was the fashion. She believed in reincarnation and was very liberal." He agreed with our choice and said he looked forward to seeing our first screens.

The more I thought about it, the more amazing the entire task became. It seemed as though it was as profound as I was able to perceive, for the deeper I looked, the more it unfolded. Obviously, it involved computers. Anything we could learn about computers would further our careers. Second, it would give us an opportunity to work with a small group of students. Third, it meant I would be able to learn more about astrology. If Rama were pleased with our work, he would teach us things about astrology that weren't in any books. Fourth, we would be spending hours and hours in front of our computers, working on a task from an Enlightened Teacher. Computing would become a form of meditation.

All of the packages were to be IBM compatible. I immediately leased a cheap clone so I could get started on our project. One of the happiest moments of my Buddhist practice was dragging my old Apple IIC computer out to the trash pile and smashing it beyond recognition. It had been the single item from my past that I felt I couldn't get rid of until I got a replacement. Disposing of it was more powerful than burning any letters or photos. Not only was it used when I got it, but I had been writing on it for six years. It was way past time for it to go.

The Passionate Heart

My team met many times that month to discuss such fun things as colors, planets, signs, stars, titles, and fonts. The possibilities were endless. Six very independent women had to reach consensus on hundreds of issues. We were constantly confronted with our egos, our wills, our selfishness. We laughed. We argued. We panicked. The days were quickly passing and the deadline was not negotiable. We got it together and went to the next meeting with a disk in hand.

The most magical component of magic is that it never stops spilling over the limitations of the human mind. Even if the boundaries of the mind expand, magic fills it to the brim and always floods over the edges. I am the one who limits the possibilities by trying to control it with my puny perceptions. Never had I been so overwhelmed with wonder and admiration for my Teacher than when I was watching him review his student's software.

As the graphics were projected on a huge screen, Rama stood on the stage and went through them, one by one. On the surface, his comments were intelligent, artistic, and constructive. Rama noticed everything. He talked about shading, colors, proportion, balance, form, and clarity. He was conversant on every topic, offering suggestions on content, design, depth, and research.

But below the surface, beyond the surface, it was sheer magic. Rama was viewing screens and *feeling* what each student had done with their attention for the entire month. Listening with ears, with hearts, with feeling, each student was given a personal opportunity to practice Self-Discovery. Each of us was shown exactly where we stood and what was necessary to progress.

At first, I found the process utterly confusing. I looked at a screen and thought it was very nice. Yet Rama was abrupt, cold, untouched. Another screen that I found quite ordinary, Rama generously complemented. It took me several meetings to realize what was happening. If we argued all month, if we had not worked much, if we were careless, Rama reflected it right back. He was somber, flip, and looked bored. If we had worked hard, overcome egos and really tried, Rama took extra time, made detailed suggestions, and paid more attention.

The Passionate Heart

All of the women on my team were powerful and clever. I didn't know any of them very well, but I always had a special feeling for Marcie. Although I had only spoken with her a few brief times over the last six years, I loved her from the instant I saw her. There was something regal about her. She was graceful, articulate, wildly funny, and sometimes downright blasphemous. Physically, she was impeccable; make-up, shoes, suits, especially her brilliant red hair. Marcie preferred the truth to the trivial, though she could ramble effortlessly for hours about anything and everything. But it was none of that. Marcie had a resonant depth. Marcie had heart.

We were about the same age. When each of us walked in the door and found our Teacher, we had very busy and full lives. We were involved in living. In contrast to many of the younger students, we had mileage on us, we had been around, we had built lives for ourselves. Although quite different from each other, we had a certain worldliness and sophistication. Marcie was interesting. There was something about both of us that was intense and, so we were often told, intimidating.

I found it curious that students described me as intimidating. From my point of view, they hardly knew me. How could they form any opinion? But many times I heard that I intimidated people. I asked several students how I won such a reputation and the answer I got most was the questions I had asked Rama over the years. The words, the phrases, the tone were all straightforward. The questions were personally revealing and honest.

I finally understood it when I remembered questions Marcie had asked. She always spoke to Rama as if they were the only two people in the hall. She would joke and laugh, but always with a deep and abiding respect. While other students tried to couch their questions in such a way as to deflect scrutiny, Marcie welcomed it. There was no shame, no guilt, no pride. Marcie loved Rama and let it show at any cost. Having heard her questions over the years, I welcomed this opportunity to be friends at last.

Marcie had been an actress, a very successful actress. When the rest of us made the shift to computer science, it was hardly a sacrifice. For the overwhelming majority of us, it had been a significant upgrade, professionally and financially. This career change was a giant leap for Marcie. Being the grand woman she was, she braced herself and was ready for anything. She bought a computer and dug right in with the rest of us.

A systems analyst position opened up where I was working. I knew Marcie could easily do it. I only had to convince her. She gave me her resume. The next week, they called Marcie for an interview. To my surprise, I was scheduled as one of three people who would interview her. She came in for the interviews, looked smashing, and spoke intelligently. Afterwards, all three of us agreed; Marcie was our first choice for the position.

The project manager had no idea that we knew each other. He asked me to help Marcie get oriented. Her cube was only two away from mine. We ate lunch together. We laughed. We giggled. We worked hard. But the best part was that now each of us had someone at the office who knew. Our work was our practice. We were Buddhists. And we had an Enlightened Teacher.

Chapter 34

As the years passed by it felt as though, more and more was occurring within the stationary boundaries of 365 days. Watching the lives of many people who were not students, it appeared that a year held a few memorable events and the rest of the time simply rolled by. I would call an old friend to inquire about the last few years and, on the whole, not too much had happened. "Oh, same old thing."

The Buddhist teaching is that a soul is on a cyclic journey of birth, life, death, and rebirth; called the Wheel of Life. A soul incarnates into each lifetime to learn certain lessons. The number, content, and speed of these lessons depend on one's karma. The process is a natural unfolding of circumstances that present the soul with experiences that call for detachment through struggling with desire and aversion.

When an Enlightened Teacher accepts a student, the evolutionary process is sped up. Because the Teacher lifts the student's state of awareness, raises their vibratory frequency, and mitigates their karma, a student processes the lessons of many lives within one lifetime. Through the guidance of Enlightenment, they actually are born, live, and die to a new attachment or a new aversion on a regular basis. It may sound mystical and technical and it most certainly is. To a student, it can be both exhilarating and exhausting.

By 1989, it felt as if the lessons of a single lifetime were occurring within a month, sometimes within a week. As quickly as I adjusted to one thing, another was demanding a new level of detachment and flexibility. I found the typical Monday morning office question, "So, how was your weekend?" completely unanswerable. Even if I could articulate it, they would never believe me. I might have looked the same as I did on Friday, but inside I hardly recognized myself.

My mind had grown both in depth and breadth. My concentration span was significantly longer and wider. I could hold much more information in the fore at one time. It was becoming easier to discard eroding or unpleasant thoughts. Even more interesting was that, through meditation, I was beginning to actually know my mind. I could watch it expand. It was like watching a high-rise building under construction, floor by floor, room by room. I was able to distinguish where I was, where I had been, and where I wanted to go.

I remember vividly that before I meditated on a regular basis, my mind took *me* where it wanted. I would surface from time to time and say, "Where am I?" Now I was directing my mind. Now I was realizing that I am separate from my mind. Now I was becoming aware enough to ask, "Who is the *I* that is directing my mind?" Such understandings must have been noted passages in a student's evolution because on January 23, Rama announced that he was going to initiate us into the Holy Order of Buddhists.

Two hundred and fifty women and men were going to become ordained members of the American Buddhist Society. Rama told us only the night before. He asked us to wear our very best. It would take place in a hotel ballroom in Westchester, New York. A hotel might seem like a strange choice for such an occasion. But then, there is no proper place in the West for such an event.

Parking the car, going through the revolving door, walking past the lobby as I had so many times before, I never expected to find what was inside the main ballroom. Hundreds of elegant balloons floated throughout the room. Dozens of gorgeous pastel roses lined the front of the stage. Twenty exquisite Thangkas were hung on the walls with the most beautiful one behind Rama's chair. I walked through the doorway and paused to drink it all in. I felt as though I was standing on the steps of a temple in Tibet or great monastery hall in Nepal. It certainly was not a hotel ballroom.

It wasn't that we were transported to the Far East. It wasn't that we left the West. We were clearly Westerners engaged in an ancient Eastern tradition. Within those walls that had known their share of weddings and network selling was the energy and attention of our ancestors. Every ordained Buddhist -- past, present, and future -- was there in spirit, wishing us well.

A formality surfaced effortlessly, as if we had all done this before and knew the correct etiquette. Everyone looked very beautiful. The entire room and everything in it was living in the attention field of beauty. It felt reverent and graceful. The universe had stopped on its axis. It was the moment to which all previous moments had led. It was the outcome of every task, every hardship, every joy, every seminar, every step on the path, every meditation. And yet, it was utterly and infinitely undeserved.

Rama arrived and wanted to begin right away. He laughed and said that he did not want to explain the nature of this initiation until it was over. "Better not to know," he said with a Yiddish accent. He explained that he would call us up in groups, according to age, with the youngest first. We should form a single file line in the center aisle. When we stood in front of him, he would place his thumb on our third eye and meditate for a few moments. While standing there, we should try to clear our minds. He added that if we couldn't stop our thoughts, even if it was the grossest thought in the world, he would understand. When he finished, he would hand each of us a rose. Finally, we should place the rose on our chair and leave the room.

The youngest members of the community were two eighteen-year-old women. They walked up the aisle and stood in a single line. Rama touched the first woman's forehead and after a minute handed her a rose. She walked away to the left. The next woman stepped forward. Rama meditated for a while, with his thumb on her sixth chakra and then, gave her a rose.

This was not fast. It was not careless or carefree. It was a deep and meaningful moment between Teacher and student. In the past, there had been many occasions when Rama stood at a doorway or table to say hello to each of us, but he always directed us to pass by quickly, as if the physical greeting was merely a formality. This time was eternally different. The physical placing of his hand was important. The seconds spent in the exchange were important. This time there was a sacred transference from Teacher to student that required time and space to stop.

The Passionate Heart

Rama called for those who were nineteen. Again a line formed in front of him. With some he spoke a few words. To all he said hello. If the student said thank you, he replied, "You are welcome." And to each person he handed a rose. The room was completely silent. Every woman and man sat as they never had before. As Naropa stood before Marpa and Marpa before Milarepa, we would stand before our beloved Teacher, Rama.

I was sitting on the far left about six rows from the front. I sat watching students line up and wait their turn to meet with Eternity. After a moment with Rama, students would quietly turn to the right or the left, place their rose on a chair, and leave the room. But who were they now and who was I going to become? What was this procession and where did it lead? My attention was razor sharp and totally present. I sat perfectly still as if I had no body at all. There was no disease, no old age, no death, only ecstasy.

After a very long time, I heard Rama call out, "Forty." I stood and walked to the center aisle. A woman motioned graciously for me to go ahead of her and I stepped in line. There were probably six people in front of me, allowing me time to feel what was happening. But what did I feel? It was more a sense of not feeling. Whatever feelings the earth foists upon us had disappeared. I was floating between the worlds. Pleasure, pain, climate, taste, excitement; every feeling I could ever list had wholly vanished. What I felt did not live in the world of words, in the world of feelings. It was beyond safe. It was beyond subtle or delicate. It was unfamiliar, but it was home.

The student in front of me stepped to the side and suddenly I was facing my Teacher. Rama said, "Hi, Zoe. How's it going?" I said, "Fine." I stood as still as an oak tree. He raised his hand and touched my forehead for a long time. There was a smile on his face and he had gone very far away. I looked at his necktie trying to decide if I should shut my eyes. I didn't want to shut my eyes and miss this chance to see him up so close. I should have been trying to stop my thoughts, but I didn't want to get caught up in some juvenile internal argument. So I just stood there. Then he opened his eyes and handed me a pink rose. I said, "Thank you very much." "You are very welcome," he replied as I walked away to the left. I put my rose on my chair and left the room.

The Passionate Heart

When the meeting reconvened, Rama asked us to talk about our perceptions of what happened while standing in front of him and his touching our third eye. There were many answers, but one stands out so deeply it has wiped away all of the others.

A woman said that when Rama touched her third eye, the entire room transformed into a Buddhist temple. She saw all of the Teachers and initiates from the Holy Order standing behind Rama, watching the ceremony. There were men and women dressed in various traditional Buddhist robes. Many had shaved heads. They were Chinese, Japanese, Indian, and Tibetan.

Rama said yes, it was true. They were all here. "Just like the Buddhists in this picture, we were all in a Thangka," Rama said, pointing to the Thangka hanging behind his chair. Like an eternal snapshot - the room, the ceremony, all of us, every member of the Order, and Rama were now in a living Thangka.

As I listened, I wondered how many of the Teachers or monks standing behind Rama were women. How many Teachers had ordained women to be full members in the order? I imagined that Yeshas was standing next to her Teacher, Padmasambhava. Regrettably, she was the only Enlightened woman's name I knew. In my search through Buddhist literature, she was the only one I had found anything written about.

Like a bolt of lightening, it struck me -- there were more women in front of Rama than behind him. Rama had ordained more women in this single ceremony than had been ordained in all of our history. Rama had broken with tradition entirely. He believed in the Enlightenment of women. He was working tirelessly for the Enlightenment of women. He was taking responsibility for the Enlightenment of women in his lifetime. Regardless of the centuries of oppression, conditioning, and tradition, Rama was not going to be held to the past. That night he changed the future. That night he created an unprecedented present.

Rama explained that there are many types of initiations. Each one has a certain power. A Teacher gives them to a

219

student at a very specific time - sometimes because the student has earned it, sometimes because the student needs it, sometimes both. An initiation leaves an indelible mark on the student's occult body and carries the "signature" of their Teacher.

On this night Rama had given us two initiations: Vadra and Dharma. The Vadra initiation was the initiation of power. It gave the initiate the ability to defeat any opponent. This included breaking through conditioning and past life tendencies. It was extremely important for the women in particular, who are trying to overcome centuries of repression, degradation, bondage, torture, and misery. Finally, this initiation conferred the power to break through the ultimate opponent, thought.

The second initiation, Dharma, imparted the gift to teach about the Holy Dharma and meditation. Rama said that we were not ready to formally teach, but now our lives should be examples of the Dharma. Now we carry the imprint of this initiation and our lives should reflect the Holy Dharma. Rama told us that when he dies, it will be our duty to carry on the Teachings of the American Buddhist Society. While he is alive, we should talk about meditation to anyone who genuinely asks.

Rama said we had no idea what just happened to us and wouldn't for a long time. It was something that would unfold and express itself as life presented the necessary circumstances. Suddenly we would simply find ourselves doing things we never could do before. Now we would be able to conquer things that held us up in the past.

Certainly we were not prepared to receive these elevated and advanced initiations. Rama said he couldn't wait any longer; he wanted to be assured that the line of initiated Buddhists would continue. When we needed them, when it was the Dharma, we would be able to access the powers of these initiations. It was permanent. It was forever.

Chapter 35

We Americans love to measure things. We want to know where we stand, where we have been, and where hard work will take us. We want to know there is someone behind us, less than us, shoring up our status. We have report cards, IQ tests, SAT scores, and class ranking. We watch mortgage rates, credit card fees, the national debt, the GNP, and the stock market. We compare our lives with the divorce rate, the percentages predicting the probability of criminal violence, and the insurance actuarial charts. In the world of religion, we use volunteer hours, indulgences, sin, grace, tithing, commandments, and even assigned seating in a place of worship to clearly illustrate one's position in the congregation. In Buddhism, the sign of progression is increasing happiness.

Rama put it quite simply, "If you are not becoming happier everyday, you are not doing it right." Daily meditation, if done correctly, always leads to happiness. Even if it isn't possible to meditate every day, sitting on a consistent basis is bound to increase personal happiness. The release from earthly attachments and aversions opens the door to build a relationship with the inner self. I remember on a cassette tape Rama made years ago that he said if you meditate and look across the great river, you will see someone waving back. It is you in a different world where everything is perfect and you are eternally happy.

I have often called on this image to carry me through. As a little girl, I believed deeply in my guardian angel. It is a Catholic phenomenon in which each girl and boy has an angel assigned exclusively to safeguard their welfare. To a child, who had no safe harbor it was a lovely image. Now, I think of this consistently cheery, innocent, and vigilant being who has only my best interest at heart as my higher self. She is not tainted or jaded by life in cosmopolitan USA. She is my ideal - the guardian of my ideals. She meditates perfectly. She is infinitely happy and I only wish I was aware of her all of the time.

I can't see her across the great river when I amble from thought to thought. I forget her completely as I crash head on from fear to fear. I disown her entirely as I lose myself in the

latest desire or mourn the loss of the most recent attachment.
Those rare moments when I have found her deep within I think
that she *is* the great river. She is the stillness of the water
and, as the *I Ching* says, the joy of the lake.

It could be argued that this is merely a projection or at least
wishful thinking. But the reality of my own experience tells
me that whenever I do settle my body down, shut my mind off,
and elevate my attention, she is very much alive, hardly a
phantom. She is unruffled and so very contrary to my
habitual mode of operation that she didn't even notice that I
had left for any amount of time.

This is not an imaginary friend who feels no pain when I am
battered. This is not a mental paper doll who cannot be raped.
This is not the bionic woman who seizes equality. This is not
an island to which I escape when the agony of life is
suffocating me. This is the constant and real self who lives
outside of desire and aversion, outside of pleasure and pain,
outside of the Wheel of Life. She is ecstatic. I am happy when
she is me and I am she. My Buddhism and my Teacher are
always pointing, "She is here. She is already liberated. She is
right here."

My life had developed facets that I never would have
created for myself. At the age of forty-one I was knee-deep in
studying computer science, making more money than I had
ever imagined and wielding a level of professional authority
that I never would have sought for myself. Instead of
frequenting women's or spiritual bookstores, I was pouring
over shelves of computer books. Instead of living in a tiny
pond of limited expression, I was managing the development,
testing, and production of an international mortgage system.
Instead of protesting the inequality of women, I was living a life
that far surpassed most American men in education, income,
responsibility, and potential advancement.

My roommate and I had long outgrown the log cabin. Our
careers made it possible to make a considerable change in our
living conditions. Both of us were analysts working on Wall
Street - I for a bank and she for a brokerage firm. We rented a
gorgeous condominium in Connecticut. It was three stories
and situated on a river. We each had our own bedroom and

bathroom. I had a study on the lower level with a sliding glass door facing the river. Mary, Alice and I spent hours wandering in and out of the house watching the moonlight on the water.

Nights and weekends were nothing but astrology. I was totally absorbed in working on the astrology software. I adored every minute of it. Fortunately the work I was doing at the bank did not require any time away from the office, so I was free to read, create charts, and design screens. The only thing that got me to stop was the unflagging knowledge that the alarm was going off at 4 AM.

Rama surprised us and offered to meet with the software teams at dinners held in our homes. There were at least twelve different software packages, each one designed by two competing teams. Rama was going to have one dinner for each of the packages. Nancy, a woman on my team, volunteered her house. Rama planned the entire event, right down to the menu. He told us that he wanted ours to be a fondue party. He even knew what kind of cheese and bread to buy. Desert was to be chocolate fondue served with fruit and pound cake.

I had only been with Rama at general community gatherings. I had heard that long ago, Rama met with small groups of students in restaurants or went to movies. But I had never been to any select event. I had no idea what to expect. All I knew was that the house and the dinner had to be as perfect as humans could provide. All together there were twelve women working on astrology software and now we went to work on Nancy's house.

Besides the pure good manners of having a nice party, this was a very special situation. When one meditates well, one develops psychically. It doesn't mean that one can see the future, although that sometimes happens. It means that as you slow down the torrent of your own thoughts, you can feel the thoughts of others. You can get into a taxi and feel the thoughts of the people who just got out. You can go to a project meeting at work and feel the hostility or frustration of everyone in the room. Spiritual advancement includes expanding one's psychic abilities.

The Passionate Heart

An Enlightened being can feel everything that has ever happened in a room, in a vehicle, or just walking down the street. (Not that Nancy's house was better or worse than any of ours, we still went to work.) With the same etiquette as we were hoping to express in our software, we wanted to give Rama the very best. All of the tasks were divided among the women: shampooing the carpet, cleaning, shopping and decorating.

Nancy's apartment was small which was an advantage - there was less to clean. She also had known Rama longer than any of us. She is a Libra with a Virgo moon and an expert in relational databases. Until the astrology project, I really didn't know her very well, but I had heard about her dogs. More precisely, I had heard about Nancy's abiding dedication and affection for dogs.

Many times over the years Rama brought his dog to a seminar. He would let his canine pal wonder around while the meeting continued as usual. The only direction Rama gave us was to leave him alone and let him decide where he wanted to go. In the course of the evening, Rama would pause a couple of times, look out into the group and ask where his dog was. Without fail, he would be sitting with Nancy. Sometimes he was sitting on the chair next to her. At others, he had jumped on her lap and made himself at home. Nancy had some kind of magic. She loved dogs: moreover, they adored her.

Nancy had two dogs of her own. Samurai was the oldest. He was from a kennel in Massachusetts. He was handsome, quiet, very well-mannered, and wise. The younger one's name was Joy. I had met them both at the log cabin when Nancy brought them over to an astrology meeting. Joy and Mary got into a rhubarb. I tried to intervene and Joy nipped me. I love dogs, but after that I was always careful with Joy. He seemed aggressive and unpredictable.

When Rama drove up, everything was absolutely perfect. The veggies were cut, the bread was cubed, the fondue was bubbling, the tables were set, the candles were lit, and it didn't even show that perfection had happened two seconds before he rang the bell. Rama took off his shoes and headed for the kitchen. He bid everyone to sit down and await our feast.

The Passionate Heart

Nancy's kitchen was small, certainly not built for two grown adults. Rama called me in to help him find something. There I was rifling through cupboards, back to back, with my Teacher and chef for the night.

Our dinner tables were arranged Japanese style, low to the floor with seating on the ground. I took my place in a far corner, wedged in, unable to move at all. Impishly, I said to Marcie, "I'll pay you a thousand dollars in a future life if you get me some more cherry tomatoes." Before Marcie could reach for them, Rama said, "You better not joke like that, those promises are real." I leapt for the tomatoes myself.

When all the food was ready, Rama walked over to a clear space on the floor and sat in a half lotus. Samurai came by and offered his hellos. Rama called Joy over. When Joy came within reach, Rama swept him up and held him in his arms. As Joy tried to escape, Rama tightened his grip, drawing him even closer to his body. The more this strong and willful dog fought to flee, the more intensely Rama held him. All the time Rama talked to Joy. Sweetly and gently, Rama told him you'll be okay, settle down, relax. Throughout this twenty minute conversation between Rama and Joy, no one else made a sound or moved an inch. We were mesmerized.

Nancy told me later that Rama had sensed that Joy was filled with fear. As a puppy he had a difficult time before Nancy found him. Rama held Joy. Rama pushed out all of the fear, consoled him, and assured him there was no reason to be afraid any more. From that moment forward, Joy was a different being. Each day his aggression diminished. He grew calmer and more responsive. Until eventually Joy actually became attentive and affectionate.

Rama filled each and every plate, serving us individually. We ate fondue until we thought we were going to burst. Rama didn't eat until everyone had twice as much as they originally wanted. He was the ultimate host. Then Rama sat and talked to us about astrology. He recommended that we seriously look into Hindu astrology. It is completely unlike the system followed in the West. The principle difference is the understanding of the cycle of reincarnation. In the Hindu system, a chart is seen as a single reflection in a series of

225

lifetimes. We asked lots of questions and Rama patiently answered them. We meditated for a short time and Rama said goodnight.

Rama never stopped encouraging us to improve our careers. The human tendency is to reach a plateau and settle in for the long winter. People get comfortable and complacent, forgetting that change is the natural course of life. Adults look at children and admire their tenacity, flexibility, and sense of adventure as if it is the sole property of youth. The fact is that youth never ends for women and men who move through winter, inviting spring's return.

In the corporate world, employees are expected to embrace other workers as a family. They have parties, picnics, sporting events, and holiday gatherings. They want to know one another and prefer that others have lives similar to their own. Fundamentally, they want to operate as a unified group, agreeing on tempo, morality, and future plans. They are tribal.

For Buddhists there is no judgment about these choices except that they are inappropriate for ourselves. We are not seeking an extended family with a twenty-five year commitment. Our lives are about being fluid and detached. Going to the same job every day, interacting with the same people every day can become difficult as others hope and need to find the same person sitting across the aisle. The entire system is counter productive.

We work hard and try to express perfection in our careers, but maintain an unspoken distance. On every job I've made friends who became very close. I think they liked how present I was for them. I was always genuinely interested in their lives. But I believe if I had told them that I was also aspiring to a level of detachment, they would have felt unnecessarily suspicious and distrustful.

And so there was the puzzle. How could we responsibly live and work in the world, and yet move, change and grow? How could we begin and finish a job, enjoy our professional relationships, and be true to our principles of detachment? Rama proposed that the solution was contracting. We would be hired for our skills, perform the tasks with dedication, and when the job was done, be free to begin anew elsewhere.

This shift was not as simple as it sounded. As employees, there was a grace period in which a person was oriented, trained, and given some amount of slack. A contractor had to hit the ground running, ready to tackle any task with authority and expertise. This new challenge meant that we would have to reevaluate how we thought about ourselves. We would have to see ourselves as capable and accountable. Certainly we had the skills; it was a matter of self-esteem.

At the next seminar I sat in the balcony. Marcie was a few rows in front of me. Rama talked about how becoming a contractor would create important internal changes for us. He knew that the only thing we lacked was self-confidence. Many women and men had taken his advice and landed contracts. Their self-esteem had significantly and visibly increased. Rama looked directly at Marcie and challenged her to find a contracting position before the next meeting. He said that she was definitely capable; she just needed to believe in herself.

At work the next day I kept my distance. I didn't want to pressure Marcie any more than I knew she was already pressuring herself. But I did watch. Marcie wasted no time. She polished her resume and called some agencies. She arranged a series of interviews. That night she got a whole new hairstyle. She pulled in her energy and focused on what she wanted. Basically, I saw Marcie create and collect personal power. Within just five days she had signed a contract, given notice at the bank, and accomplished her goal.

I couldn't let it go by. I had worked at the bank much longer than Marcie. I followed the steps, simple and plain. I faxed out my resume and made an internal decision that I was going to sign a contract before the next meeting. Nothing less would do. I went on one interview. The job was to test a very complex insurance system that was being developed with state-of-the-art graphical software. As the interview progressed, I realized that I actually did know a tremendous amount about testing, far more than I had thought back at the bank. Not only did they offer me the contract, but they were also happy to have found me.

227

The Passionate Heart

When the next meeting began, Rama asked if anyone had landed a contract. Marcie put her hand up. Rama congratulated Marcie. She had believed in herself as much as he believed in her. As always, everyone applauded to show their support. "Anyone else?" Rama asked. I raised my hand. Rama told me to stand up. Then he motioned for Marcie to stand up too.

Jittering from head to toe, I felt as if I was going to explode. Rama told the other students how proud he was of both of us. He explained, "This was not an easy thing for these two women to do. They are older than most of you. They had more conditioning to confront and overcome to make this break through. This shift was much more difficult for them than it was for you. They are troopers."

Chapter 36

The mark of a good teacher is a thorough understanding of the material and the ability to impart it to a specific student. The mark of a great teacher is that they provide a student with whatever is needed to accomplish a mutually agreed upon goal combined with exemplifying the result of that study. One of my favorite university professors taught a course in Eastern religions. Not only was he deeply fluent in the subject matter, but he had also spent many years studying in several monasteries in Japan and India. What more could a student ask? His class was genuinely unforgettable.

Rama is so much more than a teacher; he is the study itself. In addition to being a successful businessman, computer scientist, music producer, composer, author, martial artist and spiritual Teacher, he demonstrates through his example the impeccability that he seeks to teach his students.

In Rama's dedication to the professional success of his students, he presented a computer science program that far surpassed those offered by any college or university. A typical undergraduate degree program in computer science requires two years of general academic classes and the real course of study doesn't begin until junior year. Most of the upper level classes are in computer methodology and hardware architecture, often taught by people who have never worked in the industry. Before graduation from a four-year program, a student may learn one or two programming languages and possibly one actual database package. Clearly, this is not oriented towards actually working in the computer industry, at least not without many more years of study.

Rama created a fast-track computer science program that was intentionally designed to develop technical expertise and business knowledge directly applicable to career advancement. Courses were taught by women and men who had graduate degrees in mathematics, chemistry, engineering, and philosophy and had worked in the industry. Classes included C, Expert Systems, Artificial Intelligence, and Relational Databases: DB2, Informix, Oracle, Sybase, and Ingres. Ancillary courses were business accounting, legal concepts, negotiation issues, marketing, discrete mathematics, set theory, and calculus.

Students did not pick and choose which classes to take. Every woman and every man took them all. Obviously, if Rama had told us seven years ago that we would be taking classes in advanced math or artificial intelligence, none of us would have believed him. But even more astonishing was the fact that seven years ago our minds would not have been able to comprehend and hold all of that information. The last seven years of reading, lectures, gradual career improvements, and most of all, meditation had created the discipline and mental structures that made this monumental course of study possible. While most Americans were watching videos or partying on Friday and Saturday nights, we were in a lecture hall learning the most advanced computer science.

In the never-ending pursuit to teach us all about the world, Rama began holding formal blacktie dinners. This graduation was from navy blue suits to evening dresses and tuxedos, from theater seating to table conversation, and from coffee breaks to elegant cuisine.

Our first dinner was remarkable. The men were positively dashing. Most of them are accomplished martial artists so their posture and demeanor were pure polish. Bow ties, patent leather shoes and cufflinks never looked this good. The women were smashing. Black floor length and cocktail dresses, peau de soie, exquisite tiny beaded bags floated across the dining room. Neither Perry Mason nor Shana Alexander could have ever guessed that under all of the fashion, style, and savoir faire lived ordained Buddhist students. That is, until dinner was served...

Our Teacher never missed an opportunity for a bit of spontaneous and raucous fun. It is safe to assume that the majority of us had been vegetarians most of our lives. The soup and salad were identifiable and easy to maneuver. Then the food servers headed out of the kitchen with the main course. Suddenly, as if invaded by aliens, each of us was staring directly into the eyes of our very own full size lobster. Making the switch from broccoli to chicken is difficult enough, but at least the bird isn't glaring back at you. Reactions rippled throughout the room -- gasps to nervous giggles.

Rama graciously attended to every single table, every single person. He stopped and showed each circle of eight diners how to crack the shell and use the tiny fish fork. He was not just a host but the docent of the feast. He was the epitome of abundance. He wanted nothing but the best for us.

Once again, we were radically changing. We were sitting at formal dinner tables. We were enjoying some of the finest food in the world. We were developing a level of refinement that rivaled the royalty of Europe. You could dress us up. You could take us out. You could have never guessed that we were just silly Buddhists playing with the Wheel of Life.

At the end of dinner, Rama sat and talked for a couple of hours. He explained that we had been students for many incarnations. We do the same thing in every lifetime. We build structures as we live and work in the world as occultists. In the past we painted mandalas and transcribed sacred writings. Now it is programming computers. This is what we do. We incarnate forever. Our pain comes from not accepting who we are and what we do.

Rama said that this was a special time in our evolutionary process and we needed to focus on purity. It was time to access power from our past lives and begin to live as pure occultists. Although we walk in this world, our souls are somewhere else. He told us that to begin the new year with a renewed purity, we would fast from Christmas to New Years and start our morning meditation by chanting *Sring* five hundred times.

By this time, my career began expanding exponentially. My new job introduced me to the latest computer technologies: client / server architecture and graphical user interfaces. Because these concepts and development tools were so new, there were no traditional testing procedures. I had to invent my own. In addition, the project was not using the accepted development methods, so I was exposed to prototyping and rapid applications development procedures.

The Passionate Heart

I was participating in the data processing cultural revolution. The industry was evolving from huge mainframe, character-based systems to downsizing and graphical desktop computing. The changes were radical and often met with destructive opposition. I saw that there was a need for a methodology that made this transition smooth, easy, effective, and reliable. I wrote a workbook and offered a one-day course, "Graphical User Interface Project Management." It included everything from forming project teams, designing graphical screens and joint application development sessions to version control, testing methods and maintenance procedures.

Teaming up with two other students, we parlayed this single workbook and seminar into three books and over a dozen courses. We taught seminars in Boston, New York, and Washington DC. Through the encouragement of a friend, we contacted The Computer Channel and made three television shows; *CUA '91*, *GUI Project Management*, and *Screen Design and Human Factors*. In just these few jammed packed years we had learned so much that we were already on the cutting edge of computer technology.

Tracking the progress and accomplishments of two hundred and fifty students was no small task. It's size and complexity did not deter Rama. He kept up with us through our monthly reports. The headings were simple, which gave us the latitude to be as concise or explicit as we wished. They were: Meditation, Economics, Health, Special Projects, and Fun.

Meditation
Meditation has become integral to my life. I am positively unable to navigate a day without it. Regrettably, it was through the experience of skipping it that I realized meditation is no longer an option. On the days I did not meditate, my mind was cloudy, organizing my life was impossible and the most elementary task took twice as long.

Economics
I finished my first contract and found a new one. I was hired to manage forty-two people who are developing an insurance claims workstation. It pays $72.00 an hour. The project is

creating a multiple platform, integrated workstation with a graphical user interface.

Health

Fighting my natural proclivity towards laziness, I am taking a high impact aerobics class three times a week at a health club in lower Manhattan.

Special Projects

The workbooks and seminars are doing well. We presented the management class to one of the largest software development companies in the country and they are considering purchasing license rights.

Fun

Nothing is more fun than my little companions. Mary the amazing poodle and I went to a kennel in Massachusetts and got a new friend, Annapurna, the smallest Scottie in the world. She is brilliant and much too cute. Alice thinks that the three of us are very immature and wishes we would just grow up.

There was some discussion among the students as to whether or not Rama read all of the monthly reports. I had no idea if he did or not, but I definitely knew that he read some of mine. On a few occasions Rama made pointed comments to me that directly referenced something I had included in a monthly report. There would have been no other way for Rama to have known. With Rama, everything was a surprise. From dissecting lobster to fasting through the Christmas holidays, Rama was consistently unpredictable with one notable exception: he was always perfectly, impeccably in the present.

Marking four years in New York, there was a very special meeting. Instead of a formal dinner or an evening of Rama talking and meditating with us, we spent an entire seminar on one single question. Rama asked us to survey all of the years each of us had been a student and tell him what inspired us the most. It could be a desert trip. It could be a private moment with Rama. It could be something that happened at work or even on the subway. The circumstances didn't matter. The only thing that mattered was that it be the truth.

The Passionate Heart

The room immediately flooded with light because each of us was reaching for that single moment of greatest inspiration. Many raised their hands right away, instantly sure of their selection. Others fell into reflection, sorting through the myriad of possibilities. For each of us there was one perfect answer and it was important to find it. I just listened for quite a while.

The answers were very diverse. For some, it was their first big contract and making more money than they ever expected. It shifted their opinion of themselves so radically that they finally saw how the world had imposed the limitations they had been carrying around for years. Many talked about a personal conversation they had with Rama that changed them forever. Others relayed stories of how the applications of Rama's teachings in their everyday life had created whole new realities for them; work was not just work any more. Some talked about their experiences while developing the software packages. One woman said it was getting her black belt.

There were many who shared their perceptions of miracles in the desert or at meetings. They saw golden light pour out of Rama. They talked about the night Rama danced and what they saw. A woman relayed how she had seen images of Rama's past lives, superimposed on him while he was meditating in front of us. In the desert they had seen the moon travel across the sky or the stars shift and swirl in perfect geometric designs. They watched the world dissolve.

There were so many, how could I ever decide? I felt pressured. What if I regretted my choice later that night? What if I forgot something and missed this chance to tell Rama how much I appreciated him? Without knowing what I was going to say, my hand went up.

"When I walked in the door almost nine years ago, you were always talking about empowering women. I knew it was important to you. Then a few years ago, you seemed to stop talking about it. At first, it really bothered me and I wondered if you had lost interest. But tonight I looked around and saw that some of the most powerful women in the world are sitting here. Many of these women are in the first percentile of wage earners in the entire world. They are technical experts in their field. There was nothing more for you to talk about - you simply did it. The transformation of the lives of these women is the greatest miracle to me."

Finally, after many, if not most, had their say, one man raised his hand and asked what we all should have asked, "What inspires you, Rama?"

"A long time ago, when this adventure first began, we were all very poor. To keep expenses down, about ten of us rented a big house where we could live and hold meditation classes. We had no furniture and most of us didn't have cars. We spent every last penny on posters advertising our first Friday night meditation class. One man knew that our living room was bare and on Friday afternoon he sold his car and bought a couch. I will never forget what he did. He understood something. Selfless giving always inspires me."

Chapter 37

On November 18, 1991, I celebrated my ninth anniversary of being a student of Rama. In that time, I had attended 549 classes and meditated for 6,404 hours. While that might sound impressive to some people, it is merely a pittance compared to the hours and hours that women and men living in monasteries or ashrams spend in meditation. My daily average is under 2 hours and many monks around the world sit for five or six hours a day.

Disregarding our unabashed lack of qualifications, in November, 1991 Rama announced that we were going to be tested for certification as Buddhist monks. The test was "open book," and we would have one month to complete it. If the work was accepted, we would be officially ordained as monks in the Rae Chorze-fwaz Society of Tantric Buddhist Enlightenment on January 1, 1992. The test included seven questions. The recommended length of the answers was ten to twenty pages in all.

There was a certain magic in writing for Rama. We would get essay assignments from time to time. After working on a few of them, it dawned on me that they were hardly about the pages that came out of the printer. It really meant that we would spend the allotted time contemplating the topics. When the essays were finished, we had changed. Sometimes, when we had totally forgotten what we were doing and why we were doing it, Rama would ask us to write a paper about our first desert trip or a special memorable experience. Holding my attention on the subject all month and thumbing through the pages of my mind it would inevitably rekindle my wonder and innocence.

The next thirty days of my life were focused on one thing; I was going to be a monk. The answers to these seven questions had to be perfect. They had to reflect all of my aspiration, all of the wonderful things Rama had taught me, all of my hope for an order of women in equal proportion to men. Rama was going to break the chain, break tradition, break new ground, and hand the baton to women. We turned in our papers at the December meetings and prepared for the New Year.

The event was blacktie. Dinner was a buffet. It was held at a beautiful private restaurant in Westchester, New York. The decorations were spectacular. A student who had visited Nepal recently and brought back hundreds of Tibetan Prayer Flags. They were strung throughout the room and on each table. There were shiny metallic balloons, holiday flower arrangements, and magnificent Thangkas. Everyone and everything was elegant.

Rama arrived wearing a tuxedo and the most amazing blue velvet vest. Following him into the dining room were two students carrying pet crates. Rama had a surprise. He was going to raffle off two puppies. He opened one of the crates and took out a three month old terrier. As he talked about the night and the ceremony, he held the adorable puppy in his arms. The longer he talked, the more the dog relaxed, until finally she was lying on her back, paws drooping in every direction, obviously in utter bliss. "This is how I am holding each of you, all the time," he said. "I love you."

I was sitting at a table close to the front on the left side of the dais. Rama explained that he would call a few names at once, we would come forward in the order called, and after a moment in meditation with him, he would hand us our certificate of ordination. As usual, first names would be called in alphabetical order. Thus, I would be last.

Four names were called. A woman was first. Rama put his right hand on her head and his thumb on her forehead. He closed his eyes for a short time. Then he began to talk about her past lives. He mentioned three or four of them. It was fascinating. This was a woman I had known for years and, although I was sure that all of us had countless past lives, I had never really put them in a personal context before. In a few minutes, she was no longer an American Buddhist student; she was an ordained Buddhist monk who traveled lifetimes to get to this particular moment. She had been in other countries, other centuries. As surely as I looked upon her differently now, I could only imagine how differently she must have viewed herself.

Man after man, woman after woman, student after student, rose from their chair to learn about their journey, their past, their previous associations, and return to their seat a monk. They were no longer lay people, hoping one day to be accepted into the order. This was the day of days. So many times I had seen Buddhist monks in New York: in front of the UN, wandering the Japanese garden at the Metropolitan Museum of Art, or creating mandalas at the Museum of Natural History. I saw their robes, their smiling faces, and their camaraderie. I had felt a longing to be admitted to my order. This was my wish come true.

Rama spent two or three minutes with each person. I sat for hours, positively mesmerized with wonder about the past life stories. I couldn't wait to hear about my own. I had many fantasies about my past lives. Tonight, I hear about a few of them. I wanted him to tell me that I would be a teacher. I wanted him to tell me that I had known Gandhi. I wanted him to tell me something that would confirm my fantasies.

Well into the morning hours, I heard my name. I stood and walked to the center of the room, awaiting my turn. A man named Zen moved aside. I was next. I stepped forward. Rama placed his hand on my head and his thumb on my third eye. He closed his eyes. "She is French. She is *very* French." With that, Rama opened his eyes, looked around the room and said, "In every lifetime, she has been an artist." He lifted his hand off my head and held out my certificate. I bowed slightly and said thank you.

The night was over. I went home to Mary, Anna, and Alice. I was a Buddhist monk. Thirty-eight years ago, in my parents' basement, I had promised God that I would join a convent. Although this was quite different from the simple vision of that five-year-old Catholic girl, it was my deepest dream come true. I had kept my promise. Maybe my promise had kept me - kept me safe, kept me on the path, kept my eyes on the heavens.

Along the way, there were so many distractions, so many opportunities for cynicism, indifference, or hopelessness. Many times I was sure I would have to let my intense longing for God fade just a bit, as if it was going to consume me. What if I had been accepted in the convent at eighteen? What if my marriage had been tolerable? What if my search through the religions of the world had provided plenty of room for feminism? What if my failed political activities had embittered me forever? After offering my life in exchange for an elementary and obvious piece of legislation, where does one go? What if I hadn't gotten over that my Teacher is a man? On this night, all of these moments had led me home. I loved them all.

I was not the least bit surprised to hear that I had been French. My mother's parents were from Paris and I had always felt some type of connection with France. Although my family vacation to Europe at fifteen had been a total disaster, there was one notable exception: the trip to Lourdes.

In my mother's usual crass fashion, she booked a trip to visit twenty-one countries in just as many days - all on one big red American Express bus filled with Americans. I spent most of the twenty-one days smoking Marlboro cigarettes, endlessly cussing, and dedicating myself fully to my mother's abject disgust. We went from cathedral to church in a strange empty pilgrimage to validate mother's Catholicism. Forget the art. Forget the history. It was a scavenger hunt for postcards and Papal paraphernalia. The high point, illustrating mother's comprehension of where we were, was when she actually lit a cigarette in the Sistine Chapel and was dismayed when the guard had a stroke.

In the midst of my adolescent outrage, I found myself inexplicably moved when we took a four day side trip to Lourdes. We left the big red bus, took a train to Southern France, and visited the place where Bernadette had seen the Virgin Mary. Whenever in my mother's presence, I was obstinate and escalated disrespect to an art form.

But when I was alone, watching the people stream back and forth from the shrine, I was speechless. In the morning, those who could walk stopped at one of the three hospitals and helped the miracle-seekers reach the grotto. There were hundreds of women and men in wheelchairs and on cots, asking God for a favor. At night, every night, there was a candle-lit procession as visitors said the rosary. All around the actual shrine, where Mary is said to have appeared to Bernadette, hung discarded crutches and canes. Surrounded by all of this and to my unprecedented shock; my disdain, my foul mouth, and my Marlboro cigarettes seemed vulgar.

I had always wanted to go back to Paris to find out what I had been so drawn to. Since I had not even looked at a painting until my twenties, I knew that I had missed almost everything Europe had to offer. Now that Rama said that I had been an artist and French, I wanted to go even more. I had no recollection of being an artist. In the current incarnation, I bought the box of 96 crayons only to compete with the others in my class. I never really used them. When there were art projects, I was quickly passed over as I could never draw a Spring Elm tree with even a single raw umber trunk supporting emerald green clouds. My entire artistic repertoire was cutting paper snowflakes and the limited use of stencils.

A friend and I booked a flight to Paris. We stayed in a very cheap hotel on the Left Bank. Neither of us was any good at being tourists. We spent much of the first few days trying to find electric outlet converters so we could use our laptop computers. We were not accustomed to so much free time. For me, wandering the streets, looking at all of the people, and all of the stuff in the shop windows became boring almost instantly.

On the third night, I had a vivid, terrifying, and unforgettable nightmare. I dreamt that I had been raped by two men. It was in Paris, at the turn of the Century. I was a young and attractive girl. It happened on the street just outside the hotel where I was actually staying. Every detail was real: the scenery, the feeling, the screams. As if in a movie, there was a sudden switch to a courtroom. I was standing in the witness box telling the judge and jury what had happened. The defense attorney asked me if I could identify the men who raped me. I said, yes, most definitely. With that, the double doors opened and two uniformed policemen entered the courtroom. It had been these two men. It had been these two respected policemen. Within a matter of minutes the men were cross-examined and declared innocent. I woke up crying and unable to catch my breath. I fell to the floor and sobbed as if it had all just happened that very night. My friend tried to console me. It took an hour or so for me to calm down and explain what had happened. We left the hotel that morning.

Finally, the moment I had been waiting for arrived; the Louvre. I wanted to see absolutely everything. I wanted to see Raphael, DaVinci, Michelangelo, Durer, van Eyck, de la Tour, Caravaggio, Vermeer. I paged through my guidebook, following the signs from room to room. Walking through the second floor corridor, I was overcome with a pain so deep, so wide, so ancient; I wanted to die. It was an awareness that flooded through my soul and spilled over the entire earth.

All my work, all my beautiful work was gone. All the lifetimes of painting were gone. Every woman's work was gone. There was no building for the women's paintings from the Renaissance. There was no docent pointing to the work by women from the Fifteenth or Sixteenth Century. Where were the paintings that filled the hearts of women over the last thousand years? Did they even get on a canvas? Could the women buy oils and gesso? Where was the art that women bore, that longed to be seen, that told their story? It was gone.

Maybe there is one crystalline moment in the life of a heart when everything comes roaring together. This was such a moment. This was why I cared so deeply about the liberation of women. This was why I had been driven to speak of a pain that was not conceivably mine. This was why I simply devoured the arts when I finally discovered them. This was why I loved so many artists and their work. It didn't matter if it was poetry, literature, sculpture, or painting; once I felt it, I loved it. For twenty-three years I had loved the *School of Athens, Repentant Magdalene*, the *Last Supper, Melancholia*; but where was the work by women? It was gone.

Chapter 38

"Remember tonight for the rest of your life. Everything you have ever done has brought you to this moment." Rama told us what I had waited ten years to hear. We were going to become teachers. We were going to teach beginning meditation. We were going to become representatives of Enlightenment.

It was optional, but each and every one of us could apply to become teachers of basic meditation. We could start giving back what we had been receiving over the years. There would be a qualification process of writing a thesis on Buddhism and making a video of a sample class.

Rama began teaching over twenty years ago. He taught meditation classes across the United States and Europe: in public libraries, school classrooms, churches, all the way to Rockefeller Center. He began with taping posters in store windows and then one day bought a full-page ad in the New York Times. Rama had taught hundreds of thousands of people all over the world to meditate.

Rama recommended that we start the way he did. He rented rooms near college and university campuses. He made beautiful but inexpensive posters and posted them himself. He handed out flyers during lunch time while lots of students were milling around the union and cafeteria. His research revealed that students were more likely to attend classes on Mondays or Tuesdays and the best time was early evening. Everything was designed to accommodate the students' schedules. Even though Rama was a struggling university student, he paid for the printing, rental spaces, and advertising himself. Classes were always free.

I have probably heard Rama teach beginning meditation over a hundred times. Although we might have felt buried in the world of computers, software, and databases, Rama never let us forget that meditation is the primary component in Buddhism. Even though one doesn't have to meditate after reaching Enlightenment, Rama loved it so much he had never stopped. At the center of it all - the career development, the software, or the miracles - Rama radiated pure respect for the art of meditation. It is the pillar of our practice.

For centuries, people have tried to slow down their thoughts. Every type of spiritual seeker and artist uses some form of focused concentration. Catholics say the rosary. Christians sing hymns. Jews recite the scriptures. Hindus chant. Composers and painters long for that sacred moment when they slip away and the infinite takes over. Even repetitive activities like knitting or sanding have a certain meditative quality. It is as if we all know, deep down, that eternity is on the other side of thought.

Rama taught us many forms of meditation. Ten years ago we sat mid-day in silence for a half hour. For several years we concentrated on a yantra for an hour every day. Occasionally we chanted or said japa. One year we sat for an hour in the morning and an hour at night. While we were experiencing a variety of meditative practices, our Teacher was on a mission.

Rama was looking for the best meditation method for modern Americans. We were hardly sitting on a mountain top, in a desert, or on a quiet shore. We certainly did not live in a remote village where everyone supported a secluded garden and temple. We lived in big cities where aggression and violence were inescapable. We had apartments and condos surrounded by families and lots of diverse people. We were trying to meditate in the center of society, immersed in the densest human aura the earth has ever known.

Rama explained that in previous eras, meditation was a lot easier. There were fewer people and fewer thoughts. Today, the earth is glutted with people and barraged with thoughts; thus, meditation is much more difficult. Being psychic is not a carnival game or just a skill marketed on the 900 lines. It is one of the senses, like taste or sight. In this age, being psychic can be a problem, a serious problem.

Since all of us are psychic, over ninety percent of the thoughts we have are not our own. Ninety percent of the feelings we have are not our own. On a walk in the woods, a trip to the shore, or a retreat in the mountains, one hardly thinks. But, working and living in the city we are inundated with an ocean of thoughts, thoughts that belong to everyone else. Meditation was easy when people only had to stop their own thoughts, but now it is nearly impossible.

Rama wanted to find a way for us to meditate in the middle of Twentieth Century cosmopolitan life - in the middle of the anger and violence in the middle of our own minds.

Rama didn't stop searching until he found a solution. Rama composed music specifically for meditation. Instead of concentrating on a flower or a yantra, we sat and listened to every note, every feeling in the music. Instead of leaving the city to sit in a power spot, we could leave through focusing on the music. Listening to it creates an auric shield that blocks out the thoughts and impressions of the world.

Spiritual seekers have always known it was easier to meditate in the presence of an Enlightened Teacher. It is easier to feel the planes of light, feel what it is like to be outside of thought, feel the higher planes of consciousness. Since this music comes from Rama's mind and from the worlds he accesses in meditation, listeners are actually lifted to higher planes, as if they were sitting and meditating with him.

Rama developed several albums. Among them is one for morning and another for evening. Each of them reflects a different world, a different dimension. Even Rama said he couldn't explain how it is done. He composed the music, his band recorded it, and, after dozens of mixes, Rama would meditate to remove any traces of human impressions.

Somehow (I didn't care *how*), Rama traveled to the planes of light and brought back perfect, pure music. After meditating to it for several months, the difference was significant. I could sit longer without fidgeting or inventing an excuse to get up. My incessant internal arguing stopped. With the music, I could always find something lovely, majestic, and wonderful. I simply moved my focus back to the songs, like a compass point floating back to North. It was gentle and graceful. Most importantly, I could feel Rama's energy field. It wasn't as powerful as actually sitting in the same room with him, but it was much different from sitting in silence. If I really tried to stop my thoughts and listened to the music, I could feel Rama.

The best way to learn to meditate is to sit with someone who meditates perfectly and that certainly wasn't any of us. But now, with our Teacher's music, we would be able to teach basic techniques and know that our classes would carry the energy and light of eternity.

To make sure we did know the basics, Rama asked us to write a thesis on Buddhism. The topics were: Meditation, Buddhism, Power, Wisdom, Enlightenment, Personal Happiness, Reincarnation, Career Success and Miracles. Fortunately, I had a lot of experience with long papers. I spent about a month on it.

The video was another issue. Although I had been teaching and speaking publicly for years, I hate hearing my voice on the phone machine and I never watched myself on film or TV. I focused on the information and decided to worry about the shooting later. I made a series of queue cards for the topics and spent a couple of weeks filling in the spaces. I made the video in one shooting, glad that it was over.

In Spring 1992, Rama certified his students to teach beginners' meditation. We were responsible for our own posters, advertising, and room rentals. We had Zazen music to play and freely distribute. We could speak on special topics, such as astrology, computer science, or general meditation. We would be able to bring our guests to hear Rama speak and meditate with him.

I was ecstatic. It was the most exciting thing that ever happened to me. In the first month, I spoke at three women's colleges in New York. I started designing posters with the name *Women & Light*. Although there clearly was a focus on women, anyone and everyone was welcome with one notable exception. The classes were open only to people under twenty-nine.

It made perfect sense to me. I guess sometimes, when you understand the logic and wisdom of something, it is easy to forget that others might find offense. I was really taken off guard when I got the first of many phone calls from irate people accusing me of ageism. My self-righteous indignation was instantly ignited and my inability to eloquently explain it inside a phone call brought my ego back down to earth.

Astrologers would immediately recognize and admire the intelligence of teaching people under twenty-nine. They would know that there was a compassion in it, a kindness to it, and most of all, a wise person had made such a determination. Because astrology is not respected and universally accepted, people presumed it was discrimination. Admittedly, I was embarrassed to be judged as an ageist. I struggled to explain something I had studied for years.

Saturn, the Great Lord of Karma, travels around the earth in a cycle of twenty-eight to twenty-nine years. At the time of one's birth, Saturn is sitting in a certain place in the sky, designing a template for one's evolution. At the very moment of a baby's first breath, there is a contract drawn up, an agreement is struck between the person's soul and Saturn. All the lessons of life are perfectly lined up. All the things that this particular soul needs to touch and experience are put in perfect order. Everything is awaiting the native's journey to guarantee as much humility, patience, and responsibility as this soul can handle: no more, no less.

Then the pilgrimage begins. The new soul ventures forward and Saturn transits through the Zodiac. With each step and each degree in the circle, the two continue accumulating experiences and solidifying the native's character. Saturn's goal is perfection. It brings tests, imposes limitations, and creates definitions. If the native tries to avoid responsibility, Saturn will make the decision for them. Saturn destroys the old and familiar to make room for the new and more useful. Some images of Saturn are Father Time, the reaper, and Lord Shiva, the Hindu God of destruction.

Generally, Saturn is known to be the architect of character and maturity. But there is a window of time, a sliver of time in which the person sheds all of the definitions they picked up along the way. Just before Saturn comes back to the exact placement of one's birth, the soul passes by a doorway. It is a chance to discard the thoughts, expectations, definitions, and conditioning of the world while reaching for a higher plane.

When the circle is complete, the person has made their choice and the cycle begins all over again.

I had read about this special time in a person's life in a book, *Cosmic Consciousness*, by Dr. Richard Maurice Bucke. This Canadian doctor became interested in the Enlightenment process and researched the lives of several hundred people whom he felt had made great leaps in the evolutionary process. One noticeable similarity was that they reached the greatest awareness in their twenty-ninth year. He wrote about the lives of Siddartha, Jesus, Thoreau, Bacon, Socrates, the Brontes, and at least thirty more. Although Dr. Bucke did not make the astrological connection, it seemed obvious to me.

As with most things in life, it was all conjecture until personal experience beats us over the head. I had read about Saturn returns for six years before I had my own and still, at the time, I had no idea what was going on. When I was twenty-eight I began feeling as if I was in a tunnel crushing in on all sides. Actually, it felt more like a tube of toothpaste and I was the paste. The world was closing in on me and I was having trouble maintaining my space, my sense of self, my identity.

I was living with a brilliant woman at the time. She was a pianist and painter. She walked into the bookstore one day, spent the night, and stayed for seven years. She was moody, intense, beautiful, and I loved her. When I started feeling as if the world was going to squeeze me to death, she went to the store and bought me a very special present. It was a box filled with thousands of tiny pieces of wood, a quart of glue, and blueprints in Japanese.

I spent the next four months building a fantastic Victorian doll house. It was a perfect replica: one inch to one foot. It had two stories, a staircase, a fine porch, and a shingled roof. I installed parallel wiring and working light fixtures. I papered the walls and put wainscoting in the hall. I made the furniture, the decorations, and even the food inside the refrigerator. In the splendid vision of retrospect, I realized that while I was building this intricate house, I was building myself.

Once Saturn completes its conjunction, it is more difficult to discard conditioning and imposed definitions. Something inside is crystallized, like Jell-O hardening, and people have made their decision about defining the next twenty-eight year cycle. Teaching people before their Saturn return was easier. They hadn't made their final decision about whom they will be "when they grow up." It is easier to make internal changes. It is easier to practice Self-Discovery.

I have read many charts and watched people deal with their Saturn return with varying degrees of composure. There is no question that the students who began meditating and studying with Rama before their Saturn return found the whirlwind of changes much easier, much more comfortable. Besides the fluidity of the native during the months of their Saturn return, it is also an important time in the Teacher-student relationship. When the window of change opens, the Teacher can provide a boost, a nudge, or even a big kick towards self-realization. Like the lead snow goose creating an easier flight for those who follow, the Teacher clears the way. Like a great gust of wind, the Teacher can increase a soul's velocity.

Chapter 39

To promote my classes, I put together a brochure about the fast, the questions it raised, and the answers I had found.

Women & Liberation
A 10 Year Perspective

I have sent this brochure to introduce myself to you. I have learned much in the last nine years and would like to share some of it. Maybe you are asking, why now? Because it is time.

The Wall Street Journal recently printed articles about women in the workplace as if the Women's Movement just happened yesterday. Anita Hill has been humiliated in front of the nation. Helen Gurley Brown finally exposed her IQ. Women have never been in more serious trouble. It is time.

A close friend of mine, who teaches women's history, told me recently that her students have never heard of the ERA. They think the Women's Movement is a failed social event in the 70's that had no effect on their lives. They have no idea about potential losses that await them with the new Supreme Court. It is time.

At 25, I thought it was going to be a slow but steady string of gains for women. At 34, I risked it all, because I truly believed in what I was doing and moreover, that we could not fail. At 43, it is the glass ceiling, the silent conspiracy, the flagrant oppressors sitting in national government and a new wave of young women who have no sense of continuity in their history. It is time.

Now men don't have to do much; they have convinced women to oppress themselves. They have taught women to accept the images presented in media and advertising, forget the past, and limit their dreams for the future. It is time.

There is a way out of this oppression. It happens in the mind and heart first. It happens within the spirit, where no one can stop true liberation. If the mind and spirit are free, then media, marketing, and courts don't have a chance. It is time.

The Passionate Heart

> My presentation includes over 70 slides from my summer vacation in Illinois during 1982 and readings from my own diary recounting those 42 days. I hope that you will consider inviting me to speak to your group.

The brochure included pictures and quotations from 1982 and 1992. I was glad to be using something from that strange summer which seemed to simply evaporate. As I was picking it up from the local quick print shop, the young woman who was waiting on me asked if she could have a minute of my time. We stepped away from the counter and the other customers. She said she rarely reads the papers as they fly through the copier, but she had read my brochure and hoped I didn't mind. "Certainly not," I assured her. She wanted to talk, so we made dinner plans.

Over Caesar salads, my new friend, Elizabeth told me that she was an incest survivor and a member of a family who includes and loves an alcoholic. Why do we live in a world where such news is not a shock? I put down my fork and my eyes. Maybe chances were that having dinner with any woman twenty-three years old would lead to a similar revelation. But how do we honor the tragedy, the unthinkable reality, and go forward in hope, knowing that most of us carry such news in our hearts? Does the fact that it is *common* place make it any more tolerable? If we turn our pain to forgiveness and our scars to fading memories, are we valiant, just trying to cope, or erasing the truth?

Although I hardly knew her, I wanted to tell her that I am her witness, her family, her sister, her confidant. I wanted to say that I shared her pain, but that phrase bears a hidden insult that somehow her pain would be less. After participating in countless women's groups, meetings, seminars, conventions, round tables, I have come to the conclusion that all one can really do, at this point, it not turn away in shame. There is bravery in listening and not crumbling. There is courage in not hoping it will just disappear. The strength is in being present.

We sat for hours, until they were closing and threw us out. We were both raised Catholic. We talked about twelve step programs. We talked about being women. We talked about everything and anything. By the time coffee arrived, I knew why Elizabeth had read my brochure. She was looking for liberation and I could take her to see Rama the very next week.

For ten years I had sat in the hall with familiar faces. I knew exactly what it felt like. I would walk in, take a seat, open a book, seldom look around, and wait for Rama to arrive. Although we were quite different from one another, there were similarities, at least on the outside. We wore expensive suits, carried briefcases, looked like professionals. At first, I might have gotten heady about my tailored and polished professional appearance. But now it was more like being impersonal or invisible. Seville, Chanel, Armani, Claiborne, Bernard, Brooks Brothers might have made our ochre robes, but the effect was the same: it erased personal importance.

Saturday night, as I sat next to Elizabeth, everything was different. While I had on my sturdy navy suit, she had on a white blouse and black trousers. They were perfectly pressed and obviously chosen with great care. She whispered questions and I whispered answers. The music, the stage, the registration table, the briefcases, the tickets; everything was brand new. I was seeing everything for the first time -- through Elizabeth's eyes. Rama accepted questions from the guests. They were innocent, excited, interested, and curious. They were us ten years ago and we were them, remembering our first night.

One day, while parking the car in front of my apartment, I noticed a young man with a map in his hand. He was confused. The street he was looking for was on the other side of town. I offered my phone and invited him in. Upon entering my tiny house and surveying the living room, he appeared quite surprised. "Are you a Buddhist?" he asked. "Yes, I am," I replied. He proceeded to tell me that he was a graduate student in Buddhist studies. We talked about my posters and statues. We ran through a list of authors and books. We couldn't get over the *coincidence*. Obviously, he too, was looking for liberation.

The Passionate Heart

My band of apprentices was growing. I was teaching classes on Tuesday, Wednesday, and Thursday evenings at two universities and a Unitarian church on Saturday mornings. I ran ads in local papers for classes on Beginning Meditation, Women's Special Issues, and Astrology. Within three months, there was a strong group of nine women and men who became my apprentices. Being a Virgo, a school teacher, and natural mother hen, I was in love with them all.

Once a month, we all saw Rama. I was very proud of them. They had a million questions. They wanted to know absolutely everything. Meditation was changing their lives right before my eyes. They loved the practice of Self-Discovery. They loved Rama. With every meeting, more and more women and men were discovering that, "Samadhi is loose in America."

Twice a week we met at my house to meditate and talk for several hours. As they were on a great new adventure in meditation, martial arts, and computer science, I was having my own realizations. First I noticed that, as I answered a question, I could no longer waffle on the issue myself. They would ask about impeccability and as the answer came rolling out of my mouth, I was refining my commitment. I could no longer back out of my own changes as I was extolling the vicissitudes of change. If I was going to tell them about the importance of an immaculate house, I had to do it first. My house had never been so clean.

Secondly, and more importantly, I had to deeply examine what was my proper role with these aspiring students. What could I really offer them? I knew ours was a fleeting relationship. One day they would be direct students of our Teacher and I would drift away. I was their tour guide - someone to provide an orientation. I concluded that the greatest service I could contribute was to teach them about etiquette. If I could teach them proper etiquette, they could avoid many of the mistakes I had made. Of course, I would have to learn it first.

We made a mutual agreement: 1) I would correct them, it would be instantly forgotten, and we would move on, 2) when I was wrong, I would openly admit it as fast as possible, and 3) we would treat each other as we would treat Rama, but never take it personally -- knowing that we were using each other as practice.

▣ The wonder of etiquette is that it is infinitely complex and beautifully simple. I once heard about a professor at Long Beach State University who said that all genuine truths boil down to an irreconcilable paradox. Etiquette is one such truth. As the layers of etiquette are peeled back, there is always another of deeper subtlety and grace. Without question, the greatest resource of my study on etiquette was watching Rama.

Everything Rama does is an expression of etiquette. Because of his state of attention, because he comes from the World of Enlightenment, he is the epitome of etiquette. The magic of it is that the depth of the revelation is in direct ratio to one's ability to perceive it. It is like a great book or movie that never ends. It becomes more intricate and meaningful as one's comprehension expands. The best way to *read* this book of etiquette is to watch and note everything Rama does: music, tickets, posters, tapes, videos, clothes, food. They all reflect pure, perfected etiquette.

▣ The political masters of etiquette are the Japanese. I told all of my apprentices to read *Shogun*. I love that book. It explains some of the basic principles of etiquette in a social hierarchy. The Shogun knows everything about his society, but comports himself in such a way as to grant face to everyone who is loyal. (Not to overlook the fact that the lead Samurai is a woman)

Manners are the rudimentary rules of etiquette. It is a system of increasing and diminishing favors. The more you give, the more you receive. The less you give, the less you receive. It may sound familiar, but there is a fundamental difference in how Westerners and Easterners begin this cycle. Here in the West we perform an action and then await the reward. In the East it is just the opposite. The reward is given first. A Japanese houseguest offers a present upon arrival, not after the departure. They make it known up front that this will be a lovely visit, rather than sending a gift later to indicate how lovely the visit had been.

The Passionate Heart

In a relationship the same principle applies. Instead of holding out and waiting to see if the other person is "worthy" of respect, respect is immediately given. If it is not met appropriately, then it is gradually withdrawn. The diminishment continues until the behavior is corrected or it is removed completely as the other person proves not worthy. It is assumed from the start that everyone is worthy of respect. The intent is that no one stands in judgment, holding back their best behavior. Both parties meet and from the start each is respected and respectful.

There is a beauty and grace in this method of exchange. Immediately awarding the other person "face" places them in the right. If you are incorrect, it can be withdrawn. If you are right, it is in place from the start. But better yet, if the other person reaches and ascends to a new level of worthiness, you have contributed to their growth. The consideration is to always place the other person in the right. How can I participate in this situation so that they will be right, be first, be respected? It calls for taking a position of selflessness.

Why? Why bother? That is the question. A Buddhist practices etiquette because it is graceful and selfless. In every transaction, each party is elegant and in the right. In fact, an even higher understanding is that the receiver's perception is incidental. If I step aside, as you thoughtlessly stumble through the door, my awareness has saved us both. Eventually it becomes completely irrelevant if it is perceived or received at all. It is done because it is a gentle, mindful, and elegant way to live.

Rama would never lower his level of etiquette because we were too thick headed to comprehend it. One time he told us that his impeccability was so refined that no one on earth could ever perceive it. He does it for God. It shows a respect for life itself, for the Holy Dharma, for Eternity.

Another aspect of etiquette is holding in one's energy. In the over-populated world, as people are spewing their energy in every conceivable direction, it is a simple courtesy to keep one's energy in check. Rama calls this "not pushing it out." If you are in a room with a dozen people and one is getting all the attention, they are pushing it out. Obviously, it is a waste of energy that might be well used in a better way and they certainly aren't considering that all of that attention might not be so desirable.

In addition, pushing it out is a form of egotism. Holding one's energy in allows a sensitivity. It is easier to feel danger, dishonesty, or beauty if one is in check. Watching a sunset is a much better movie if one isn't trying to impress the sun. I heard a story once that God is like a little mouse waiting in the corner. If you are very quiet, the mouse will come out and walk freely throughout the room. But if you make a lot of noise thrashing about, the mouse will stay hidden from sight.

As I was learning about this amazing system of etiquette, I tripped over the easiest rule of thumb. I realized I always knew what to do if I imagined that Rama was with me. If I pretended that the Light of Eternity was all around me, my natural instinct was to be graceful. If I shut my eyes and focused on the feeling of meditating with Rama, I could find my better self. When I had acted like a jerk, been totally self-obsessed, or made someone else look like a fool, I had been wandering around in my mind, all by myself.

After working my way through this process, I began to understand what the Buddhist teachings mean by saying that a teacher "loans" their attention field to their students. Years ago Rama said that he would show us different levels of attention and we would be able to reference them in the future. They would be recorded in our attention forever. Anywhere, anytime, I could pause for a moment, remember what it felt like meditating with him, and move my mind to that point. It was like holding paint chips against a clear and sunny summer sky.

Chapter 40

In April 1992, I went to the National Women's Freedom of Choice March in Washington DC. It had been almost ten years to the day that I went to the national ERA march. Strolling among the half million women and men, my mind traveled many lands. While working in the Women's Movement, I knew people in five or six states. So I searched under their state banners for a familiar face. Although I felt much different than I had in 1982, the people seemed to look the same. Some were hopeful. Some were determined. Some had just discovered activism and were inspired. Some were having a fine Sunday afternoon out. I felt sheltered under the friendly green and white of NOW.

As thousands of faces streamed past me, I could hear the speeches in the distance. Suddenly it occurred to me that most of the women I had known years ago were now on the stage. I mused that, had I continued in the Women's Movement, maybe I would have been one of those speakers. I could have been influential and well known. I asked myself: what had I done in the last ten years? I zigzagged to the edge of the stage and listened carefully.

Just as fast as I had slipped into the last state of attention, I flipped into the next. Within twenty minutes, I realized that none of the speeches had changed. It could have been the 1980 Mother's Day March, any Freedom of Choice march, any Women's Rights march in any city, at any time. The words, the ideas, the phrases, the anger, the determination, the hope: nothing had changed. "We will win, because we must." "We will seize our rights if we have to." "We will remove our opponents from office." There was a litany of Senators and Congress people who were put on notice for re-election. Many were the same names I had heard ten years ago.

There was so much I wanted to tell everyone. I wanted to jump on the stage and grab the microphone. I wanted to shout and weep and warn them. I wanted to crack open my mind and heart, like a big ostrich egg, to spill out my love, my pain, my vision. "You can't stop it that way!" "We are caught in a global web of lies." "They will only allow us enough latitude within the system to placate us. And if we go too far we will be harnessed again." "I know a way out. Please listen, I know a way out." I wanted to show them the mechanics of oppression and liberation, but how would I ever find words to describe something that was visceral and intuitive?

The traditions, conditioning, ideologies, and thoughts of the earth cover us with a great blanket of intricate and resolute knots. We sustain this network with our beliefs, our definitions, and our language. We inherit it without question just as we accept one Sun and one Moon in the sky. It is all we know and regardless of the consequences or pain we have agreed to hold this firmament in place like a giant chupa.

There is nothing on earth that is not woven into this network. It is in our religions, in our cultures, in our governments, in our schools. It is in our language. No matter how we try to weave, unweave and re-weave again, we are always working with the same material that is available to us. If the lie unravels a bit, we become uncomfortable standing in the debris and scurry to braid it back together again.

Theorists lace and unlace with research and intelligence. They say it is rooted in racism or classism. It is about ageism or lookism. It is about gender roles and homophobia. It is about the definition of family. It is about economic imbalance. They posit that women must have reproductive rights, equal wages, and equal opportunity.

Psychologists knit and purl about archetypes and childhood conditioning. They work tirelessly to assist survivors of incest, rape, abandonment, and battering. Educators pour over history and sociology books trying to eliminate the "isms." Legislators reorder the laws protecting women and their property rights. Lawyers take it to the courts. Activists take it to the streets.

Academics argue that we must change the language. And so we rewrite the dictionary and the bible. We rearrange the words and debate the rules of spelling. Be it history or herstory, womyn or women, we reticulate the knots, like shifting tiles on a scrabble board.

The Passionate Heart

In anger we point to suttee, infibulation, foot binding, pornography, the Feminine Mystique, and the Beauty Myth, as if dissecting the knots will reduce the pain. In hope we report that more women are going to college and entering the male-dominated professions, not recognizing (or unable to tolerate) these puny conciliations for what they really are. We rejoice over women in the Supreme Court and the redefinition of sexual harassment while we bow our heads over Clarence Thomas and Senator Packwood jokes.

Within our ranks, we splinter and organize. We divide over words such as "feminist" and "radical." We debate about fighting in the streets, in the courts, in the Congress, or at the grassroots level. We analyze solutions such as women's credit cards and women in the ministries. We are patronized with glamorous magazines for every woman, from under eighteen to over forty. We have replaced the *Ladies'* section of the Sunday paper with the *Women's* section, but it is still paid for by furriers, cosmetic companies, and grocery chains. Finally, we deliberate on whether or not men can be feminists, as if it were voluntary service.

I wondered if in ten more years I could return to the Ellipse and hear the same speeches. In 2003, will Ms. Magazine have a cover story on how feminists don't think alike? Will women make 52¢, 62¢, or 59¢ on the dollar? Will abortions be regulated by legislation and will we still be arguing if life begins in one trimester or another? If I am promised full coverage for mammograms will I be lulled to not care about the women in Bosnia or the latest publicized site of torture?

Secretly, I worry that we will become exhausted from watching, trying, fighting, or caring, and we will have to spend our last gasp of energy on ourselves. What is America going to do with so many women over sixty? Our life expectancy has never been greater or our numbers higher. And so, new knots are invented. The pharmaceutical companies have planned our menopause. The cosmetic companies have declared war on our wrinkles. The plastic surgeons promise us endless youth. But what of our income and our social security?

We have become experts in macramé. Some of us have learned to untie a half-hitch and replace it with a bowson. Some of us have rearranged the knots to access more oxygen and sunlight. Many of us have no idea that the knots can be rearranged at all. A few of us insist there are no knots and we only need a fair chance. Just as many believe that the knots are a good idea and stand firm, guarding their safety. But the reality is -- no matter our expertise, the depth of understanding, the ability to tie a surgeon's knot, or untie a figure-eight -- we remain inside, underneath, drowning in, and suffocated by this mantle of intertwined deceit.

If we are to ever discover who we really are, we must begin to reach beyond this interwoven canopy of beliefs, traditions, ideologies, and conditioning. We must face the lie. We must admit the enormity of the deception. We must move outside the web of duplicity. To remain inside is to continue in our pain, our grief, our oppression.

This is not an issue of religion. This is not about Gods or Goddesses, sects, denominations, churches, heroes, afterlife, or reincarnation. This is not about converting or discarding one's current philosophy. This is about reaching for, and living in worlds where there is no oppression. They exist. They are now. They are vibrant, real, and radiant. They are inside our mind waiting to be discovered.

On the other side of thought is liberation. Above, beyond, outside this familiar and ancient cloak there is no oppression. There is no division. There is no discrimination. There is freedom. There is eternal awareness. There is timeless perfection. We can break through. We must break through.

This is the ultimate revolution. This is not time or energy spent in rearranging the knots to decrease the pain. This is not writing and reading book after book, exposing our reprehensible history. This is not another political campaign to elect someone who *may* vote for women's rights. This has no dependence on the physical circumstances of one's life: economics, education, race, class, orientation, age, or appearance. This does not even require that we name the oppressor or punish the perpetrator. This does not create division, for each woman would be practicing her own Self-Discovery.

This is beauty, grace, will and power in a world that no one can corrupt. This journey unfolds gently and privately. The understanding is within every woman's reach, she has only to begin. Each woman who sits in meditation will find her truth, her freedom, her liberation, in exact measure. The practice is simple. It is our passage out of the slavery of thought to a world of endless clarity, pure perfection, unimagined power, and eternal liberation.

I felt a sadness because even if I could cross the stage and have five minutes at the microphone, the knotted network of doubt and suspicion would oppose the wisdom and purity of meditation. My Teacher and my community have been the target of profiteers who prey on the fears of people who do not want to understand. They feel the power of the truth and their weapon is to ridicule anyone who ventures beyond what they accept as possible. Regardless of their inability to wish us well on our journey outside their comfort zone, once ignited the desire for liberation cannot be stopped.

As with any revolution, it will require education and patience. But, here the outcome is eminent. Each step on the path is eternal. There are no knots to tie or untie. There are no ideas to scrutinize or conditioning to overcome. As each woman meditates, she will become more creative, more aware, and more powerful. She will find her life more manageable and her happiness invulnerable.

I have no idea who we will ultimately become. The definitions of "woman" that reside within the world of thought have no bearing on our true potential. I do know that it is not *equal* to "man." The true nature of both woman and man are shrouded in this world. They are greater than the knots could ever contain.

Standing by the stage, listening to these wonderful, brave, and resilient women, I ruminated through my memories of the last ten years. I began by asking for an amendment to the U.S. Constitution. I wanted to build a society where women and men were equal. Without a moment's forewarning, I applied to study with a Teacher. It took me almost two years to realize that the world he lives in bears no limitations based on gender.

From bookstore to Free Clinic to auto-body shop to Wall Street, I transformed again and again but was still confined to the earthly definitions of woman. All the while my Teacher kept telling me that there was more; even equality was not enough.

As I learned the ways of a Buddhist - from student to monk to teacher - bigger and brighter worlds opened up to me. As the horror of life on earth, with all of its violence and anger, became more apparent, my Teacher was encouraging me to find the worlds of liberation. Each moment spent in meditation illuminated the way.

Ten years ago, I wrote a letter and insisted that he give me the Blueprints. "He had something that was mine by necessity. He had something I had earned by wanting it so badly."

Now that I have them, how will I tell the others?

Afterword

Touch softly, hold them in esteem. They are made of the same fabric as saints. They have a burning desire to live with purpose, to know no meaningless breath, to wake every day as a warrior in battle. Rama once told us that there are four great loves; one of which is that between a student and a Teacher. While in love it is fully magnificent: no holes, no idle moments, no second thoughts. Leaving that love is next to impossible and life after that love will always pale in comparison.

As many passionate women and men have died for their beliefs, people have asked me if I would have sacrificed my life. To the idealist that is not the question. The entire quality of life depends on having something worth dying for. To the idealist, if there is not something worth dying for then life is not worth living. Everyday is lived in the zone, fully awake, filled with purpose and part of a whole. Sure there is fresh air out here, the view is wider out here, but never will love be felt like that again.

This is a passion that runs deeper than desire. This is not a passion fueled by pheromones. This is not a passion content with occasional service. This is not a passion satisfied in patchwork fashion: one hour a day, one day a week or one step at a time. This is a passion that demands a lifetime of either fulltime dedication or fulltime mourning. This is fulltime passion.

Surprisingly this passion is neutral. This passion is a matter of depth. A great friend who works in social services told me that she could have chosen working with battered women, homeless people, the disabled; the form is insignificant. Passion must be filled. Passion must be spent.

A passionate soul must create a life that never seeks rest from their spirit. The body must dance and the mind must spin in deference to the spirit. The spirit is ruler, supreme choreographer, beloved whisperer. The passionate heart always chooses to listen. Do not be fooled. It is not that they have no choice. They have every choice and they choose spirit.

Urgency, intensity, originality, fury, depth, focus, impatience with the trivial, unending patience with the important, quiet in the midst of chatter and emboldened in the presence of danger. And there is the danger. And there is the bewilderment. And there is the challenge. And there is the mystical, magical, miracle of such humans. What shall we do with such humans? What shall we do with such passion? For it will be spent. It will be expressed. This rich element of the human condition will find its expression.

Ten Years Later

Waking up on September 1, 1993 was a massive shock. My exit the night before was a passionate action that did not pause to evaluate consequences, depend on associates or even hope for agreements. The next morning was bleak, scary and lonely. No ashram, no Teacher, no plan.

As certain as I was about applying in 1982, I was certain about leaving in 1993. As certain as I was that Rama was my Teacher, I was certain that it was not true anymore. I had to be certain as the stated and maddening price was never seeing him or his students again. The only thing which wasn't certain, whatsoever, was what I would do now.

The temporary exception which anchored me for 75 nights was the completion of the task I had accepted; writing about my time with Rama. Over the last five months as a student I had given him one chapter at each of the monthly meetings. His first response, in March, was that chapter one was "well written but hopelessly episodic." (I had to look up *episodic*) Nevertheless, with the four that followed, he spoke both privately and publicly with sumptuous praise, encouragement and promise.

My character demanded that I finish the book. Even though I left for a lot of serious and troubling reasons; I had to finish the book. I never considered, for one moment, writing about judgments, accusations, manipulation or regrets. There were enough books written about that. A negative expose was not a book I cared to read and definitely not one I cared to write.

Besides, this was a task. Even if Rama never received it or read it; finishing it was my soul's requirement. It was a task. I was a student. I accepted a task. I was given the gift of a task and I would return the gift of a book.

Even today, ten years later, I wonder how I did it. At the time, I was living in a huge home in Lake Forest, Illinois. To make my world as small as possible, I moved the couch, TV and desk to one corner of the dining room and never sat anywhere else. I woke up at dark, wrote until the sunlight flickered and then went to bed. From September 1st to November 15th, I wrote. I wrote the book, all 40 chapters in their entirety. My two dogs and I stayed there until it was done. I forwarded the finished book to Rama and packed.

On December 23rd, I moved into my convent for one. A tiny and darling house in Southern California. I got a call on New Year's Day 1994 and heard that Rama had walked up to a particular student at the Christmas dinner to ask, "Were you one of Zoe's apprentices?" "Yes," she said. He continued, "Last night I gave myself the Christmas present of reading her book. It was very beautiful. When I finished it, I threw it into the fire." Then he walked away.

And so the manuscript sat in my file cabinet; unnamed and unread. I could not read it. I could not look at it. As time wore on, I agreed with fewer and fewer of the teachings. With each awareness, each brave reflection, I chanced anger, despair, confusion. I fell into a terrible long depression. Ultimately I sought and found help.

Why now? Why tell the story now? The answer is that it took me ten years to see what this experience actually held. It took ten years to face that I had called Rama to my life. He was complex, brilliant, dynamic, demanding. He taught me about lineage, Tibetan Buddhism, the Teacher - student relationship and Eastern etiquette. He showed me the pitfalls, the temptations, the heartbreaks. He showed me the size of his heart. He showed me the size of my heart. The intention of my heart. The Passionate Heart.

Lune Soleil Press
Order Form

Internet   www.lunesoleilpress.com
Phone   866 298-1080
FAX   949 642-8560
Mail Order Lune Soleil Press
            3419 Via Lido, Suite 614
            Newport Beach, CA 92663

_____**The Passionate Heart**
(quantity)   *($21.95 each)*

_____ **Matri,** Letters from the Mother
(quantity)   *($8.95 each)*

add 7.75% if mailed within California
shipping: $2.00 standard or $5.00 priority

Payment options:
❑Check
❑Credit Card   ❑Visa   ❑MasterCard
Name on Card_____
Card Number _____
Exp.date_____

Shipping Information
Name   _____
Address _____
        _____
City_____ State _____ Zip _____